Social Protection, Economic Growth and Social Change

Social Protection, Economic Growth and Social Change

Goals, Issues and Trajectories in China, India, Brazil and South Africa

Edited by

James Midgley

Harry and Riva Specht Professor, University of California, Berkeley, USA

David Piachaud

Professor of Social Policy, London School of Economics, London, UK

Edward Elgar

Cheltenham, UK • Northampton, MA, USA

Published by
Edward Elgar Publishing Limited
The Lypiatts
15 Lansdown Road
Cheltenham
Glos GL50 2JA
UK

Edward Elgar Publishing, Inc.
William Pratt House
9 Dewey Court
Northampton
Massachusetts 01060
USA

A catalogue record for this book
is available from the British Library

Library of Congress Control Number: 2013936179

This book is available electronically in the ElgarOnline.com
Social and Political Science Collection, E-ISBN 978 1 78195 395 2

MIX
Paper from
responsible sources
FSC® C013056

ISBN 978 1 78195 394 5

Typeset by Servis Filmsetting Ltd, Stockport, Cheshire
Printed and bound in Great Britain by T.J. International Ltd, Padstow

Contents

Tables and figures

TABLES

FIGURES

Contributors

Francesca Bastagli is Research Fellow in social protection at the Overseas Development Institute (ODI). At the time of writing the chapter on social protection in Brazil for this book she was research fellow at the Centre for Analysis of Social Exclusion (CASE) at the London School of Economics (LSE). Her main research interests are in the design, implementation and evaluation of social policy, with a focus on income, employment and gender inequality outcomes. Her most recent research examines the role of targeting and conditionality in public cash transfers, employment trajectories of women with children and trends in the distribution of wealth. Prior to joining the LSE, she worked at the World Bank's Poverty Reduction Group. She holds a Laurea in Economics from Bocconi University, and an MSc and PhD in Social Policy from the LSE.

Anthony Hall is Professor of Social Policy at the London School of Economics. During 2003–05 he worked for the World Bank in Washington DC as Senior Social Development Specialist for Latin America. His recent books are: *Forests and Climate Change: The Social Dimensions of REDD in Latin America*, 2012; *Global Impact, Local Action: New Environmental Policy in Latin America*, 2005; *Social Policy for Development* (with James Midgley), 2004; *Amazonia at the Crossroads: The Challenge of Sustainable Development*, 2000; and *Sustaining Amazonia: Grassroots Action for Productive Conservation*, 1997. He has published a number of papers on the impacts of conditional cash transfers in Brazil.

Ruth Kattumuri is Co-Director of the Asia Research Centre and the India Observatory at the London School of Economics (LSE). She is responsible for developing multi-disciplinary research and programmes related to Asia. Her research interests include growth and inclusion, climate change and environmental sustainability. In over 25 years of experience in higher education, research and policy engagement, she has pioneered several innovative international knowledge and skills development programmes. She is advisor to various educational institutions in Asia and is actively engaged in promoting south–south cooperation. She has a PhD from LSE and is also a Cambridge Commonwealth Fellow. She was formerly Associate Professor in Statistics and Computer Science at Madras

Christian College, India, where she taught and mentored several thousand students of the 'interphase generation', who are influential professionals around the world.

John Kruger is a development economist and specialises in social and labour market policy, social policy financing and public finance. He established the South Africa office of Oxford Policy Management (OPM) in 2008 after lecturing on economics at the University of Port Elizabeth (now the Nelson Mandela Metropolitan University) and the University of Stellenbosch (1986–97) and serving as a senior manager in the SA National Treasury (1998–2006) and the Department of Education (2006–08). In government he participated in and led diagnostic, policy development and budgeting processes related to the social service departments and the Department of Labour. At OPM he has participated in a range of projects, including a public expenditure review of basic education in South Africa, a review of retirement systems in the South African Development Community and the development of policy and policy tools for the SA Department of Social Development.

Bingqin Li is Associate Professor at the Crawford School of Public Policy, Australian National University. Before she moved to Australia, she was a lecturer in social policy at the London School of Economics. She grew up in China, where she studied economics and worked in finance. She then studied social policy at LSE, and later joined the faculty there. Her research interests include housing, urbanization, migration, urban governance, social policy reform, and development more broadly. Much of her work has a China or Asia focus, but by no means all. Consulting experience includes the UN, World Bank, EU, UN Habitat, Save the Children and the Chinese government at different levels. Recent publications include: *European and American Welfare System: Challenges, Reforms and Constraints* (in Chinese), China Society Press (*zhongguo shehui chubanshe*), 2011. She has also published numerous journal papers and research reports on the issues of social policy reform and urbanization in China.

James Midgley is Harry and Riva Specht Professor of Public Social Services and Dean Emeritus of the School of Social Welfare, University of California, Berkeley. He has published widely on issues of social development, international social welfare and social policy. Among his most recent books are *Social Security, the Economy and Development*, Palgrave, 2008 (editor with Kwong-leung Tang) and *The Handbook of Social Policy*, Sage, 2009 (editor with Michelle Livermore); *Social Work and Social Development*, Oxford University Press, 2010 (editor with Amy Conley); *Poverty and Social Security in Asia*, Routledge, 2010 (with K. L.

Tang) and *Grassroots Social Security in Asia*, Routledge, 2011 (editor with Mitsuhiko Hosaka); *Colonialism and Welfare: Social Policy and the British Imperial Legacy*, Edward Elgar, 2011 (editor with David Piachaud). He is a Fellow of the American Academy of Social Work and Social Welfare and holds honorary professorial appointments at Nihon Fukushi University in Japan, the University of Johannesburg, South Africa, Hong Kong Polytechnic University, and Sun Yat-sen University in China.

Letlhokwa George Mpedi is Professor in social security and labour law, Vice-Dean of the Faculty of Law and Director of the Centre for International and Comparative Labour and Social Security Law (CICLASS) at the University of Johannesburg. Prior to joining the University of Johannesburg, he was a research fellow at the Max Planck Institute for Foreign and International Social Law in Munich from August 2003 to July 2006. He lectures on social security and labour law to Diploma, LLB and post-graduate students and has delivered papers at numerous national and international conferences. He publishes on social security and labour law.

Rohit Mutatkar is Assistant Professor at the Centre for Study of Social Exclusion and Inclusive Policies, Tata Institute of Social Sciences (TISS), Mumbai. He has been a visiting fellow at the Asia Research Centre, LSE, as part of the LSE-TISS academic collaboration. He holds an MA in Economics from Jawaharlal Nehru University, New Delhi, and a PhD in Development Studies from the Indira Gandhi Institute of Development Research, Mumbai. His broad areas of research interest are poverty, inequality and human development.

Kinglun Ngok is the Pearl River Scholar Distinguished Professor of Social Policy at the School of Government/Centre for Chinese Public Administration Research, Sun Yat-sen University, Guangzhou, China. Prior to joining Sun Yat-sen University in 2004, he taught at the Department of Public and Social Administration, City University of Hong Kong where he completed his PhD. His current research interests are social policy, social insurance, social management and social services. He is the founding director of the Institute for Social Policy at Sun Yat-sen University. He has authored and co-edited several books on Chinese social policy and numerous journal articles. His books include *Social Policy in China: Development and Wellbeing* (2008, co-authored with C. W. Chan and D. Phillips), *Chinese Social Policy* (2009, co-edited with C. W. Chan and K. Q. Han), *Welfare Reform in East Asia: Towards Workfare?* (2011, co-edited with C. W. Chan), and *Public Services for Migrant Workers* (2012). He is also the editor-in-chief of *Chinese Public Policy Review*.

Leila Patel is Professor of Social Development Studies and Director of the Centre for Social Development in Africa at the University of Johannesburg, South Africa. She was previously the Deputy Vice Chancellor and Vice Principal of the University of the Witwatersrand, Johannesburg and the Director General for Social Welfare in the Mandela government after 1994. Her research on the *Restructuring of Social Welfare: Options for South Africa* was published 1993 by Ravan Press. She authored the *White Paper for Social Welfare* (1997) and wrote *Social Welfare and Social Development in South Africa* (2005) published by Oxford University Press (Southern Africa). She was Editor of *The Social Work Practitioner Researcher* and has published widely in the field of social welfare and social development in the African context. Currently she leads a range of social development research projects relating to gender, social protection, poverty and livelihoods, children and youth development, developmental social work and the transformation of social welfare in South Africa.

David Piachaud has taught at the London School of Economics since 1970 and is Professor of Social Policy and an Associate of the Centre for Analysis of Social Exclusion and of the Asia Research Centre. He was Social Policy Adviser in the Prime Minister's Policy Unit (1974–79) and has been a consultant to the European Commission, the International Labour Organization (ILO) and the Organisation for Economic Co-operation and Development (OECD). He has written papers and books on children, poverty, social security, social exclusion and social policy. Recent publications include *Understanding Social Exclusion*, Oxford University Press, 2002, (editor with John Hills and Julian LeGrand), *Poverty in Britain: The Impact of Government Policy since 1997*, Joseph Rowntree Foundation, 2003 (with Holly Sutherland and Tom Sefton), *One Hundred Years of Poverty and Policy*, Joseph Rowntree Foundation, 2004 (with Howard Glennerster, John Hills and Jo Webb), *Making Social Policy Work*, Policy Press, 2007 (editor with John Hills and Julian LeGrand) and *Colonialism and Welfare: Social Policy and the British Imperial Legacy*, Edward Elgar, 2011 (editor with James Midgley).

Maria Paula Gomes dos Santos has a PhD in Political Science. She works as a planning and research technician at the Institute of Applied Economic Research (IPEA), a Brazilian federal institution located in Brasilia. In IPEA she develops studies and research on Brazilian social protection policies, as well as on social policies in comparative perspective. Before joining IPEA in 2009, she had worked in policy planning for 26 years, at both the state level and the municipality of Rio de Janeiro. She has also taught social policies at the Social Work School of the Federal University of Rio de Janeiro (UFRJ).

Manju Singh is Professor and Head of the Symbiosis Institute of Research and Innovation at Symbiosis International University, Pune, India. She was recently Ratan Tata Fellow at the London School of Economics. Her main research interests are development economics, technology transfer, inclusive growth and diversity management. She has worked on action research projects funded by the Ford Foundation and has extensive field research experience across India. She has published widely in national and international journals. She has received awards from the Indian Council of Social Science Research, the Indian Institute of Advanced Study, Shimla and the Global Network of Government Innovators at the Kennedy School of Government, Harvard University.

Fabio Veras Soares is Researcher at the United Nations Development Programmes's International Policy Centre for Inclusive Growth (former International Poverty Centre), seconded from the Institute for Applied Economic Research, Brasilia, Brazil. His principal research interest is the comparative analysis of cash transfer programmes and social protection systems in developing countries. He has also worked in impact evaluation of cash transfers and other social programmes in countries such as Brazil, Paraguay, Mozambique and Yemen. He has published his impact evaluation work in the *Journal of Development Effectiveness* and *Latin American Research Review* and has authored book chapters on the comparative analysis of cash transfer programmes.

Sergei Soares is a researcher at Brazil's Institute for Economic Applied Research. He has also worked as Senior Education Economist at the World Bank. His main interests have been labour markets, social policy evaluation, education and racial inequality. In the last five years, though, he has devoted himself almost exclusively to the study of inequality and poverty in Brazil, and the role of social protection in their surprising fall.

Yapeng Zhu, PhD, is Research Fellow at the Centre for Chinese Public Administration Research and Associate Professor at the School of Government, Sun Yat-sen University (Guangzhou, China). He was visiting scholar at the University of Glasgow and University of California at Berkeley. His research interests focus on the policy process and social policy in China. He has published both in Chinese and English. His publications include *Housing Reform in China: Policy Innovation and Housing Inequality* (Sun Yat-sen University Press, 2007). His papers have appeared in journals such as the *Pacific Review*, *The China Review* and *Journal of Contemporary China, Politics and Policy*.

Acknowledgements

This book is based on a symposium held at the London School of Economics in March 2012. We are grateful above all to the symposium participants who gave freely of their time and knowledge. Their presentations – for many in an unfamiliar language – were enthusiastically discussed and ideas were exchanged. Authors then prepared their chapters for publication and patiently responded to editorial questions and suggestions. Their contributions are gratefully acknowledged.

The symposium was generously assisted by the Jamshetji Tata Trust which supports the research collaboration between the London School of Economics and the Tata Institute of Social Sciences. Ruth Kattumuri, Co-Director of the Asia Research Centre was instrumental in securing funding for the symposium and in the organization of the event; we are very grateful to her. Kevin Shields and Keith Tritton provided excellent logistical support.

Outstanding editorial assistance was provided by Ché Ramsden who immeasurably increased the intelligibility of the final manuscript.

We have received exceptional support and encouragement from our publishers and we thank Edward Elgar, Alex Pettifer and particularly Emily Neukomm who has supervised. We thank Sarah King for efficient copy editing and Madhubanti Bhattacharyya for managing the book's production.

Finally, we would like to pay tribute to the contribution of Professor Chandan Sengupta of the Tata Institute of Social Sciences in Mumbai, India, who participated in the planning of the symposium. Ill health prevented him from attending and, very sadly, he died in September 2012. His wisdom and cheerful enthusiasm will long be remembered.

James Midgley
University of California, Berkeley

David Piachaud
London School of Economics

PART I

Introduction and overview

1. Introduction

David Piachaud

At the start of the twentieth century only three countries had any form of national social protection. By the end of the century almost all nations had legislated some form of social protection. Thus social protection is very much a creation of the twentieth century. The form and extent of social protection differ greatly between nations but the fact that nearly all countries, differing greatly in their economic, social and cultural circumstances, have introduced social protection is of itself remarkable.

Now, early in the twenty-first century, social protection remains a highly contested area of public policy. Some nations are looking to cut it back, others to expand it, many are concerned about its future cost and sustainability. Some politicians, policy analysts and citizens see social protection, or welfare generally, as unaffordable and undesirable, creating dependency and undermining economic and family life; others see it as a force for good, liberating the most disadvantaged, reducing poverty and inequality and underpinning a modern economy.

Yet while social protection is a huge worldwide phenomenon – the ultimate determinant of the level of living of a large proportion of the world's population and the largest component of public spending in many countries – it is often regarded as boring and complex, totally lacking the glamour of, for example, health interventions, which have spawned countless television shows. Discussion of it tends to be very local and detailed, reflecting national histories and institutions, often focussing on the short-term impact of marginal changes. There is little focus on wider dimensions – the global picture and the long-term issues.

This book attempts to redress this neglect. It does not attempt to consider all nations but is focussed on four of the largest and most rapidly changing nations in the world: China, India, Brazil and South Africa. Together they contain almost half of the world's population.

Each of these nations is experiencing rapid economic growth, rapid urbanisation and fundamental social change. Some indications of the extent of development are shown in Table 1.1. The challenges and issues

Table 1.1 Comparison of four countries

	China	India	Brazil	South Africa
Population in millions, 2011	1 344	1 241	197	51
Growth of population, 1991–2011	+17%	+39%	+30%	+41%
GDP per capita, 2011 (PPP current $)	8 400	3 627	11 640	10 960
Growth in GDP per capita, 1991–2011	+462%	+167%	+43%	+25%
Agricultural employment (% of all), 2009*	40%	51%	17%	5%
Urban population (% of total), 2009	48%	31%	84%	61%
Female labour participation, 2009	68%	31%	59%	45%
Life expectancy at birth, 2009	73	65	73	52
Poverty (% below $2 per day), 2009*	30%	69%	11%	31%

Notes: *Indicates 2008 for China, 2010 for India.

Source: World Bank, *World Development Indicators*, downloaded 27 December 2012.

these changes have posed and will pose for social protection are the subject of this book.

The structure of the book is simple. In the next chapter, the background and philosophy of social protection is reviewed. Then for each country in turn we consider the past, the present and the future.

How social protection will develop clearly depends on the economies, the social structure, the cultural traditions and the political system of each country. Whilst it is impossible to consider all of these in detail in one volume, it is important to consider the past and the present before considering the future. Therefore each country is reviewed: how has social protection developed, who have been the main beneficiaries, what types of support have been provided, how has it been paid for, what have been the principle goals?

Then we consider current approaches to social protection, the provisions for different groups – children, people of working age who may be low paid or unemployed, and older people. What is the role of social protection in tackling poverty and reducing inequality? How does social protection impact on urban and rural populations, on men and women, and on richer and poorer?

Third, we consider possible future developments. What are the implications of current and planned policies? How might economies and societies change and what are the challenges to social protection and what are possible responses? The aim is not to forecast the future but rather to consider the likely influences on future developments in social protection and the implications of possible future trajectories.

Finally, we attempt to draw together and compare the evidence from each of the four countries; what common issues arise and what can be learned from this comparative approach.

This is a broad canvas and no one individual can claim expertise on social protection throughout the world. The study therefore brings together experts on each country. All the authors attended a joint symposium held at the London School of Economics in March 2012 and made a presentation to it; there was an opportunity to discuss each presentation and review general concerns and conclusions. These presentations were then developed into the chapters that make up this book. While all follow the same broad structure, national concerns differ and chapters reflect these differences. (For Brazil, the redistributive impact of social protection and its politics are considered in separate chapters.)

In preparing chapters, the editors have offered comments and suggestions, but the content of chapters remains the responsibility of individual authors and there was no attempt to enforce conformity of structure, analysis or conclusions. The concluding chapter is the responsibility of the editors alone and should not be read as indicating an agreed consensus.

'Social protection' is a broad term used to include many things ranging as far as handguns and deodorants. Even within the field of public policy there is no one agreed definition. Here, to make the scope of the study manageable, we do not consider the financing or provision of health care or of education. We have concentrated on children, working-age people and older people; given the complexity involved, we have not attempted to compare policies for people with disabilities. The focus here is on policies that in some countries are grouped under the heading 'social security' – primarily social insurance, social assistance and categorical or contingency-related benefits. Some types of benefit, such as housing allowances or tax credits, may also be a form of social protection. We are also concerned with other policies aimed at altering the distribution of incomes and protecting people from poverty, such as food subsidies, employment guarantees and obligations on employers to pay minimum wages or meet pension requirements.

There are many issues that arise with social protection. Not all can be exhaustively discussed. But it may be helpful to distinguish some of these issues to help clarify subsequent discussion.

First, there are issues of *coverage*. Does social protection cover the whole population or only the urban population? Is coverage limited to the formal sector of employment or does it include informal employment? How far are women covered as well as men?

Second, what is the *basis of protection*? Is social protection targeted or means-tested to benefit the poorest, as with most social assistance? Or is it based on contribution, as with social insurance schemes? Or is it available to all who fall into certain categories as contingencies? Or is it some combination of these?

Third, if it is based on categories, what *categories or contingencies* are covered? These may include old age or retirement, unemployment, sickness, the presence of children, or simply citizenship.

Fourth, there are issues about *benefits*. Are these based on individual circumstances or household circumstances? They may be linked to current income (means-tested) or to past earnings (earnings-related). There may also be conditionality, with benefits linked to satisfying certain tests, for example whether children attend school or adults seek employment. What are the rates of benefit paid?

Fifth, there are issues about *finance*. Who pays for social protection? Is it contributions from employees, employers or the state? Is it general taxation or a special social security tax? Are benefits paid for out of current revenues on a pay-as-you-go basis or is a fund built up? How do revenues and benefits adjust to inflation and to changes in the level of earnings?

Sixth, there are issues of *administration*. How efficiently and fairly is social protection administered? Does it reach those it is intended for and not those it is not intended for? With what delays and costs to those eligible? How costly is it to administer?

Finally, there are issues about *consequences*. How does social protection affect economic and social change? And how do economic and social changes affect social protection?

Some of these issues are questions of fact but some, such as the last, are contentious issues on which there are deep disagreements and no definite answers. Yet, despite the difficulties, all these issues are important for the lives of individuals and the state of nations, indeed for the welfare of the world.

2. Social protection in countries experiencing rapid economic growth: goals and functions

James Midgley

The recent expansion of social protection in countries experiencing rapid economic growth such as Brazil, China, India and South Africa has focused attention on its role in economic development. This issue has become increasingly relevant as academics and policymakers in these and other rapidly developing economies have recognized the need to formulate social protection policies that are compatible with economic development. Although this topic has not received the attention it deserves from social policy writers, a variety of arguments on this issue have been formulated. These range from the idea that social protection should be based solely on non-economic welfare criteria to the view that social protection should be specifically designed to serve economic objectives.

Academic debates on the role of social protection in economic development have not been widely used to inform policy and often goals have emerged incrementally or have been uncritically inserted into national legislation or adopted from international treaties without careful thought being given to their feasibility or appropriateness. Sometimes social protection policies and programmes do not have well-defined goals. Also, few countries have a comprehensive, national social protection plan that adopts what the World Bank (2012, p. vi) calls a 'systems-oriented approach that knits together a coherent portfolio of programmes . . . that addresses the problems of fragmentation and lack of harmonization that hamper the effectiveness of social protection programmes'. Concerns about this problem have previously been expressed in many documents by the International Labour Organisation (ILO) and the International Social Security Association (ISSA). In addition, it is widely recognized that much more needs to be done to integrate social protection with economic development efforts.

Another problem is that debates on the role of social protection in development have often been highly polarized. Some writers have claimed that growth is more likely when governments refrain from sponsoring social protection, while others insist that government responsibility for promoting the well-being of its citizens should override economic considerations. Although these positions oversimplify the arguments and fail to provide a viable basis for policy, the academic literature can help to clarify issues and promote the emergence of a coherent policy approach to social protection and economic development. The wider literature on the functions and goals of social protection is useful since it has uncovered the unstated or hidden goals of social protection programmes. It is also interesting for revealing hidden or unintended goals and enhancing understanding of how social protection actually operates.

The literature on the functions of social protection addresses social, economic and political issues. It is based on attempts by social policy writers over the years to determine what functions social protection serves in modern societies. Although it draws on scholarly analyses of social protection's actual functions rather than desirable goals, the distinction between goals versus functions is not always clear, and many accounts of what social protection actually achieves as opposed to what it is designed to achieve have been published. However, accounts of the functions of social protection are not always dispassionate and instead many advocate for particular goals. In some cases this is quite explicit, reflecting normative preferences in social policy scholarship. In addition, these accounts present a variety of complex and sometimes overlapping arguments. Nevertheless, they can inform policy debates about social protection's goals in the development context.

By reviewing the academic literature on the functions of social protection, this chapter seeks to contribute to debates about its proper role in countries experiencing rapid economic growth. Although not limited to rapidly growing developing countries, this review shows that a variety of social, political and economic functions are served by social protection and indeed wider social welfare interventions. Hopefully, it will be useful when social protection policies appropriate to conditions of rapid economic growth are formulated. The chapter concludes by arguing for a balanced view that integrates both economic and welfare goals in a comprehensive social protection policy. However, this requires that appropriate political arrangements are made to foster the integration of social and economic goals and serve the interests of the population as a whole.

THE GOALS AND FUNCTIONS OF SOCIAL PROTECTION

Academic inquiry into social protection has expanded exponentially over the last half century. Prior to World War II, relatively few studies of social protection were available, reflecting the fact that these programmes were still in their infancy. Previously, numerous polemical tracts on the subject had been published but these were generally designed to inform public opinion and gather political support for the expansion of statutory social protection. The work of Rubinow (1913) in the United States, who campaigned for the introduction of social insurance based on Bismarck's innovations in Germany, illustrates this approach. These studies were subsequently superseded by more rigorous academic research which became common as social protection programmes expanded rapidly both in Western and developing countries after World War II. Although most focused on domestic developments, some drew comparative lessons from a number of countries for domestic policy purposes. One example is Armstrong's (1932) comprehensive documentation of social insurance and other social protection programmes in Europe, which formed the basis for the retirement pension provisions of the American Social Security Act of 1935. After the 1960s, comparative studies appeared with growing frequency but generally focused on Western countries (Rodgers et al., 1968; Jenkins, 1969); however, studies of social protection in the developing countries also became available. These included countries which are the focus of this book such as Brazil, (Malloy, 1979), China (Dixon, 1981) and India (Srivastava, 1964; Hasan, 1972). More generalized studies dealing with the developing countries as a whole (Kassalow, 1968; Midgley, 1984; Ahmad et al., 1991) also appeared.

As in other fields of social policy inquiry, research into social protection has been largely interdisciplinary in nature, drawing on the insights of legal scholars, historians, political scientists, economists and sociologists, and in time became associated with the broader interdisciplinary field of social policy. More recently, social protection has become a major topic in the interdisciplinary field of development studies. Here, the term social protection rather than social security has been popularized and broadened to transcended social security's focus on statutory programmes operating at the national level. This has fostered a wider definition of social protection to include a variety of projects and programmes managed not only by governments but by non-profit, faith-based and international development organizations at both the local and national levels.

Early research into social protection often employed a descriptive, case study approach to document the features, history, legal basis, scope and operations of social protection in different countries. This approach was subsequently augmented by analytical accounts which drew on the insights of sociologists, political scientists and economists to discern social protection's broader functions and to uncover its unintended and hidden effects. These studies go beyond accounts of social protection's official goals and have offered many complex interpretations which suggest that documentary analyses of social protection's declared goals do not adequately explain the way they actually operate.

Although, as was noted earlier, it is not always easy to distinguish between the goals and functions of social protection or between different normative preferences, some studies do not espouse a particular normative predisposition for particular goals and have instead dispassionately sought to identify actual functions. This research has identified a number of sometimes overlapping and even contradictory functions which can be loosely grouped into three major categories. They are: first, studies associated with the analysis of welfare functions; second, with the identification of political functions; and finally, with economic functions. Each will be discussed in turn.

THE WELFARE FUNCTIONS OF SOCIAL PROTECTION

Many studies of social protection have focused on its welfare functions. These studies are usually based on analyses of the official goals of social protection contained in national legislation or the constitutions of different countries or in international treaties and human rights instruments such as those adopted by member states of the ILO and the United Nations. These instruments are clearly committed to using social protection for welfare purposes. However, the situation is complicated since very different types of welfare functions have been identified. These range from preventing and alleviating poverty to using social protection to create socially just societies.

The most common and obvious welfare function identified in the literature is the protection of people's income against contingencies or risks that interrupt, reduce or terminate income. These contingencies include work injury, sickness, maternity, unemployment, retirement and death. Social insurance, employer mandates and social assistance are widely used to give expression to this function. Since these programmes are primarily concerned with maintaining income, they are also known as income protection or income maintenance programmes. The term 'safety net' is also employed to connote the way these programmes provide a minimum income for those affected by hardship. It is for this reason that these programmes are believed to play a major role in preventing poverty. By guaranteeing an income when certain contingencies arise, they prevent people from becoming destitute. International treaties often give high priority to social protection's income maintenance function. For example, the ILO Minimum Standards Convention of 1952 explicitly states that social protection's objective is to 'maintain income in case of the involuntary loss of earnings'. This Convention and similar international instruments are based on the notion of collective rather than individual or household responsibility for managing risk. Unlike commercial insurance, which requires individuals to assess their exposure to risk and purchase appropriate protection, the collective model assigns responsibility for this task to the state, even though individuals contribute to funding pools and are subject to other conditionalities. As will be shown later, a risk management framework based on rational choice has been popularized by market liberal scholars.

In addition to maintaining income when certain contingencies arise, social protection is also used to supplement or subsidize income, and in this way, to fulfil an income support function. Social assistance programmes that provide additional cash benefits or food vouchers to poor families are generally employed for this purpose. In the developing world, social assistance, in the form of conditional cash transfers, nutritional supplements and public works programmes, have become a popular means of supplementing the incomes of poor families. In Western countries, different approaches including tax credits and minimum wages are more popular. Social insurance is also widely used around the world for this purpose. Although primarily adopted to maintain income, social insurance can be used to subsidize household income through, for example, paying child benefits, which is quite common in francophone countries. These examples reveal that by supplementing incomes, social protection has a poverty alleviation function which helps to meet basic needs and raise standards of living. This function has been a major topic of interest in development studies where, as noted earlier, social protection is often associated with community-based poverty alleviation projects. In addition, social protection is now being extensively used by governments in many developing countries to meet the Millennium Development Goal of halving the incidence of poverty by 2015. Many have recognized that cash transfers have a direct, immediate impact and are an effective way of achieving this goal (Hanlon et al., 2010).

Many studies have confirmed that social protection does indeed have a welfare function. This was a common conclusion in the 1950s and 1960s when academic publications often adopted what Baker (1979) called the 'social conscience' approach to analyse social protection's functions. Although these studies generally concluded that social protection gives expression to society's deeply felt desire to provide for those in need, some writers have pointed out that benefit levels are too low to effectively reduce poverty, or otherwise that social protection programmes are administratively ineffective or poorly targeted or limited in coverage. Limited coverage has been a major concern, particularly in the developing world where statutory social protection has generally favoured urban workers in regular wage employment, with the result that the rural majority as well as those living in urban informal settlements have been excluded. This problem has been recognized by international organizations such as the ILO and ISSA which are encouraging their member states to expand coverage to the population as a whole (Reynaud, 2002; van Ginneken, 2007).

The problem of limited coverage is closely associated with equity concerns. While agreeing that social protection does indeed have a welfare function, some writers have pointed out that these programmes fail to address fundamental social inequalities and some have even concluded that they actually exacerbate these inequalities. Research of this kind has been fairly common in Western countries and although many studies of social security in the developing world initially confirmed its welfare function, others drew attention to the failure of these programmes to reduce poverty and inequality. Midgley (1984) showed that social insurance and employer mandates provide only for a small proportion of the population in regular wage employment, neglecting the wider problem of mass poverty, especially in the rural areas. Because of government subsidies, these programmes have sometimes accentuated social and economic inequalities. Similarly, despite being officially available to everyone, social assistance is largely limited to urban areas, again accentuating urban rural inequalities.

Over the years, feminist social policy writers (Gordon, 1990; Pascall, 1986; Sainsbury, 1996; Wilson, 1977) have drawn attention to the problem of gender inequality, pointing out that social protection, and particularly social insurance, has catered primarily to a male-dominated labour force and disadvantaged women. While this is partly a consequence of the occupationalist nature of these programmes, which emerged in the context of rapid industrialization and the expansion of wage employment among men, they also believe that social protection reflects wider social and economic inequalities. Although the governments of several Western countries have sought to remedy the problem, gender inequality still persists and many feminist scholars remain sceptical that much has changed. Gender inequality in social protection is also found in other parts of the world. Borzutzky's (2002) research into Chile's privatized social insurance scheme reveals that it discriminates against women, and particularly low-income women, who are unable to accumulate sufficient funds in their personal retirement accounts to meet their basic income needs.

Analyses of the inegalitarian consequences of social protection have often been accompanied by a normative commitment to use these programmes to create an egalitarian, socially just and solidaristic society. Titmuss (1974) is among many scholars who have been critical of the limitations of conventional social protection programmes, arguing not only that their shortcomings should be addressed but that they should be redesigned to redistribute resources to foster greater equality, promote altruism and social solidarity and create what Townsend (2009) called 'decent' societies. This theme has also been taken up by writers in development studies, such as Sabates-Wheeler and Devereux (2007), who are critical of social protection's narrow focus on poverty alleviation, arguing that it should serve a wider 'transformative' function.

A somewhat different analysis of social protection's welfare function focuses on human rights. Although much of the academic discourse on this topic is overtly normative, it reflects a wider conceptualization of a welfare system based on principles of democratic participation and consensus around a social contract between citizens and their governments. Derived from Marshall's (1950) seminal work, this approach goes much further than the narrow concern with poverty alleviation associated with the welfare approach. Because of its widespread appeal, this interpretation has not been subjected to extensive critical debate, although some detractors, such as Mead (1986), have argued that rights should be circumscribed by obligations and conditionalities. It is also clear that the right to social protection is in fact politically determined and that it is not always justiciable despite being enshrined in both international and domestic law. In addition, the successes of the welfare rights movement in a number of Western countries have been tempered by the statutory imposition of more conditionalities. Nevertheless, the notion of a rights-based approach to social security derived from a theory of natural rights continues to exert a strong influence in social policy circles and efforts to secure access to social protection through redress to the courts has enjoyed some success in some countries.

SOCIAL PROTECTION AND POLITICAL POWER

Some scholars have dismissed the idea that social protection programmes have a welfare function. They have deconstructed the officially stated goals of social protection to uncover its hidden or unintended goals and many have emphasized the way social protection's official goals actually serve political ends. While some have narrowly interpreted the term 'political' to focus on the use of social protection for electoral purposes, others have been more broadly concerned with the issue of power and the way social protection contributes to consolidating and reinforcing entrenched power structures.

Academic inquiry into the historical evolution of social protection, particularly in Europe and North America in the nineteenth and twentieth centuries, often emphasized the way these programmes reflected interest group power politics. For example, Rimlinger's (1971) pioneering analysis of the development of social protection in Europe and North America showed that while Chancellor Bismarck's government paternalistically introduced social insurance in Germany in the late nineteenth century, it did so for political purposes and particularly to outmanoeuvre the Social Democratic Party which was gathering electoral support from industrial workers. In the United States on the other hand, the expansion of social security was driven to a large extent by middle-class interests; while in Russia political support for the Communist Party played a crucial political role. Subsequent studies of the expansion of social security in European countries (Korpi, 1983; Esping-Andersen, 1985; Stephens, 1979) stressed the role of trade unions, industrial workers and social democratic political parties in advocating for these programmes. In Latin America, Mesa-Lago (1978) showed that interest groups shaped the region's social security systems. The most powerful interest groups such as the military and civil service successfully campaigned to create the first and most generous social security programmes, while groups with less influence only secured social security coverage and less generous benefits at a later stage. More recently, the effective political mobilization of domestic servants in South Africa resulted in their inclusion in the country's social insurance programme, demonstrating yet again the role of interest group politics in social protection (Ally, 2009).

Marxist accounts have made a major contribution to the analysis of social protection's political functions. As is well known, Marx and Engels believed that governments introduce social welfare programmes to serve the interests of the capitalist class. However, they also recognized that the working class can engage in political action to secure concessions even though these concessions are likely to have a minimal impact on social conditions. It is only with the transition to socialism, they argued, that social programmes will serve an authentic welfare function. These ideas were resurrected in the 1970s by neo-Marxist social policy scholars who stressed the role of social protection in exerting social and political control, managing political discontent and promoting the interests of capitalism. O'Connor (1973) formulated one of the most influential accounts of this kind, contending that capitalist societies use social protection to serve accumulation and legitimation functions. The former enables capitalists to make profits, while the latter engenders the acceptance of capitalism among ordinary people. Subsequent analyses by Gough (1979) developed this theme, offering more nuanced analysis of the role of social protection in maintaining political and economic power.

Although Marx's theory has been widely invoked to explain the use of social protection for political purposes in conditions of social unrest, numerous other examples that are not explicitly based on a Marxist interpretation have also been published and these have shown that governments have often used social protection in response to political disturbances. Perhaps the best known comes from Piven and Cloward (1971), who claimed that governments expand social protection during times of economic recession to placate popular discontent, and contract social protection during times of economic growth to promote labour force participation. Although these examples are often drawn from Western countries, social protection was also introduced in developing countries by colonial governments to ease political tensions over the years. The introduction of workers' compensation by the British colonial authorities in India in the late nineteenth century came about because of demonstrations among industrial workers in Bombay who were infuriated by the summary dismissal of injured employees by factory owners (Srivastava, 1964). Similarly, the introduction of social security in the West Indies in the 1940s owed much to the recommendations of the Moyne Report which, as Harrison (2011) reports, was appointed to investigate the causes of widespread riots in the British Caribbean territories in the late 1930s.

These studies of the role of interest group politics have been augmented by a growing body of literature that shows how political elites purposefully use social protection for electoral purposes. These have demonstrated that political advantage can be secured in pluralist democratic systems by increasing benefits or extending coverage or by improving delivery systems. This is the case in both Western and developing countries. For example, Hall (2008) has analysed the way the expansion of the Bolsa Família programme in Brazil enhanced President Lula da Silva's popularity and contributed significantly to his electoral success. Another example comes from de Neubourg (2009), who reveals that political elites in some low-income African countries are securing electoral support by vigorously advocating for the expansion of these programmes.

A somewhat different interpretation comes from studies that show how political elites have secured electoral support by adopting positions on social protection that exploit racist stereotypes or anti-immigrant sentiments. In the United States, for example, politicians have over the years vigorously denounced the payment of benefits to immigrants, and in the 1980s and 1990s racial innuendo was widely used to attack the country's social assistance programme for women with children. While the Democratic Party had historically secured electoral support by marketing its compassionate stance and use of social assistance (or 'welfare') to alleviate poverty, this approach was successfully undermined by President Reagan who presented an image of welfare recipients as feckless women of colour with numerous illegitimate children. His characterization of the 'welfare queen' who drives a 'welfare Cadillac' resonated with many voters and contributed to his electoral success. It was only when President Clinton famously declared his intention to 'end welfare as we know it' that the Democrats were able to discard the negative imagery associated with their traditional position. His firm but compassionate 'welfare reform' programme, which was devolved to the states, solved the electoral problem and discarded the negative imagery associated with the Democratic Party's traditional position on social welfare (Midgley, 2008b).

Another example of the way social protection functions to exercise power is given by feminist writers, who point out that these programmes are used to exert control over women and maintain their subjugation in patriarchal societies. It is not only that these programmes discriminate against women and heighten inequality, but that they reveal deeper, oppressive gender relations. Numerous feminist social policy scholars (Gordon, 1990; Pascall, 1986; Sainsbury, 1996; Wilson, 1977) have drawn attention to the way social protection functions, as Abramovitz (1998) argued, to 'regulate the lives of women'. This has been a recurring theme in analyses of the American welfare-to-work programme which, as Reese (2005) contends, is purposefully used to discipline women and control their lives. Extending this argument, a number of writers contend that social protection programmes are also used to control people of colour and that they function to maintain an institutionalized racist system (Williams, 1989; Neubeck and Cazenave, 2001).

Some studies of the use of social protection for political purposes have shown that the power dynamic also operates at the international level. In an interesting historical account, Semmel (1960) showed that political leaders in Britain in the late nineteenth century were very concerned that the expansion of social insurance in Germany would harm Britain's global imperial prestige and that this contributed to the Liberal government's decision to introduce social insurance. A similar dynamic is currently at work in the developing world as the Millennium Development Goals put pressure on national leaders to expand social programmes and reduce the incidence of poverty. Failure to do so is likely to attract negative comment and weaken the international status of their governments and countries.

SOCIAL PROTECTION'S ECONOMIC FUNCTIONS

As noted at the beginning of this chapter, social policy scholars have not paid sufficient attention to social protection's economic functions, preferring instead to emphasize the way it serves welfare purposes. The popularization of the rights-based approach and notions of altruism and social solidarity in social policy in the 1950s and 1960s contributed to the marginalization of debates on social protection's economic role. Indeed, Titmuss (1974) vigorously criticized the use of social protection for economic purposes in countries such as Germany and the Soviet Union. Attacking what he described as the 'handmaiden' model of social policy, he argued that principles of meeting social needs and promoting collective altruism rather than achieving economic success should provide a rationale for welfare provision.

However, it was clear from Titmuss' denunciation that some countries were in fact using social protection to promote economic objectives. Also, there is plenty of historical evidence to show that economic motives had previously played a major role in the development of social protection. For example, de Schweinitz (1943) revealed that the evolution of social security in Britain since feudal times had been significantly influenced by economic considerations. Various medieval monarchs had enacted formative poor laws that not only catered to the destitute but restricted labour mobility to ensure that feudal landowners had an adequate supply of workers. The Elizabethan statute consolidated these provisions as did the 1834 New Poor Law which curbed the generosity of benefits in an attempt to maintain work incentives. The writings of Marx on the issue of what Pinker (1971) calls 'social amelioration' reveal that nineteenth-century scholarly analysis was already attuned to the economic as well as political functions of social reform.

The idea that social protection functions as an adjunct to the economy was especially popular in the 1930s and 1940s as government sought to respond to the economic and social crisis of the Great Depression. Although welfare considerations were clearly present in both the New Deal and Beveridge proposals, the use of social protection to address the problem of unemployment, calm the turbulence caused by the Depression and foster long-term economic stability was given high priority. The positive economic function of social protection was recognized and promoted by both social policy and economic thinkers. Beveridge linked his proposals to full employment policies, and Skidelsky (2000) reports that Keynes was an enthusiastic supporter of Beveridge's ideas. Similarly, President Roosevelt's Brain Trust economists such as Tugwell vigorously advocated for the expansion of social protection, urging the president to integrate social policies with economic recovery measures (Leuchtenburg, 1963). As Keynesian economics became dominant in the post-World War II years, the view that social protection serves a desirable economic purpose by functioning as an automatic stabilizer, stimulating demand and minimizing exposure to risk was widely accepted. Indeed, some later social policy commentators including Jessop (2002, 2004) and Mishra (1990) even used the term Keynesian Welfare State (KWS) to connote this period of social policy development.

The close linkage between economic and social policy also finds expression in formative analyses which emphasize the role of industrialization in fostering a broad-based social protection system designed to mitigate the social effects of industrial dislocation. In Wilensky and Lebeaux's (1965) account, social protection is integral to the process of economic modernization and its expansion is driven by economic and social forces rather than ideological preferences. This claim was subsequently confirmed by Wilensky's (1975, 2002) empirical research. However, as mentioned earlier, a moral rather than economic rationale for social protection was also popular, as notions of compassion, altruism and social rights were adopted in both academic and government circles. In the 1950s and 1960s, social democratic and social liberal political parties often proudly proclaimed their welfare commitments and secured electoral advantage from voters who shared these ideals. Support was particularly strong from voters who had survived the traumas of the Great Depression and World War II.

A radically different interpretation of social protection's economic role emphasizes its harmful economic effects. As economic adversity, high unemployment and stagflation became pervasive in Western countries in the 1970s, the idea that social protection was unaffordable gained electoral support and was increasingly fuelled by academic research that claimed that an expansive social protection system had negative economic consequences. The writings of market liberal pioneers such as Hayek (1960) and Friedman (1962), which advocated for a minimalist, residual social protection system, were soon accompanied by a barrage of critical analyses of social protection's negative economic impact. As Midgley (2008a) summarized, these critiques range over a number of issues, such as the inflationary impact of social protection, its harmful effects on work incentives, its negative impact on savings and investments, and ultimately the way it undermines economic production by creating a sizable class of non-productive citizens dependent on a steadily shrinking, productive labour force. As these criticisms increasingly resonated with voters, many Western governments adopted policies that significantly modified the expansionary trajectory that had previously characterized social protection policy.

There were similar developments in the Global South where the expansion of social protection was often either halted or slowed because of economic stagnation and sovereign debt. This was exacerbated by the imposition of structural adjustment programmes as a condition for receiving credit from the International Monetary Fund (IMF) and the World Bank (Hall and Midgley, 2004). In some countries, such as Chile, radical policies that resulted in the marketization of the social insurance system were introduced. These were subsequently emulated by the governments of other Latin American and East European countries, often with fiscal incentives and the support of the World Bank, which vigorously promoted the adoption of commercial social protection provisions. Policies for creating market-based retirement programmes, establishing social funds and safety nets, and fostering 'risk management' strategies all gave expression to an approach to social protection based on market liberal analyses (World Bank, 1994; Holzmann and Kozel, 2007). Notions of household responsibility for coping with risk inspired by market liberal economics have also exerted considerable influence, especially on the emerging field of microinsurance (Midgley and Hosaka, 2011).

Although the social policy literature made frequent reference to the 'crisis' resulting from the widespread adoption of neoliberal economic and social policies, it is clear that social protection provisions have not in fact been dismantled or abolished. Nevertheless, several commentators (Castles, 2004; Gilbert, 2002; Timonen, 2003) have shown that major changes have taken place which have fostered a more pluralistic approach, restrictions on benefit eligibility and generosity, increasing use of means testing and a greater role for commercial providers, among others. These developments have undermined earlier attempts to formulate a coherent rationale for social protection, resulting in a much more fragmented approach which, as was argued earlier, needs to be addressed. In addition, the recent global banking crisis and Great Recession have created major challenges for social protection as many millions of middle-class people who have become unemployed, lost their homes and depleted their savings have become the victims rather than beneficiaries of the market liberal project.

It is in this context that some have argued that social protection's positive economic function should again be emphasized within the normative framework of what is described as a 'social investment' or 'welfare developmentalist' approach. The concept of social investment has attracted some attention in social policy circles but it is often used narrowly to connote social policy's role in promoting human capital. For Giddens (1998), the 'social investment state' is primarily focused on enhancing educational and skills development, and in a recent collection Morel (2012) and her colleagues take a similar view. However, others have articulated a broader approach in which a variety of social programmes are configured to serve an investment function. These include social capital initiatives, asset programmes, employment creation strategies, microenterprises and social protection, among others (Midgley, 1999; Midgley and Tang, 2001; Midgley and Sherraden, 2009).

Although it has conventionally been accepted that social protection serves a consumption rather than investment function, a growing body of research largely associated with scholars in the field of social development has demonstrated that these programmes can be designed to contribute to economic growth. This approach transcends social protection's conventional protective function to promote a productive function which has wider, positive economic benefits. The best known productive forms of social protection are conditional cash transfers, which have been adopted in Brazil, Mexico and other developing countries to modify social assistance programmes to ensure that they contribute to human capital formation and have a positive economic impact (Rawlings, 2005; Fiszbein and Schady, 2009). However, this investment effect can be achieved without imposing bureaucratic conditionalities. For example, Patel and Trieghaardt (2008) reveal that social assistance child benefits in South Africa have fostered high rates of school attendance and improved nutritional standards, thus contributing to economic development even though it is only recently that the government imposed attendance and other requirements. In addition, they report that many old-age pensioners have used their benefits to establish microenterprises. Local economic activity in depressed rural areas has also been stimulated by the emergence of what are known as 'pension market days', when local people, including pensioners themselves, gather around the government's distribution point to barter and trade and engage in other economic activities.

POLITICAL POWER AND THE INTEGRATION OF FUNCTIONS AND GOALS

The preceding review shows that scholarly inquiry into the functions and goals of social protection has been pursued for many years and is now quite extensive, but there is no consensus on what social protection's functions are or indeed what its goals should be. It is also the case that interpretations are frequently compartmentalized, focusing on one rather than multiple functions that often overlap. This approach reflects the tendency in the social sciences to create typologies, and especially dichotomies, that reduce complex realities to relatively simple categories. As is well known, Wilensky and Lebeaux (1965) constructed an enduring typology that classified social protection into residual and institutional types, while Titmuss (1974) and Esping-Andersen (1990) created threefold typologies. However, none of these capture the complexities of social protection policies and programmes around the world.

The tendency to oversimplify is even more marked when normative categories that reveal ideological preferences for particular goals are constructed. Titmuss, for example, juxtaposed his analysis of the goals of social protection so that his own preference for an egalitarian redistributive model rather than a residual or work performance approach was prioritized. As was noted earlier, he was also adamant that social protection should not serve an economic function. This conclusion was widely shared, not only in social policy circles but among economists as well. For example, Okun (1975) famously posited a 'trade-off' between democratic-egalitarian and market efficient social and economic policies. The former, which include extensive social protection provisions could not, he argued, be reconciled with the need for market efficiency, on which growth and prosperity depends. In both cases complex phenomena are reduced to basic, mutually exclusive categories.

Although these examples reveal that many social protection writers have a preference for a single, particular function or goal, it will be argued that social protection can serve multiple functions and goals. It is not inconceivable that social protection can foster the social well-being of the population while also being compatible with economic development efforts and that this can be achieved in the context of a democratic political system committed to social rights and enhancing people's welfare. Despite claims to the contrary, a carefully thought out social protection policy can alleviate poverty and promote desirable ideals such as solidarity and social justice while simultaneously contributing to economic development by, for example, being fiscally sustainable, enhancing economic stability and promoting social investments.

However, to achieve the integration of social and economic goals, the exercise of political power by the state on behalf of the interests of its citizens will be required. Governments need to play a positive and proactive role if social protection's multiple goals are to be achieved. Contrary to the claims of market liberals about the virtues of laissez-faire, Polanyi

(1944) showed many years ago that states invariably intervene to create and shape the social protection system. Just as the British New Poor Law of the early nineteenth century was used by the state to support an expanding market economy, so the vigorous advocacy of a market-based social protection system in the late twentieth century is designed to promote capitalist economic interests. This was certainly the case in Chile where, as Borzutzky (2002) revealed, General Pinochet's military government orchestrated and funded the emergence of the privatized social security system in the 1980s.

While the Chilean case is only one of many examples of states using political power to serve the interests of commercial, political and other elites, governments can and have used their authority to formulate social protection policies that serve the wider social good. Studies of corporatist statecraft have shown that governments have proactively promoted social protection for economic and social purposes with positive benefits for citizens (Malloy, 1979; Mishra, 1990). In addition, the preceding discussion on the role of interest groups in the evolution of social protection reveals that those with limited power can mobilize collectively to exert pressure for the expansion of social protection. Governments have also successfully harmonized economic and social development and used social protection to simultaneously serve social and economic purposes. Denmark's 'flexicurity' approach (Midgley, 2008a), various studies of East Asian social policies (Chan et al., 2002; Holliday and Wilding, 2003; Tang, 2000) and the experience of countries such as Botswana, Costa Rica, Mauritius and Taiwan all challenge the idea that social and economic goals are incompatible (Midgley, 1995). While it is true that the governments of many countries remain indifferent to the needs of their citizens or have otherwise adopted policies that are inimical to their well-being, the case studies in this book reveal that much has been achieved to extend social protection to hundreds of millions of people around the world while at the same time integrating social protection's welfare and economic goals.

REFERENCES

Abramovitz, M. (1988), *Regulating the Lives of Women: Social Welfare Policy from Colonial Times to the Present*, Boston, MA: South End Press.

Ahmad, E., J. Dreze, J. Hills and A. Sen (eds) (1991), *Social Security in Developing Countries*, Oxford: Clarendon Press.

Ally, S. (2009), *From Servants to Workers: South African Domestic Workers and the Democratic State*, Ithaca, NY: Cornell University Press.

Armstrong, B. N. (1932), *Insuring the Essentials: Minimum Wage Plus Social Insurance – A Living Wage Program*, New York: Macmillan.

Baker, J. (1979), 'Social conscience and social policy', *Journal of Social Policy*, **8** (2), 177–206.
Borzutzky, S. (2002), *Vital Connections: Politics, Social Security and Inequality in Chile*, Notre Dame, IN: Notre Dame University Press.
Castles, F. G. (2004), *The Future of the Welfare State: Crisis Myths and Crisis Realities*, New York: Oxford University Press.
Chan, K. L., K. K. Leung and R. M. H. Ngan (eds) (2002), *Development in Southeast Asia: Review and Prospects*, Burlington, VT: Ashgate, pp. 131–62.
de Neubourg, C. (2009), 'Social protection and nation-building: an essay on why and how universalist social policy contributes to stable nation states', in P. Townsend (ed.), *Building Decent Societies: Rethinking the Role of Social Security in Development*, New York: Palgrave Macmillan, pp. 63–79.
de Schweinitz, K. (1943), *England's Road to Social Security*, Philadelphia, PA: University of Pennsylvania Press.
Dixon, J. (1981), *The Chinese Welfare System, 1949–1979*, New York: Praegar.
Esping-Andersen, E. (1985), *Politics Against Markets: The Social Democratic Road to Power*, Princeton, NJ: Princeton University Press.
Esping-Andersen, G. (1990), *The Three Worlds of Welfare Capitalism*, Cambridge: Polity Press.
Fiszbein, A. and N. Schady (2009), *Conditional Cash Transfers: Reducing Present and Future Poverty*, Washington, DC: The World Bank.
Friedman, M. (1962), *Capitalism and Freedom*, Chicago, IL: University of Chicago Press.
Giddens, A. (1998), *The Third Way: The Renewal of Social Democracy*, Cambridge: Polity Press.
Gilbert, N. (2002), *The Transformation of the Welfare State: The Silent Surrender of Public Responsibility*, New York: Oxford University Press.
Gordon, L. (1990), *Women, the State and Welfare*, Madison, WI: University of Wisconsin Press.
Gough, I. (1979), *The Political Economy of the Welfare State*, London: Macmillan.
Hall, A. (2008), 'Brazil's *Bolsa Família*: a double-edged sword?', *Development and Change*, **39** (5), 799–822.
Hall, A. and J. Midgley (2004), *Social Policy for Development*, Thousand Oaks, CA: Sage Publications.
Hanlon, J., A. Barrientos and D. Hulme (2010), *Just Give Money to the Poor: The Development Revolution from the Global South*, Sterling VA: Kumrian Press.
Harrison, J. (2011), 'The colonial legacy and social policy in the British Caribbean', in J. Midgley and D. Piachaud (eds), *Colonialism and Welfare: Social Policy and the British Imperial Legacy*, Cheltenham: Edward Elgar, pp. 55–70.
Hasan, N. (1972), *The Social Security System of India*, New Delhi: Chand.
Hayek, F. von (1960), *The Constitution of Liberty*, Chicago, IL: University of Chicago Press.
Holliday, I. and P. Wilding (2003), *Welfare Capitalism in East Asia: Social Policy in the Tiger Economies*, New York: Palgrave.
Holzmann, R. and V. Kozel (2007), 'The role of social risk management in development: a World Bank view', *IDS Bulletin*, **38** (3), 8–13.
Jenkins, S. (ed.) (1969), *Social Security in International Perspective*, New York: Columbia University Press.
Jessop, B. (2002), *The Future of the Capitalist State*, Cambridge: Polity Press.
Jessop, B. (2004), 'Hollowing out the "nation-state" and multilevel governance', in

P. Kennett (ed.), *Handbook of Comparative Social Policy*, Cheltenham, UK and Northampton, MA, USA: Edward Elgar Publishers, pp. 11–245.
Kassalow, E. M. (ed.) (1968), *The Role of Social Security in Economic Development*, Washington: U.S. Department of Health, Education and Welfare.
Korpi, W. (1983), *The Democratic Class Struggle*, London: Routledge.
Leuchtenburg, W. (1963), *Franklin D. Roosevelt and the New Deal*, New York: Harper and Row.
Malloy, J. (1979), *The Politics of Social Security in Brazil*, Pittsburgh, PA: University of Pittsburgh Press.
Marshall, T. H. (1950), *Citizenship and Other Essays*, Cambridge: Cambridge University Press.
Mead, L. M. (1986), *Beyond Entitlement: The Social Obligations of Citizenship*, New York: Free Press.
Mesa-Lago, C. (1978), *Social Security in Latin America*, Pittsburgh, PA: University of Pittsburgh Press.
Midgley, J. (1984), *Social Security, Inequality and the Third World*, Chichester: John Wiley and Sons.
Midgley, J. (1995), *Social Development: The Developmental Perspective in Social Welfare*, Thousand Oaks, CA: Sage Publications.
Midgley, J. (1999), 'Growth, redistribution and welfare: towards social investment', *Social Service Review*, **77** (1), 3–21.
Midgley, J. (2008a), 'Social security and the economy: key perspectives', in J. Midgley and K. L. Tang (eds) (2008), *Social Security, the Economy and Development*, New York: Palgrave, pp. 51–82.
Midgley, J. (2008b), *Welfare Reform in the United States: Implications for British Social Policy*, CASE paper 131, London: Centre for the Analysis of Social Exclusion, London School of Economics.
Midgley, J. and M. Hosaka (eds) (2011), *Grassroots Social Security in Asia: Mutual Aid, Microinsurance, and Social Welfare*, New York: Routledge.
Midgley, J. and M. Sherraden (2009), 'The social development perspective in social policy', in J. Midgley and M. Livermore (eds), *Handbook of Social Policy*, Thousand Oaks, CA: Sage Publications, pp. 263–78.
Midgley, J. and K. L. Tang (2001), 'Social policy, economic growth and developmental welfare', *International Journal of Social Welfare*, **10** (4), 242–50.
Mishra, R. (1990), *The Welfare State in Capitalist Society: Policies of Retrenchment and Maintenance in Europe, North America and Australia*, London: Harvester Wheatsheaf.
Morel, N., B. Pallier and J. Palme (2012), *Towards a Social Investment Welfare State? Ideas, Policies and Challenges*, Bristol: Policy Press.
Neubeck, K. J. and N. J. Cazenave (2001), *Welfare Racism: Playing the Race Card Against America's Poor*, New York: Routledge.
O'Connor, J. (1973), *The Fiscal Crisis of the State*, New York: St. Martin's Press.
Okun, A. (1975), *Equality and Efficiency: The Big Tradeoff*, Washington, DC: Brookings.
Pascall, G. (1986), *Social Policy: A Feminist Analysis*, London: Tavistock.
Patel, L. and J. Trieghaardt (2008), 'South Africa: social security, poverty and development', in J. Midgley and K. L. Tang (eds), *Social Security, the Economy and Development*, New York: Palgrave Macmillan, pp. 85–109.
Pinker, R. (1971), *Social Theory and Social Policy*, London: Heinemann.

Piven, F. F. and R. Cloward (1971), *Regulating the Poor: The Functions of Public Welfare*, New York: Pantheon.
Polanyi, K. (1944), *The Great Transformation*, New York: Farrar and Rinehart.
Rawlings, L. B. (2005), 'A new approach to social assistance: Latin America's experience with conditional cash transfer programmes', *International Social Security Review*, **58** (2–3), 133–62.
Reese, E. (2005), *Backlash Against Welfare Mothers: Past and Present*, Berkeley, CA: University of California Press.
Reynaud, E. (2002), *The Extension of Social Security Coverage: The Approach of the International Labour Office*, Geneva: ILO.
Rimlinger, G. (1971), *Welfare Policy and Industrialization in Europe, America and Russia*, New York: Wiley.
Rodgers, B. N., J. Greve and J. S. Morgan (1968), *Comparative Social Administration*, London: Allen and Unwin.
Rubinow, I. (1913), *Social Insurance, with Special Reference to American Conditions*, New York: Holt.
Sabates-Wheeler, R. and S. Devereux (2007), 'Social protection for transformation', *IDS Bulletin*, **38** (3), 23–8.
Sainsbury, D. (1996), *Gender, Equality and Welfare States*, New York: Cambridge University Press.
Semmel, B. (1960), *Imperialism and Social Reform: English Social Imperial Thought, 1895–1914*, Cambridge, MA: Harvard University Press.
Skidelsky, R. (2000), *John Maynard Keynes Volume Three: Fighting for Britain 1937–1946*, London: Macmillan.
Srivastava, P. C. (1964), *Social Security in India*, Allahabad: Lokbharati.
Stephens, J. (1979), *The Transition from Capitalism to Socialism*, London: Macmillan.
Tang, K. L. (2000), *Social Welfare Development in East Asia*, New York: St. Martin's Press.
Timonen, V. (2003), *Restructuring the Welfare State: Globalization and Social Policy Reform in Finland and Sweden*, Northampton, MA: Edward Elgar.
Titmuss R. M. (1974), *Social Policy: An Introduction*, London: Allen and Unwin.
Townsend, P. (ed.) (2009), *Building Decent Societies: Rethinking the Role of Social Security in Development*, New York: Palgrave Macmillan.
van Ginneken, W. (2007), 'Extending social security coverage: concepts, global trends and policy issues', *International Social Security Review*, **60** (2–3), 39–59.
Wilensky, H. (1975), *The Welfare State and Equality*, Berkeley. CA: University of California Press.
Wilensky, H. (2002), *Rich Democracies: Political Economy, Public Policy and Performance*, Berkeley. CA: University of California Press.
Wilensky, H. and C. Lebeaux (1965), *Industrial Society and Social Welfare*, New York: Free Press.
Williams, F. (1989), *Social Policy: A Critical Introduction*, Cambridge: Policy Press.
Wilson, E. (1977), *Women and the Welfare State*, London: Tavistock.
World Bank (1994), *Averting the Old Age Crisis. Policies to Protect the Old and Promote Growth*, Washington, DC: World Bank.
World Bank (2012), *Resilience, Equity and Opportunity: The World Bank's Social Protection and Labor Strategy 2012–2020*, Washington, DC: World Bank.

PART II

China

3. The transition of social protection in China

Kinglun Ngok

China's long-documented history shows that, traditionally, the family was revered as the core unit of society and the primary provider of social care (Wong, 1998). The family kinship system functioned as the most important safety net (Chen, 2012). The influence of government was mediated through kin and local groups. Under Confucian paternalism, the imperial government and the elite were responsible for the provision of public welfare. The most vulnerable, particularly those without familial support, were eligible for government aid. Although the government played an important role in famine relief and natural disaster relief, the role of government in people's well-being was supplementary, and public welfare provisions were minimal and temporary. In the era of the Republic of China, prior to 1949, due to a lack of state authority and a poor economy, China failed to establish a solid social protection system. Although some social legislation was enacted during this period, there was neither sufficient authority nor resources to enforce it, with only small-scale experiments on workers' welfare funds and social insurance attempted. In contrast to this weak state provision, charitable bodies, especially missionaries, played a notable role in social protection, filling the vacuum created by family structures weakened by war and widespread destitution (Wong, 1998). On the whole, the pre-revolutionary social protection system in China was characterized by a residual model of welfare with Chinese idiosyncrasies, which coexisted with an economy of scarcity and subsistence agriculture (Wong, 1998).

The tradition of relying on families and local collectives in welfare provision was maintained after China was transformed into a socialist state in 1949. From this time, China's social protection system has undergone significant changes. This chapter intends to examine the changes in the social protection system since the foundation of the People's Republic of China (PRC). Aside from the introduction and conclusion, this chapter has three sections: the first discusses the social protection system from 1949 when the PRC was established to the beginning of the economic reform of the late 1970s; the second looks at the changes to social protection before 2002; the third examines new developments since 2002.

SOCIAL PROTECTION BEFORE THE ECONOMIC REFORM (1949–78)

If we use the economic reform starting from the late 1970s as a turning point, the development of social protection in China can be roughly divided into two stages: pre-reform and post-reform. The latter can be further divided into three sub-stages, which will be examined later.

During its period of planned economy, guided by socialist ideology, China promoted public ownership of productive materials and on the basis of this the government prioritized equity and stressed organized distribution. Economically, the state prioritized heavy industries. At the same time, it used the *hukou* (household registration) system to divide rural and urban populations, and set up two separate social protection systems in rural and urban areas. During this period, the state monopolized major social resources and controlled individual lives and opportunities for personal development. In a highly organized, centralized and monotonous social structure (Leung and Nann, 1995), a state-dominated social protection system that differentiated rural and urban areas was set up. This became the foundation of a Chinese society that was characterized by dualism. In this dualistic 'socialist China' the state's role in providing social welfare had two branches: an institutional branch in which the state provided relatively comprehensive welfare and services to urban residents, especially workers based on the work unit, the state-owned enterprise (SOE) system; and a residual branch in which the state only provided very limited assistance and support to urban and rural residents who were not part of the work unit system. The provision of social protection was mainly through urban work units and rural people's communes.

In cities and towns, the state set up a social protection system for urban workers based on the labour insurance system, which was set up in the early 1950s. Labour insurance initially covered only industrial workers in state-owned enterprises, but later extended to employees in service industries. According to Wong (1998), the labour insurance system for the urban workforce had three salient features. First, it offered comprehensive benefits, including protection for sickness, invalidity, maternity, medical care, retirement and death. Second, benefits levels were generous. Third, they were non-contributory and were funded entirely by employers. These features made labour insurance 'comparable to the most advanced social insurance systems in the world' (Wong, 1998, p. 190). The labour insurance system, along with other collective welfare facilities provided by enterprises such as dormitories, canteens, bath houses, nurseries, clinics, libraries and schools, meant that SOE – also called the 'work unit system' (Lu, 1989) or 'work unit socialism' (Womack, 1991) – acted as a 'mini welfare state' (Gu, 2001). This social protection system played a key role in meeting the basic needs of workers and their dependents, and was considered to be the masterpiece of socialism. Like state workers, cadres, party employees state organizations and other public institutions were protected comprehensively by publicly funded social programmes such as free medical care, pensions, housing, and other benefits in cash and in kind.

In rural areas, the population was organized in people's communes, 'multi-functional units for production, consumption, residence, social services, and development entrepreneurship' (Shue, 1988, p. 60). As collective institutions, communes provided protection for peasants from many risks, such as bad weather, poor harvests, natural disasters and deprivation arising from disability (Wong, 1998). In this sense, communes gave rural families a measure of material security. The welfare arrangements made by communes included cooperative medical care, the 'five guarantees' scheme, relief for households suffering from hardship, disaster relief and aid to veterans (for details, see Wong, 1998). The 'five guarantees' system, established in 1956, provided the most basic social protection in rural areas. Under this system, rural collectives guaranteed food, clothes, health care, housing and burial services for the elderly, disabled, widowed and children without income, working ability and family support (Wong, 1998). This basic social protection system was still in use in 2012. Compared with their city-dwelling counterparts, peasants in rural areas had a very low level of social protection and the types of risks covered were also very limited.

In sum, during Mao's era, China developed a dualistic collective-based social protection system which offered differential treatment to rural and urban residents through work units and rural communes. Though collectivism made minimal state welfare tolerable (Wong, 1998), the state did directly or indirectly play an important role in providing social protection. Of course, compared with rural residents, those in cities, especially state workers and officials, benefited much more from the state-dominated social protection system. While the level of welfare benefits between rural and urban areas was vastly different, there was no serious social inequality within urban and rural areas. During this period, China was considered to be one of the most equal societies in the world. It is generally believed that prior to the economic reform of the late 1970s, the Chinese government successfully guaranteed the basic needs of the population despite the economy not being developed, with the social system being more developed than the economic system (Guan, 2008).

CHANGES IN SOCIAL PROTECTION POST-ECONOMIC REFORM (1978–2002)

Since the inception of the 'reform and opening' policy in the late 1970s, in order to change the backward status of the national economy, China engaged in a large-scale socio-economic transformation oriented towards economic development. During this transition, the state focused on economic development. The government's role in creating economic policies was stressed, and social protection policies were adapted to serve the economy. The purpose was to promote the enhancement of economic efficiency and economic growth. During the period from 1978 to 2002, two sub-stages in the development of social protection policy can be identified.

First Sub-stage (1978–92): The Decline of Collective-based Social Protection

The post-Mao economic reform started in rural areas in the late 1970s when the Household Responsibility System (HRS) was introduced to stimulate farmers' work incentives. With the widespread introduction of the HRS, the old commune system was dismantled by the mid-1980s. Following the initial success of the rural economic reform, the Chinese government extended the reforms to the cities in the mid-1980s, and the SOEs became the main target of reform. By the mid-1980s, many SOEs were facing increasing competition from non-state enterprises. In order to make SOEs more competitive in a market-orientated economy, the government tried to reform the rigid employment and wage system practiced in SOEs. The most significant break with the old employment system was, undoubtedly, the introduction of a labour contract system in 1986. It indicated that the government had broken the previous promise of full employment to socialist workers. As a result of the contract-based employment policy, Chinese workers had to cope once more with unemployment after three decades of job security in a communist economy (Chan et al., 2008).

In rural areas, the decollectivization of agricultural production and the death of the commune system since the late 1970s yielded great incentives to peasants' production, and brought about positive impacts on rural development. However, the dismantling of rural economic collectives and the lack of collective accumulation for welfare purposes had produced many social regressions. Without the protection provided by the collective, the vast majority of the rural population had to be responsible for their own welfare, including the support of the elderly, children and dependants. The 'five guarantees' scheme, targeted at the most vulnerable peasants, stood on the verge of collapse as peasants were reluctant or unable to pay welfare levies. Without the funding for operations, the once-praised cooperative medical scheme – a collective health insurance scheme in rural China – collapsed, leaving more than 80 per cent of the rural Chinese population not covered by any health care insurance (Wong, 2004).

Though SOEs in China functioned as important welfare institutions, their contribution to the national economy was limited as the majority of them were unable to run at a profit. Lack of production incentive, poor management, waste, overstaffing, high costs of employee welfare and low labour mobility led to the inefficiency of SOEs. To make SOEs competitive and profitable, the government decided to launch an enterprise reform in 1984. In doing so, the first strategy was to reform the employment system, which until this point was so rigid that it was known as the 'iron rice bowl'. As well as diversifying channels of employment, one fundamental reform measure was to introduce a contractual system of employment, indicating the end of the more secure 'iron rice bowl'. In line with the reform of the employment system, in particular the introduction of the labour contract system, China established an unemployment insurance system, which provided protection for contractual workers when their employment contracts expired. At the same time, pension insurance was placed on the reform agenda. Shanghai and several other cities started to experiment with social pooling for urban pensions. Though its costly welfare function was recognized as one of the key reasons for the plight of SOEs, no significant reform measure was introduced to dismantle the work unit welfare state in the 1980s.

In view of the declining welfare function of the work units, China started to turn to 'communities' for welfare delivery. In 1987, the Ministry of Civil Affairs proposed to develop urban community services. In that year, the Ministry of Civil Affairs held a community service forum and made it clear that it would encourage community members to provide social services in the spirit of mutual help and solve the social issues locally (Wong, 1998).

Second Sub-stage (1992–2002): The Formation of Social Insurance-based Social Protection

If we can claim that the 1980s was a period of declining collective-based social protection, especially in rural China, the 1990s was a period of dramatic change in social protection, as shown by the collapse of the work unit welfare system and the formation of a social protection system dominated by social insurance programmes. During this period, radical enterprise reforms forced the SOEs to gradually separate their welfare functions from their commercial activities, spelling the end of the work unit welfare system. As an alternative to the collective welfare arrangements, the Chinese government intended to establish social insurance-oriented social protection for the urban workforce. Meanwhile, due to the full withdrawal of the state from social welfare services and the growing marketization of education, health care, housing and other social policy areas (Wong and Flynn, 2001), all of the main areas of social protection policies underwent major restructuring.

After the Tiananmen Square protests of 1989 and the collapse of communist regimes in the Soviet Union and Eastern Europe in the early 1990s, the pursuit of economic growth turned into a 'GDPism' (economic growth worship) in China as economic prosperity became the key source of the legitimacy of the Communist Party. Thus, the Chinese government formulated a policy guideline of 'efficiency first, equity second'. As a corollary, economic development as measured by the growth rate of gross domestic product (GDP) became the paramount policy goal of the Chinese government. The state, resultantly, focused only on GDP growth and ignored its role in ensuring that all people benefited from the resulting economic prosperity.

To support the reforms of SOEs and minimize the fiscal burden of the state, the government took many measures to reduce welfare expense, minimize the welfare commitments of SOEs and privatize public services. Social welfare programmes which were originally attached to SOEs were gradually divested. In other words, SOEs were no longer able to provide generous packages of welfare and benefits, such as pensions, health care, housing and schooling to their employees. Meanwhile, public money for public services was gradually reduced due to the limited fiscal capacity of the state. To finance public services, government departments, SOEs and service providers in the public sectors were encouraged to make use of market mechanisms in service provision. As a result, marketization became popular in the main public service sectors, such as education and health care (Wong and Flynn, 2001). The market-oriented economic reforms and marketization of public services brought about uncertainties and risks to hundreds and thousands of people, especially those who worked in the SOEs.

The repercussions of SOE reform on the urban workforce are notable. Workers not only lost the generous package of occupational benefits, but were also exposed to the threat of joblessness. In other words, urban workers found themselves in the situation of losing job security and social security at the same time. Furthermore, no social protection programmes were set up for new workers engaged in new economic entities, such as private enterprises and foreign invested enterprises (FIEs) and people engaged in self-employment. This lack of social protection would constitute a hindrance for the development of a healthy market economy. Against this backdrop, the state decided to restructure the social protection system for the urban workforce. Drawing lessons from the work unit welfare system, the state determined to establish social insurance-based social protection with a risk-sharing mechanism and multiple funding sources.

In order to deepen the reform of the SOEs, minimize the state's financial responsibility and maintain social stability, the state decided to establish a multi-level social security system in the mid-1990s, which included a social insurance system, social assistance, welfare benefits, preferential treatment for soldiers and their family members, mutual assistance and personal saving (Zheng, 2002). The key element of this social security system was a cluster of social insurance programmes, including unemployment, retirement, occupational injury, health care and maternity. As mentioned above, unemployment insurance was initiated in the mid-1980s and improved in the 1990s. During this period, of primary importance was the construction of an old-age insurance system for urban workers. Efforts to set up a unified pension insurance scheme started in 1993; after several years of discussion, deliberation and experimentation, a basic pension insurance system for enterprise employees was formally introduced in 1997. This basic pension scheme for urban workers was composed of two tiers: social pooling and individual accounts. The first tier (social pooling) was based on a pay-as-you-go (PAYG) structure and financed by employers. The second tier (the individual account) was a defined contribution scheme financed by both employees and employers. The 1997 pension insurance reform marked the shift of urban workers' pension schemes from a pure PAYG mode to a mixed pension mode.

On top of the introduction of the workers' pension insurance scheme, in 1998 the state also established a new medical insurance system for urban workers to replace the old health care scheme based on the labour insurance system. Like the workers' pension insurance scheme, this new social health insurance system was also funded by a mixture of social pooling and individual accounts.

Although the new insurance-based social protection began to take shape in the 1990s, the emerging social insurance system was proven inadequate and inefficient in coping with the mounting unemployment and urban poverty caused by the reform of SOEs; it left more people outside of the social protection system, which posed a threat to social stability. From the mid-1990s to the early 2000s, more than 20 million workers in SOEs were made redundant and released from the production process. These workers were called *xiagang* (laid-off) workers (Wong and Ngok, 2006). Many urban people fell into poverty even though they were employed or had a pension or other benefits. The size of the new urban poor in China was estimated, based on different methods, to range from 12 million to 30 million (Leung, 2006). The majority of the new poor consisted of retirees, the unemployed, laid-off employees and even current employees from SOEs for whom benefits or wages could not be delivered on time or sufficiently (Ministry of Civil Affairs, 2002). This became a source of social instability. To pacify the laid-off workers and poor retirees, the government decided to restructure the traditional social relief system and set up an alternative welfare mechanism to address the financial needs of the new poor. In doing so, an anti-poverty policy, known as the Minimum Living Standard Scheme (MLSS) began to be instituted throughout the country from the mid-1990s.

In sum, during this stage, social protection in China went through fundamental changes, which signalled a profound paradigm shift in Chinese social policymaking (Mok, 2008). The policy objectives shifted from prioritizing social equity to economic efficiency. In order to invigorate SOEs and promote economic growth, the collective-based inclusive social protection, with its superior treatment of working men and women in general and of the industrial workers in particular, was gradually dissolved. Social insurance became the backbone of Chinese social protection. However, more time is needed for the burgeoning social insurance system to provide enough protection for workers and the general public. Meanwhile, market mechanisms were introduced in the provision of basic public services such as education, health care and housing. Individuals and households were required to share the cost of social protection with the state and work units. As a result, many people lost their basic social protections. The neglect of the basic needs of the ordinary people has led to much social unrest since the late 1990s.

CHANGES IN SOCIAL PROTECTION POST-ECONOMIC REFORM SINCE 2002: THE EXPANSION OF SOCIAL PROTECTION

The creeping social unrest and increasing social pressures caused by unbalanced economic growth and social development, especially the outbreak of the Severe Acute Respiratory Syndrome (SARS) crisis and its social consequences in 2003, made the new generation of political leadership aware of the importance of social protection and social development in China (Ngok, 2009). The swelling government purse has made the expansion of the welfare commitment of the state possible. Against this backdrop, a rapid expansion of social protection has taken place in China in the first decade of the new century.

In October 2003, the Chinese Communist Party (CCP) introduced the concept of a 'Scientific Outlook to Development' (CCP, 2003). In September 2004, the CCP proposed the idea of building a 'harmonious society' (CCP, 2004). In October 2005, social development was formally listed as a major task of the CCP, which expressed its determination to 'pay more attention to social equity and make all people share the benefits of reform and development' (CCP, 2005). In October 2006, the CCP issued the 'Decision on several major issues of building a socialist harmonious society' (CCP, 2006), which marked the beginning of a new era of social protection. The 'Decision' proclaimed that the state would make efforts to achieve social development, improve social management and push for social progression alongside economic, political and cultural progression. According to the 'Decision', by the year 2020, the trend of growing rural–urban and regional inequality would be gradually reversed; a reasonable and ordered pattern of social distribution would be in shape; and a social protection system that covers both rural and urban residents would be set up and a more comprehensive basic public services system would be developed. In October 2007, the CCP stressed that the government must

> pay more attention to social construction as it develops the economy, and make an effort to protect and improve people's livelihoods, to expand public services, improve social management, facilitate social equity and justice, to try hard to make the whole population to be educated if they attend schools, to be paid as they work, to be treated as they are ill, to be provided as they become older, to be housed as they need to be sheltered, and to push for the construction of a harmonious society. (Hu, 2007)

This was the most comprehensive statement by the CCP on reconstructing the social protection system in China.

Some salient features of this round of social protection expansion can be identified:

First, the development of rural social protection has increased the social inclusion of peasants, who were previously excluded by the urban-biased social protection regime in China for a long time. Under the policy of building a new socialist countryside, the central government has made many efforts since 2003 to promote social development in rural areas, especially to increase the income of peasants. As a result of the reform of rural taxes and fees, the agricultural tax was completely rescinded throughout the country in 2006. Meanwhile, the state has dramatically increased its budget expenditure on agriculture, rural areas and farmers. The MLSS was extended to cover the rural population in 2007. The New Agricultural Cooperative Medical System was established in 2003 and covers almost all peasants in villages. A new type of pension insurance for rural residents has been progressing since 2009. Children in rural areas have been entitled to nine years of free education since 2007.

Second, social protection for migrant workers, the farmer turned new working class in the making (Mok and Ngok, 2010), has been increased. For a long time, migrant workers did not have access to the social protection available to urban residents. To give more protection to rural migrants, the urban social insurance schemes have been extended to cover migrant workers since 2003. More public services, especially labour market services, have been open to migrant workers. Many cities have carried out new policy measures to accept migrant workers as urban residents. Education services for the children of migrant workers have become a top priority in the education policy agenda.

Third, voluntary services and philanthropy have been encouraged as a way to increase participation in social protection. More and more voluntary associations and philanthropic agencies and charitable foundations have been created to boost community-based welfare and services.

Lastly, the social work profession has been created to develop community social care and services. Until the beginning of the 2000s, the social work profession, social work posts and social work services did not exist in China. With the development of social care services in urban communities, social work has been recognized as a profession and social workers have become an important force in social service provision.

Of these developments, the most important one is the expansion of the MLSS throughout the country. The first decade of the new century has witnessed a rapid growth of both the urban and rural MLSS. The number of urban MLSS claimants increased from 11.7 million in 2001 to 23.1 million in 2010. More than 52 million peasants were beneficiaries of the rural MLSS in 2010, an increase from three million in 2001 (Ministry of Civil Affairs, 2011).

Besides providing cash benefits to poor residents, the state also became more active in addressing the medical, educational and housing needs of poor people: in 2003, the rural medical aid system began to be established in China; in 2004, the government started to set up an educational assistance system; in 2005, the urban medical assistance system began to take shape. China has established a social assistance policy framework which consists of the MLSS for both urban and rural residents, the 'five guarantees' scheme for the poorest rural residents, emergency aid for the victims of natural disasters, aid for homeless people in urban areas, and some special programmes to supplement the MLSS, such as educational aid, medical aid and housing allowance. Even legal aid is regarded as an integral part of the social assistance system in China (Ngok, 2010a).

The social insurance system is also in the process of expansion and improvement. In 2005 the state decided to expand the coverage of basic pension insurance for urban workers, and to gradually turn the personal accounts from a PAYG system to a partially funded accumulated system. In 2008, migrant workers, non-public sector employees and people in flexible employment were also encouraged to participate in social insurance schemes. With the enactment of the Social Insurance Law in 2010, the state sought to speed up fund-pooling at provincial level, and to develop a unified and transferable social insurance entitlement nationally. China has established three basic pension schemes to provide social protection for workers, civil servants and farmers. They are: a budget-financed pension scheme for civil servants and employees of public institutions, a basic pension scheme for urban workers, and a newly developed rural social pension scheme for rural residents. Civil servants and employees of public institutions enjoy generous pension benefits that amount to 88–90 per cent of their salary at retirement (assuming an overall career length of 35 years or longer). Recently, in order to alleviate the financial burden, the Chinese central government launched pilot reforms of the pension scheme for employees of public institutions in several provinces. However, this effort has encountered strong resistance from those with vested interests.

CONCLUSION

Going through the history of social protection since 1949, we can see that the social protection system in China has changed in line with the changing social and economic environments. Before the economic reform of the late 1970s, the state, by making use of the collectives, such as work units in cities and communes in villages, dominated and even monopolized social protection provision. There was no market provision or non-government donation. In this period, the nascent socialist nation launched major social reform and introduced a series of progressive social protection policies, among which of primary importance was the labour insurance system for urban workers. Though the state emphasized social equality and welfare redistribution and took on major responsibilities in the provision of social welfare services, a dualistic social protection framework was created for urban and rural China. As social rights were tied to household registration status and employment status, there were serious discrepancies between rural social protection and urban social protection in terms of coverage and benefit levels. Even within urban social protection, social rights were conferred according to the ownership structure of individual work units and the employment status of workers. As a corollary, there was no uniformity of social protection in China. In addition, social protection before the economic reform was characterized by the fusion of social welfare services with the employment system. This important feature led to the formation of the work unit welfare system, which had a significant impact on the work and life of urban workers (Lu, 1989; Walder, 1986).

The advent of a market economy from the end of 1970s has undermined and overturned the existence of collective-based social protection in the planned economy. To replace and augment the pre-existing social protection framework, the state sought to establish in the 1990s a multiple-level social protection system with social insurance schemes as its core. The efforts to build a comprehensive social insurance system had some success in the 1990s, with four insurance schemes gradually established, including unemployment, pension, work injury and health care. Unlike the old labour insurance system, which actually became an enterprise insurance scheme in 1969 when its risk-sharing mechanism was broken down during the Cultural Revolution, the emerging social insurance system aimed to be accessible to the whole of society, with unified funding and universal coverage. Notwithstanding, the new social insurance system still suffered from limited coverage, fragmented and overly decentralized management and insufficient funds, and could not satisfy the huge social needs of workers brought about by the market economy. In light of this, the state decided, in the late 1990s, to establish a modern social assistance based on the MLSS. However, these efforts were confined mainly to providing protection for state workers who were negatively impacted by the collapse of the work unit welfare system. The new workforce created by the market economy, especially the huge number of migrant workers, was not adequately protected.

More importantly, in the 1990s, as economic development became the major state goal and social policy had to serve economic growth, the state directed fewer resources towards social protection; many welfare and social services that used to be provided by the state (via SOEs) were shifted to individuals, households, communities and the market. In the provision of basic services such as education, health care, employment and housing, there was a trend towards marketization. As a result, despite significant economic growth, a massive socially disadvantaged population also emerged due to a lack of effective social protection, placing huge pressure on social stability.

At the start of the twenty-first century, in light of a series of social issues, such as rural and urban disparity, regional inequality and unbalanced social and economic development, the Chinese government decided to prioritize social protection and strike a balance between economic growth and social development. Thus, an expansion of social protection came into practice in 2003. As a result, many old social programmes have expanded their coverage, particularly the social insurance programmes, and a number of new social policy programmes have been launched, moving China's social protection regime beyond the occupation-based social insurance model. By 2012, China's social protection covered not only urban workers, but also migrant workers, and those outside of the formal labour market as well as within it, albeit with different degrees of protection.

China's social protection during the planned economy era was designed to 'serve the economic goals' (Ngok, 2010b). Social protection was regarded as part of the production process: it was a means to satisfy workers' rather than citizens' needs. The state did not really address citizenship and social citizenship; on the contrary, it used the household registration system to institutionalize the differences between rural and urban identity and the entitlement to welfare (Shi, 2009).

Although China's social protection has been undergoing rapid expansion since the dawn of the twenty-first century, social citizenship has not become a policy issue in the development of social protection. To a large extent, the current social protection expansion is not a result of a strong social welfare movement or a labour movement existing as part of a strong civil society. Instead, it is the result of the response of the Chinese leadership to the social crisis brought about by the all-out development approach practiced in the last two decades of the twentieth century. In other words, these changes are related to the imperative to maintain social and political stability. Though the coverage of social protection is enlarged, and more of the population is included, China's existing social protection is still under the influence of the *hukou* system, the localization of social spending and the over-decentralization of social administration. Even the social insurance system is suffering from financial and administrative fragmentation. The central government's efforts to upgrade the management of the funding for the basic pension insurance for urban workers have been fruitless due to resistance from local areas, especially those which are well off. As local governments, under political pressure from the central government, have put much more effort into developing social protection, a strong trend of localization or regionalization of social protection based on local citizenship and local finance is taking shape, which will lead to a proliferation of local welfare states in China (Ngok and Zhao, 2011). If this trend persists, it will be more difficult for China to develop nationally unified social protection. As Wong (1998) points out, for the Chinese population the prospect of universal social rights is a distant vision.

REFERENCES

CCP (Chinese Communist Party) (2003), *The Decision on Several Issues about the Improvement of the System of Socialist Market Economy*, 14 October, Beijing: CCP Document.

CPP (2004), *The Decision on Strengthening the Building of the Party's Governing Capacity*, 19 September, Beijing: CCP Document.

CPP (2005), *The Suggestions on the Formulation of the Eleventh Five-year Plan of National Economy and Social Development*, 11 October, Beijing: CCP Document.

CPP (2006), *The Decision on Several Major Issues of Building a Socialist Harmonious Society*, 11 October, Beijing: CCP Document.

Chan, C. K., K. Ngok and D. Phillips (2008), *Social Policy in China; Development and Well-being*, Bristol: Policy Press.

Chen, J. Y. (2012), *Guilty of Indigence: The Urban Poor in China, 1900–1953*, Princeton, NJ: Princeton University Press.

Gu, E. X. (2001), 'Dismantling the Chinese mini-welfare state? Marketization and the politics of institutional transformation, 1979–1999', *Communist and Post-communist Studies*, **34**, 91–111.

Guan, X. P. (2008), 'Forewords', in D. W. Xu (eds), *Towards a Developmental Social Policy: A Study of the Transition of Social Policy in China*, Beijing: Social Sciences Academic Literature Press, pp. i–v.

Hu, J. T. (2007), *Hold High the Great Banner of Socialism with Chinese Characteristics and Strive for New Victories in Building a Moderately Prosperous Society in All Respects, a Report to the Seventeenth Party Congress*, 15 October, Beijing: CCP Document.

Leung, J. (2006), 'The emergence of social assistance in China', *International Journal of Social Welfare*, **15**, 188–98.

Leung, J. and R. Nann (1995), *Authority and Benevolence: Social Welfare in China*, Hong Kong: The Chinese University Press.

Lu, F. (1989), 'The work unit – a special type of social organization', *Chinese Social Sciences*, **1**, 71–89.

Ministry of Civil Affairs (2002), *China Civil Affairs' Statistical Yearbook 2002*, Ministry of Civil Affairs of the People's Republic of China, Beijing: China Statistics Press.

Ministry of Civil Affairs (2011), *China Civil Affairs' Statistical Yearbook 2011*, Ministry of Civil Affairs of the People's Republic of China, Beijing: China Statistics Press.

Mok, K. H. (2008), 'The paradigmatic shifts of China's social policy since the inception of reform and open door policy', *Chinese Public Policy Review*, **2**, 1–21.

Mok, K. H. and K. L. Ngok (2010), 'A new working class in the making? The rise of the peasant workers and implications for social policy in China', *Work: Journal of Prevention Assessment and Rehabilitation*, **38** (3), 241–56.

Ngok, K. L. (2009), 'State capacity, policy learning and policy paradigm shift:

the case of the institutionalization of the "theory of scientific development" in China', *Korean Journal of Policy Studies*, **24** (2), 1–23.
Ngok, K. L. (2010a), 'Social assistance policy and its impact on social development in China: the case of the minimum living standard scheme (MLSS)', *China Journal of Social Work*, **1**, 35–52.
Ngok, K. L. (2010b), 'The changing role of the state in welfare provision: sixty years of social policy development in China', *Chinese Public Policy Review*, **4**, 39–69.
Ngok, K. L. and H. Zhao (2011), 'The development of localization of social security system and its constraints: a case study of the integration of social pension insurance systems in Dongguan City, Guangdong Province', *Public Management Research*, **7**, 39–52.
Shi, S. J. (2009), 'Sub-nationalization of social protection: the spatial-politics transformation of social citizenship in China', *Taiwanese Sociology*, **18**, 43–93.
Shue, V. (1988), *The Reach of the State: Sketches of the Chinese Body Politic*, Stanford, CA: Stanford University Press.
Walder, A. G. (1986), *Communist Neo-traditionalism: Work and Authority in Chinese Industry*, Berkeley: University of California Press.
Womack, B. (1991), 'An exchange of views about basic Chinese social organization – transfigured community: neo-traditionalism and work unit socialism in China', *The China Quarterly*, **126**, 313–32.
Wong, L. (1998), *Marginalization and Social Welfare in China*, London and New York: LSE and Routledge.
Wong, L. (2004), 'Market reforms, globalization and social justice in China', *Journal of Contemporary China*, **13** (38), 151–71.
Wong, L. and N. Flynn (eds) (2001), *The Market in Chinese Social Policy*, London: Palgrave.
Wong, L. and K. L. Ngok (2006), 'Social policy between plan and market: "xiagang" (off-duty employment) and the policy of the re-employment service centers in China', *Social Policy and Administration*, **40** (2), 158–73.
Zheng, G. C. (2002), *The Changes and Evaluation of China's Social Security System*, Beijing: Renmin University Press.

4. Current approaches to social protection in China

Yapeng Zhu

Alongside profound economic, social and demographic changes, the Chinese social protection system has also undergone profound changes in the past decades. In order to address various social problems and poverty resulting from the transition to marketization and social transformation, the government has introduced several new social protection measures, especially after the global financial crisis. This chapter examines current approaches to social protection and reviews their preliminary impacts on meeting social needs of vulnerable groups and to poverty alleviation.

SOCIAL TRANSFORMATION, SOCIAL NEEDS AND SOCIAL PROTECTION IN CHINA

The last three decades have witnessed China's phenomenal economic growth and remarkable social transformation. During this period, the country's economy has been growing by an average rate of 9.8 per cent and it is now the second largest in the world after that of United States. China's rapid social transformation has generated great demand for social services and social security, which has required a major shift of social policy. First, the large-scale rural–urban migration and consequent risks and social problems have posed a major challenge to the social policy system (Cook, 2002; Li, 2006; Nielsen et al., 2005). Second, the accelerating trend towards an aging population, rural–urban migration and the undermining of the traditional role of the family in social service delivery have created unprecedented social problems. Third, market reforms and economic globalization have had an uneven impact on different social groups, regions and industries (Han, 2005), re-stratifying social structures and aggravating social polarization and inequality (Lu, 2004; Sun, 2003). New forms of urban poverty have emerged and a new urban underclass, mainly comprised of low-income households, laid-off workers and rural migrants, has been created (Leung and Wong, 1999; Liu and Wu, 2006).

Fourth, like most developing countries (Leisering, 2009), many Chinese citizens, and especially those in the informal sector, have been exposed to new forms of insecurity during the marketization reform (Cook, 2002). Last, despite great efforts made by the government and remarkable improvement in livelihoods as a whole, there is still absolute poverty in rural China: increasing social needs in the countryside have posed a big challenge to the social policy (Zhu, 2012). In response to these social needs and social risks, the Chinese government has in recent years advanced a new policy goal of building a 'harmonious society'. This represents a paradigmatic shift from the excessive emphasis on economic growth to a balanced development of economic development and social equality (Ngok and Zhu, 2010). Following this goal, a series of policy adjustments such as a rapid increase in social expenditure, more state commitment to education, public health and housing, and noticeable changes in social protection, have been carried out.

FABRIC OF THE CHINESE SOCIAL PROTECTION SYSTEM

The social protection system in China has undergone development, restructuring and improvement. Broadly, the current institutional framework of social protection mainly consists of two basic systems: first, social insurance and social assistance and, second, labour market policy. These systems are administered and implemented by different government ministries. The social assistance system includes separate minimum livelihood security schemes for urban and rural residents, the 'five guarantee' scheme in rural areas, medical assistance, educational assistance, housing assistance, legal assistance and poverty relief. The social insurance system includes basic pension insurance for urban employees and residents, basic medical insurance for urban employees and residents, and unemployment insurance, injury insurance and maternity insurance for urban workers; there is also new rural cooperative medical insurance and rural pension insurance for peasants. In addition, there is also interim assistance available to help those temporarily trapped in hardship or at risk of falling into poverty.

MAJOR SOCIAL PROTECTION SCHEMES IN CHINA

Responding to the poverty problem and other social needs, the Chinese government has introduced various measures designed to promote social protection. Developments in social protection policy can be seen in five fields, namely social assistance, social insurance, child welfare, labour market participation and an allowance for old people.

Social Assistance

Social assistance is a safety net or the last resort when people fall into poverty. It is designed to provide cash transfers to those in temporary financial difficulty or who have no means of income and livelihood. Several social assistance programmes are carried out in both urban and rural areas in China.

The most important social assistance programme is the Minimum Living Standard Scheme (MLSS). This scheme aims to provide material aid to residents and their families once their income is below the official set minimum living standard. It was first introduced in Shanghai in 1993 and targeted at only the urban poor, being extended to pilot cities in the mid-1990s. In 1999, the State Council promulgated Regulations of the Urban Minimum Living Program (The State Council, 1999).

This marked the establishment of this programme throughout the country. Starting from 2003, the government widened support for the target group and provided its members with medical assistance, educational assistance, housing subsidies (both in cash and in kind) and an allowance for heating, and gradually established a comprehensive social assistance system for the urban poor. In May 2012, more than 21.6 million urban citizens or 11.1 million households were benefiting from this programme with an average monthly subsidy of 240 yuan per capita (Ministry of Civil Affairs, 2012b).

In rural areas, there are two main social assistance programmes. The Rural Minimum Living Standard Security Scheme (RMLSS) is a means-tested arrangement that provides assistance to those most in need in rural areas. Although this programme was originally adopted in urban areas, the idea of ensuring a minimum living standard for low-income rural people was first proposed in 1990 and initially tested on the rural poor in Shanxi province (Tang, 2006). It was expanded in 1999 after pilot projects were carried out. However, the programme was selectively implemented and only benefited about four million people or 0.4 per cent of the total rural population by 2003 (Tang, 2006). It was only in 2007 that the scheme was extended over the whole of China. By May 2012 it covered more than 26.9 million rural households, around 52.4 million people. The average monthly benefit was about 108 yuan (Ministry of Civil Affairs, 2012a). A significant factor in the expansion of this programme, besides reducing poverty, was to alleviate conflict between local officials and farmers and compensate those peasants who lost their farmland (Chan, 2010) because of expropriation for development.

The other form of social assistance in rural China is the traditional 'five guarantee' programme, targeted at the poorest and most vulnerable social groups in the countryside. Introduced in the 1950s, this programme aimed to provide 'five protections' of basic life necessities, including food, clothes, accommodation, medical and funeral services and education for eligible groups. It was mainly financed by resources from each rural collective until the central government committed itself to funding the scheme in 2006. This has meant that the programme has transformed from a collective mutual welfare arrangement into a formal modern social policy (Zhu, 2012). By the end of 2010, the 'five guarantee' scheme had been extended to 5.3 million rural households totalling 5.6 million rural residents (Ministry of Civil Affairs, 2011) and provided basic coverage for almost all eligible rural residents. This programme has played a very important role in protecting the poorest and most marginalized people in the countryside.

In addition, temporary social assistance programmes, including medical aid, education assistance and housing assistance have also been established. Eligible families – namely target groups for the MLSS in both cities and the countryside and the 'five guarantee' programme in rural areas – are entitled to apply for educational assistance, medical assistance and housing assistance when needed.

Social Insurance

In order to protect Chinese citizens from various risks in the marketized and globalized world, several social insurance schemes have been formulated or reformulated in China. In the past, comparatively speaking, urban residents benefited from a more comprehensive contributory social insurance system, including pension, health, unemployment, maternity and occupational injury, while rural China had long been neglected. Rapid developments in social security have taken place in both urban and rural China, in health and old-age pensions in particular.

(a) Pension insurance

The Chinese pension insurance system is characterized by distinctive fragmentation. It mainly consists of three programmes, namely rural social pension insurance, basic social pension insurance for urban employees, and basic social pension insurance for urban residents. In addition there are generous arrangements for retirement tailored for civil servants.

In rural areas, the old pension insurance was dismantled with the introduction of economic reform. To respond to the challenges of a rapidly aging population, urbanization, family planning policy and migration, the state strove to reintroduce pension insurance in the countryside. In 2009, a national framework for rural pensions was formulated and pilot reforms were carried out in one-tenth of the country's counties. The reform is planned to be gradually extended across the country by 2020. The new scheme is co-financed by three parties: individual participants, the rural collectives and the state. Learning from previous lessons, the state plays a major role with clearly defined responsibilities for the central and local governments in terms of finance and administration. Central finance subsidizes all the basic funds for old-age pensions for the middle and western regions in line with the standards decided by the central government, and subsidizes 50 per cent of such funds for wealthier eastern regions; local governments were required to subsidize at least 30 yuan per year for each participant in 2011. All rural people who are not members of the government's urban social pension system are eligible to join. Each participant has a lifelong account. The pension consists of two components, the base pension and individual contribution. Both belong to the account holder. Normally participants are eligible to receive a pension at the age of 60 years if they have contributed for 15 years. By 2011, 1914 counties in 27 provinces and four municipalities directly under the central supervision had implemented the programme and about 326.4 million farmers had enrolled (Ministry of Human Resources and Social Security of the People's Republic of China, 2012). Thus China's pension system has made steps to benefit broad rural areas.

There are two pension insurance programmes in cities. One is social pension reform for urban employees. It was established in 1997 and underwent adjustments in 2000 and 2005. The programme is based on a combination of a social pooling account and an individual accumulation account. The contribution rates were 20 per cent of the total wage for enterprises and 8 per cent for employees. Individual accounts were originally established with a contribution rate of 11 per cent of a worker's wage, into which individuals contributed 8 per cent and enterprises 3 per cent. In 2000, the size of the individual account was reduced from 11 per cent to 8 per cent to be solely paid by individuals. Enterprise employees who have reached retirement age as provided by law (60 for male employees, 55 for female cadres and 50 for female workers) and who have contributed their share of the premiums for 15 years or more are entitled to receive a basic pension every month after retirement. The basic pension consists of two parts: base pension and pension from the personal account. The amount of the base pension is about 20 per cent of an average employee's monthly wage in that area in the previous year. The monthly pension from the personal account was equivalent to the funds in the individual account divided by 120 (months). In 2005, the state adjusted the benefit formula. The amount of pension from an individual account was recalculated taking into account life expectancy, retirement age and interest accumulated in the account. Participants are now entitled to receive a monthly payment equivalent to the accumulated funds in the individual account divided by 139 instead of 120. The base pension also takes into account both the average and individual wage prior to retirement and the years the participants had contributed (Xu and Zhang, 2012). Initially, the pension insurance programme mainly covered employees in formal sectors, namely state-owned enterprises, urban collective enterprises, foreign-invested enterprises and urban private enterprises. Since 2003, it has been extended to those who are employed in a flexible manner in urban areas. By the end of 2011, 283.9 million urban employees were participating in pension insurance for urban employees (Ministry of Human Resources and Social Security of the People's Republic of China, 2012).

In order to guarantee provision for retirement for urban residents who are not affiliated to employers, a Pilot Social Pension Insurance for Urban Residents was announced in 2011 and planned to be extended nationwide by 2012 (The State Council, 2011). Basic principles for this new initiative include broad coverage, protection at the basic level, flexibility and sustainability. It is targeted at urban residents over 16 years old (students excluded) who are not eligible for basic pension insurance for urban employees. It is non-compulsory. The framework is quite similar to the rural basic social insurance programme. The scheme is funded by individual contributions and governmental subsidy. Individual participants are allowed to choose from 10 annual contribution rates ranging from 100 yuan to 1000 yuan (The State Council, 2011). The central government provides the base for insurance while local governments are required to provide a subsidy of no less than 30 yuan per year to each participant. Each participant has a pension insurance account, and individual contributions and the state subsidy belong to participants. The pension benefit consists of two components: base insurance and individual account. The standard of the base insurance set by the central government is 55 yuan monthly, which can be improved by local governments according to the local situation. Participants aged over 60 years are eligible to collect monthly pensions. By the end of 2011 this programme had been implemented in 1902 counties and 5.4 million urban residents were enrolled, of which 2.4 million had begun to receive pensions (Ministry of Human Resources and Social Security of the People's Republic of China, 2012).

In addition, experiments have been carried out to establish a specific pension insurance system for the huge number of rural–urban populations in pilot cities such as Guangzhou, Shenzhen, Beijing and Shanghai, where migrants have concentrated.

(b) Medical insurance

Currently, there are predominantly three basic medical insurance schemes in China, aiming to cover all Chinese citizens and provide them with a basic medical service. Since 1994, the government has re-established a comprehensive, rural community-based medical system, namely the New Rural Cooperative Medical Scheme (NRCMS), in rural areas. The premium is contributed by farmers, supported by collectives and subsidized by the state (the central government and local governments). In 2003, the annual premium was 30 yuan per person (10 yuan each from central and local governments, and 10 yuan from individual residents). The government rapidly raised its subsidy to this scheme. In 2012, the central government further increased its contribution to 240 yuan and the contribution of farmers was also elevated to 60 yuan. Along with these developments, the coverage of the NRCMS and the utilization of medical services has increased, while the cost of medical services has been reduced. By the end of 2011, more than 831 million farmers, or 97.5 per cent of the rural population, were enrolled in the NRCMS (Ministry of Health, 2012). The total expenditure of the NRCMS amounted to 111.4 billion yuan, benefiting 840 million farmers (State Statistical Bureau of People's Republic of China, 2012). Despite these achievements, excessive personal expenditure on medical treatment is still a significant financial burden for many rural households (Sun et al., 2009). Despite advancements, one study emphasized the need to improve the management capacity of the scheme and review the overall policy design (Zhang et al., 2010).

In cities there are two main health insurance schemes, namely the Urban Employees' Basic Medical Insurance scheme (UEBMI) and the Urban Resident Basic Medical Insurance (URBMI) scheme. The UEBMI was established in 1998 after drawing on local experiments. All urban employers, including enterprises (state-owned enterprises, collective enterprises, foreign-invested enterprises, private enterprises), governmental agencies, public institutions, social organizations, private non-enterprise units and their employees are required to participate in the basic medical insurance scheme. Both employers and employees jointly pay the premium, at rates of 6 per cent and 2 per cent respectively of the employee's salary. The premium is based on a combination of two parts: social pooling funds and individual saving accounts. The employee share (2 per cent) and 30 per cent of the contribution paid by the employer are put into the individual saving account; the remaining 70 per cent of the employer's share is paid into the social pooling fund. The social pooling fund and individual saving account are managed and used separately subject to different arrangements on the deductible amount and maximum payment of medical costs. Participants are eligible to receive medical services and to be reimbursed for their medical costs subject to different benefit and reimbursement models. By the end of 2011, 252.3 million people were enrolled in the scheme (State Statistical Bureau of People's Republic of China, 2012).

URBMI was piloted in 79 cities and the state strove to extend it to all cities from 2010. The finance source of URBMI is similar to the NRCMS scheme. The cost is jointly shouldered by the state and residents. The government share of the premium contribution in 2008 was at least 80 yuan per person, with the central government subsidising half to the western and middle regions. By the end of 2011, 220.7 million people had participated in the URBMI (State Statistical Bureau of People's Republic of China, 2012).

(c) Unemployment insurance

Along with deepening state-owned enterprise reform, a gradual establishment of a market economy and further exposure to challenges of globalization, unemployment has been one of the most serious problems facing China, especially when both the domestic and the international economy were experiencing a slowdown. In 1999 the Chinese government issued the Regulations on Unemployment Insurance, which institutionalized and standardized unemployment insurance in China. This mandatory system aims to alleviate the economic distress brought about by unemployment, to guarantee basic living standards of the unemployed and to promote their re-employment. It covers urban enterprises and institutions and their employees, including self-employment. However, farmers are not covered. Employers are required to contribute to the scheme at a rate of 2 per cent on the basis of their total salary; staff and workers in enterprise and institutions pay an unemployment insurance premium at a rate of 1 per cent on the basis of their salaries. Unlike many other countries, unemployment benefits in China are not earnings-related (Vodopivec and Tong, 2008). Instead, the benefit level is set by the local authorities and should not be lower than the locally determined minimum wage. Those who have contributed to the scheme for at least one year, been unwillingly suspended from employment and have undergone unemployment registration and requested new jobs are eligible to receive unemployment benefits. The duration of benefits varies in accordance with the applicant's period of contribution: a person who has contributed for less than five years, 5–10 years and more than 10 years is entitled to receive benefits for up to 12 months, 18 months and 24 months respectively. Contracted employees in rural areas who were recruited by urban enterprises are not required to contribute to the scheme themselves; accordingly they are given a lump sum living allowance if they have had one year of continuous service and their employer has contributed to the scheme. In response to the global financial crisis, the unemployment benefits have been enlarged to cover employment training and induction (Du, 2008). With the implementation of the Social Insurance Law in 2011, unemployment insurance has extended to peasant workers engaged in urban enterprises, who are entitled to be treated equally to their urban counterparts as regards both contribution and benefits. In addition, an unemployment monitoring system has been established so that the government can obtain exact information and accordingly organize better countermeasures. By the end of 2011, more than 141.9 million people had enrolled in the unemployment insurance scheme. The average unemployment benefit per capita was 604 yuan per month (National Audit Office, 2012).

Child Welfare

China has made a breakthrough in child protection and child welfare. A comprehensive blueprint for the coming decade for child development and child welfare entitled *Development Outline for Chinese Children (2001–2010)* (Nation Working Committee on Children and Woman under the State Council, 2001) was publicized in July 2001. The Chinese government set up the principle of 'putting children first' and proclaimed it would extend the coverage of child welfare so as to establish a universal child welfare system. In addition, a specific programme was introduced to protect orphans. In 2009, the Ministry of Civil Affairs set up a subsidy scheme to protect a minimum standard for orphans, providing 600 yuan monthly for orphans in adopted families and 1000 yuan for orphans in government-funded orphanages and nursing homes. In November 2010, the central government further promulgated a comprehensive policy framework entitled 'Opinions on strengthening the protection of orphans' (General Office of the State Council, 2010). It explicitly stipulates regulations and arrangements for proving security for and protecting and assisting orphans, including sections on displacement, basic living, education, health care, housing and other practical difficulties and problems. Crucial in the central initiative was the establishment of a cash subsidy scheme targeted at orphans. Two and a half billion yuan was allocated, benefiting 655000 orphans (*People's Daily*, 2011). This marks a breakthrough in child welfare in China, reflecting a transformation of the government's opinion on its responsibilities in child welfare: the state should step in when core family cannot effectively provide life necessities for children

(Philanthropy Research Institute of Bejing Normal University and One Foundation and Centre, 2011, p. 2).

A student nutrition improvement programme in rural compulsory education was launched in 2011. In order to improve the nutritional condition of children, especially in poverty-stricken rural areas, the central government decided to appropriate 16 billion yuan a year to provide a subsidy to every student in primary and middle school of three yuan for lunch for school days. The new initiative is benefiting about 26 million students in nearly 680 counties (General Office of the State Council, 2011). Local governments were also encouraged to take measures to improve children's nutrition. In addition, besides the exemption of fees for education in 2007, the government began to increase the livelihood allowance by 1 yuan per day for students with economic difficulties in boarding schools from autumn 2011. This means that students from poor families in primary school and middle school will respectively receive 4 yuan and 5 yuan daily allowances for living expenses (General Office of the State Council, 2011).

Despite these developments, child welfare remains residual, targeting only orphans and disabled children (Philanthropy Research Institute of Bejing Normal University and One Foundation and Centre, 2011).

Labor Market Interventions

Another social protection measure which does not involve direct cash transfer concerns occupational skill training and employment regeneration. A big breakthrough in this regard was the promulgation of the Employment Promotion Law in 2007, which emphasized employment promotion as a key responsibility of the government. It stipulates regulations relating to employment promotion, such as policy supports, employment service and management, vocational education and training, employment discrimination, employment aid, supervision and inspection. In January 2012, the State Council reasserted the active employment policy in its *Notice of the State Council on Approving and Forwarding Employment Plan (2011–2015)* (The State Council, 2012). This document specifies various measures to create jobs and facilitate employment, ranging from spurring economic development and adjusting industrial structure, to tax reduction, providing micro credits, subsidizing social insurance and jobs, encouraging business start-ups, developing public works and philanthropic institutions, subsidizing intermediate agencies, employment services and occupational training. Among these measures, the establishment of an extensive network of employment information centres and an integrative urban–rural labour market are emphasized. The employment information centres provide guidance and support to jobseekers, particularly to rural–urban migrants, so that they can find jobs in small towns without permanently leaving their hometown. Occupational training for farmers is also emphasized. In 2009 alone, 11 million rural people received job training to improve their job skills (Yang, 2010). Provinces are required to subsidize the cost of job training and establish a specific provincial-level fund for job training. The central government envisages that all rural workers should be able to receive training by 2015 (Yang, 2010). In addition, the state adopts an active financial policy, provides tax preferential policies and financial assistance to the self-employed, for start-ups and for the development of the service sector, such as elderly caring, community service and childcare.

Senior Allowance

The government has introduced a universal senior allowance for elderly people over the age of 80 years. Although this programme is not means-tested, many of the recipients are poor and many have been negatively affected because of retirement and having no source of income. In order to support them, the Ministry of Civil Affairs urged the establishment of the allowance scheme in 2009. So far the programme has developed slowly. Nevertheless, the introduction of the senior allowance is believed to be 'a significant change and innovation of the traditional residual social welfare system', realizing 'a breakthrough from temporal, irregular assistance to regular and institutionalized security' (General Office of Ministry of Civil Affairs, 2009).

PRELIMINARY IMPACTS OF SOCIAL PROTECTION

As a whole, China's social protection policy has brought about remarkable achievements. Although rural poverty is still a major problem, sustained economic growth and the great efforts made by the Chinese government in the past decades have led to what the World Bank in March 2009 described as an 'enviable' achievement in terms of poverty reduction. In terms of China's official poverty standard, the poverty rate in rural China fell from 18.5 per cent in 1981 to 2.8 per cent in 2004 (World Bank, 2009), indicating that about 126 million people had been lifted out of poverty. Along with economic growth and social development, living conditions in poor areas have greatly improved. The poverty-stricken rural population decreased from 94.2 million in 2000 to 26.9 million at the end of 2010. Even in accordance with the new national poverty line, which increased from 865 yuan in 2000 to 1274 yuan in 2010, the proportion of poor people in the total rural population decreased from 10.2 per cent in 2000 to 2.8 per cent in 2010 (Information Office of the State Council of the People's Republic China, 2011). In 2011, the Chinese government further raised the official poverty threshold to 2300 yuan (362 US dollars), an increase of more than 80 per cent compared to the standard in 2010. This sharp increase is closer to the international standard of 1.25 US dollars a day, but by this standard 128 million people are still in poverty (*Xinhua News*, 2011), 122.4 million of whom are in rural areas (State Statistical Bureau of People's Republic of China, 2012). Explicitly, poverty alleviation remains a long way ahead.

Despite the achievement, there are major disparities in income between urban and rural areas. Although the incomes of rural people have increased in absolute numbers, income inequality between the rural and urban population has widened. For instance, the annual per capita net income of rural residents increased from 3587 yuan in 2005 to 6977 yuan in 2011, while the disposable income of urban residents rose from 11 759 to 21 810 yuan during the same period (State Statistical Bureau of People's Republic of China, 2012). Due to urban bias and insufficient institutional protection in the rural areas, most of the country's poverty is found in the rural areas.

CONCLUSION

Significant improvements have taken place in social protection in China over recent years. The developments can be marked in several aspects. First, there is a trend that the very limited residual social safety net and social protection provided through rural employment collectives has evolved into a more comprehensive and inclusive system characterized by social insurance schemes jointly funded and administered by the central and local governments and by the collectives and individuals (Zhu, 2012). Second, the government is striving to re-establish a social protection system in both urban and rural areas, aiming to provide some kind of protection and security for all citizens. This can be seen from the introduction of pension insurance schemes for both rural and urban residents, the former being previously excluded by arrangements covering only urban employees. Noticeably, rural China has gained much emphasis in this new wave of social policy expansion. Third, new measures and strategies have been introduced and the scope of social protection expanded to the most vulnerable social groups, such as the very old and children. In addition, special attention has also been given to the special needs of women, such as providing a longer period of maternity leave, special treatment on occupational protection and equal job opportunities.

Despite these developments in social protection, more specific goals focused on poverty alleviation are necessary. Social protection cannot simply serve as a tool for maintaining social stability and strengthening the legitimacy of the regime (Holbig and Gilley, 2010). The Chinese government should transcend a piecemeal approach and develop a more systemic and inclusive response to risk and vulnerability so as to effectively respond to these problems. In so doing, a rights-based approach to social protection needs to be introduced in China. Social policy should be based on social citizenship and conceived as the social right of citizens rather than as a favour from the government. Steps have been taken in this direction with the introduction of a universal free compulsory education policy and a universal seniors' allowance, but much more needs to be done to achieve this goal. Last but not least, innovations in policy instruments and strategies are important. Learning from the experiences of other countries is crucial, especially in improving administrative capacity, incorporating plural actors, social organizations, businesses and the market in service delivery.

REFERENCES

Chan, C. K. (2010), 'Re-thinking the incrementalist thesis in China: a reflection on the development of the minimum standard of living scheme in urban and rural areas', *Journal of Social Policy*, **39**, 1–19.

Cook, S. (2002), 'From rice bowl to safety net: insecurity and social protection during China's transition', *Development Policy Review*, **20** (5), 615–35.

Du, Y. (2008), 'China attempts to enlarge the scope of unemployment insurance funds (zhong guo chang shi kuo da shi ye bao xian jin zhi chu fan wei)', *Xinhua News*, accessed at http://news.xinhuanet.com/newscenter/2008-11/20/content_10388014.htm.

General Office of Ministry of Civil Affairs (2009), 'Notice on the transferring of certain policies on Ningxia's Establishment of Senior Allowance Scheme (guan yu zhuan fa nixia jian li gao ling lao ren jin tie zhi du you guan zheng ce de tong zhi)', document of General Office of Ministry of Civil Affairs, No. 151, 4 June, accessed at http://fss.mca.gov.cn/article/tzgg/200906/20090600031777.shtml.

General Office of the State Council (2010), 'Opinions on strengthening the protection of orphans', 16 November, Beijing, accessed at www.mca.gov.cn/article/zwgk/fvfg/shflhshsw/201303/20130300432672.shtml.

General Office of the State Council (ed.) (2011), 'Opinions on implementing student nutribution improvement program for compulsory education in rural areas', General Office of the State Council, accessed at www.moe.gov.cn/publicfiles/business/htmlfiles/moe/s6197/201206/137685.html.

Han, K. (2005), *Economic Globalization, Social Stratification and Social Security (She hui Fen ceng He She hui Bao zhang)*, Beijing: China Labour and Social Security Publishing House.

Holbig, H. and B. Gilley (2010), 'Reclaiming legitimacy in China', *Politics & Policy*, **38** (3), 395–422.

Information Office of the State Council of the People's Republic China (2011), 'The development-oriented poverty reduction program for rural China', 16 October, Beijing.
Leisering, L. (2009), 'Extending social security to the excluded: are social cash transfers to the poor an appropriate way of fighting poverty in developing countries?', *Global Social Policy*, **9** (2), 246–72.
Leung, J. C. B. and H. S. W. Wong (1999), 'The emergence of a community-based social assistance programme in urban China', *Social Policy and Administration*, **33** (1), 39–54.
Li, B. (2006), 'Floating population or urban citizens? Status, social provision and circumstances of rural and urban migrants in China', *Social Policy and Administration*, **40** (2), 174–95.
Liu, Y. and F. Wu (2006), 'The state, institutional transition and the creation of new urban poverty in China', *Social Policy and Administration*, **40** (2), 121–37.
Lu, X. (2004), *Social Mobility in Contemporary China*, Beijing: Social Sciences Academic Press.
Ministry of Civil Affairs (2011), 'Statistical report on social service development in 2010', 16 June, Beijing, accessed at www.mca.gov.cn/article/zwgk/mzyw/201106/20110600161364.shtml.
Ministry of Civil Affairs (2012a), 'National situation of rural minimum living standard security in May 2012 above county (2012 nian 5 yue fen quan guo xian yi shang nong cun di bao qing kuang)', accessed at http://files2.mca.gov.cn/cws/201206/20120621135427139.htm.
Ministry of Civil Affairs (2012b), 'National situation of urban minimum living standard security in May 2012 above county (2012 nian 5 yue fen quan guo xian yi shang cheng zhen di bao qing kuang)', accessed at http://files2.mca.gov.cn/cws/201206/20120621135200275.htm.
Ministry of Health (2012), 'Summary of China health statistics for the year 2012 (2012 nian zhong guo wei sheng tong ji ti yao)', accessed at www.chinacdc.cn/tjsj/gjwstjsj/201206/W020120608368277572334.pdf.
Ministry of Human Resources and Social Security of the People's Republic of China (2012), 'Statistical communique of human resources and social security development', accessed at www.gov.cn/gzdt/2012-06/05/content_2153635.htm.
National Audit Office (2012), 'Audit report on social insurance funds', 2 August, accessed at www.audit.gov.cn/n1992130/n1992150/n1992500/3071265.html.
Nation Working Committee on Children and Woman under the State Council (2001), *Development Outline for Chinese Children (2001–2010) (zong guo er tong fa zhan gang yao (2001-2010))*, 22 May, Beijing, accessed at www.nwccw.gov.cn/html/08/n-121208.html.
Ngok, K. and Y. Zhu (2010), 'In search of harmonious society in China: a social policy response', in K. H. Mok and Y.-W. Ku (eds), *Social Cohesion in Greater China: Challenges for Social Policy and Governance*, Singapore: World Scientific Publishing Company, pp. 69–94.
Nielsen, I., C. Nyland, R. Smyth, M. Zhang and C. J. Zhu (2005), 'Which rural migrants receive social insurance in Chinese cities?: Evidence from Jiangsu survey data', *Global Social Policy*, **5** (3), 353–81.
People's Daily (2011), 'Orphan subsidies raised throughout China', *People's Daily*, accessed at http://english.people.com.cn/90001/90776/90882/7452272.html.
Philanthropy Research Institute of Bejing Normal University and One Foundation

and Centre (2011), 'Child welfare in China – stocktaking report 2011', Beijing, accessed at www.bnu1.org/profit/research/87.html.

State Statistical Bureau of People's Republic of China (2012), 'Communique of national economy and social development of the year 2011', 22 February, Beijing, accessed at www.gov.cn/gzdt/2012-02/22/content_2073982.htm.

Sun, L. (2003), *Cleveage: Chinese Society since 1990s (duan lie: 90 nian dai yi lai de zhong guo she hui)*, Beijing: China Social Science Publishing House.

Sun, X., S. Jackson, G. Carmichael and A. C. Sleigh (2009), 'Catastrophic medical payment and financial protection in rural China: evidence from the New Cooperative Medical Scheme in Shandong province', *Health Economics*, **18** (1), 103–19.

Tang, J. (2006), 'Minimum Living standard system in urban and rural area: history, reality and propects', *Hongqiwengao*, **18**, 14–17.

The State Council (1999), 'Regulations on guaranteeing minimum living standard of urban residents', No. 271, accessed at: www.gov.cn/gongbao/shuju/1999/gwyb199933.pdf%3E.

The State Council (2011), 'Guiding opinions of the State Council about the pilot social pension reform for urban residents (guo wu yuan guan yu kai zhan cheng zhen ju min she hui yang lao bao xian shi dian de zhi dao yi jian)', 21 August, Beijing, accessed at www.gov.cn/zwgk/2011-06/13/content_1882801.htm.

The State Council (2012), *Notice of the State Council on Approving and Forwarding Employment Plan (2011–2015) (guo wu yuan guan yu pi zhuan cu jin jiu ye gui hua (2011–2015) de tongzhi)*, 8 February, Beijing, accessed at www.gov.cn/zwgk/2012-02/08/content_2061165.htm.

Vodopivec, M. and M. H. Tong (2008), 'China: improving unemployment insurance', World Bank, Social Protection Discussion Paper (0820), Social Protection and Labor.

World Bank (2009), 'From poor areas to poor people: China's evolving poverty reduction agenda – an assessment of poverty and inequality in China', March, accessed at www.worldbank.org.cn/china.

Xinhua News (2011), 'China raises poverty line by 80 pct to benefit over 100 mln', accessed at http://news.xinhuanet.com/english2010/china/2011-11/29/c_131277041.htm.

Xu, Y. and X. Zhang (2012), 'Pensions and social assistance: the development of income security policies for old people in China', *Aging in China*, 43–59.

Yang, Z. (2010), 'State Council's report about work situations of rural labor force transfer and labor rights protection (guo wu yuan zhuan yi nong cun lao dong li bao zhang nong min gong quan li gong zuo qing kuang de bao gao)', 28 April, accessed at http://news.workercn.cn/contentfile/2010/04/29/072726878717468.html.

Zhang, L., X. Cheng, X. Liu, K. Zhu, S. Tang, L. Bogg, K. Dobberschuetz and R. Tolhurst (2010), 'Balancing the funds in the New Cooperative Medical Scheme in rural China: determinants and influencing factors in two provinces', *The International Journal of Health Planning and Management*, **25** (2), 96–118.

Zhu, Y. (2012), 'Social protection in rural China: recent developments and prospects', *Journal of Policy Practice*, **11** (1–2), 42–58.

5. Future trajectories for China

Bingqin Li

The review of the development of Chinese social protection in the last two chapters suggests that the system has been evolving over time. A key question is whether the trend of past changes will continue. And, if there are going to be some changes, then what are the factors that may bring them about? This chapter examines the trend in growing social protection spending and coverage and the factors that drive growth and possible reform in the near future. It will then examine the major social and economic changes that may affect the nature of social needs and will conclude by examining the challenges to the responses to these social needs.

FUTURE PROSPECTS FOR THE GROWTH OF SOCIAL PROTECTION ON CURRENT AND PLANNED POLICIES

Since the late 1970s, the Chinese welfare system has gradually shifted from a state-funded welfare system in cities and a collective-funded system in rural areas to a system in which the state and employers played less of a role in cities, while in rural areas there was little protection. However, this system caused lots of social and economic problems and there has been a U-turn in recent years. Starting from the early 2000s, the state began to take on greater responsibilities. A welfare state is gradually taking shape.

The major trends can be summarised as follows:

First, the total amount of spending is increasing. From 1985 to 2011, the real growth rate of the national social safety-net (SSN) was on average 16 per cent per year. The proportion of real SSN as a part of real gross domestic product (GDP) increased from about 1 per cent in 1998 to 3 per cent in 2011. Even though the proportional increase is not dramatic, considering the long-lasting fast growth in GDP, the absolute amount spent on SSN has more than doubled from 1998 to 2012. SSN clearly gained in importance in national spending as well: it rose from less than 2 per cent of gross national expenditure to nearly 11 per cent in 2011. Because of the system change in the 1990s, there was a dramatic increase in SSN spending in the mid-1990s, and the growth rate levelled out, but remained above 10 per cent. Furthermore, more types of social protection are offered to users (*China Statistical Yearbook*, various issues).

Second, more people are included in the system. In the aid sector, the total number of people that received medical aid in cities increased from 1.15 million in 2005 to 22.22 million in 2010. The numbers for rural areas were 8.56 million to 62.97 million respectively. By the end of 2011, 11.46 million households (22.77 million people) were covered by the Minimum Living Standard Scheme. The number for 2004 was 22.05 million. Another 193000 people received Three-No's Relief (for unsupported old people, the disabled and minors). In rural areas, the number of households receiving the Minimum Living Standard Scheme was 26.73 million (53.06 million people), increased from 4.88 million in 2004. Another 5.30 million households (5.51 million people) were supported by the 'five guarantees funds' (food, clothing, medical care, housing and burial expenses) (Ministry of Human Resources and Social Security of PRC, 2011). In the social insurance system, the number of people who participated in the basic urban medical care social insurance reached 473.43 million by the end of 2011. The number of people who participated in unemployment social insurance was 143.17 million. Those who participated in industrial accidence insurance numbered 176.96 million and 138.92 million joined child birth social insurance (Ministry of Human Resources and Social Security of PRC, 2011). In rural areas, the number of people who participated in the New Rural Cooperative Medicare Scheme reached 832 million (Yang, 2011).

According to the Chinese government's plan, during 2011–15 (12th Five Year Plan), the spending on the social safety net as a proportion of real GDP will continue to grow and it will take a larger share of government revenues. According to the promises made by the government in the People's Congress that took place in March 2012, the target is to increase government spending on SSN to 25 per cent of gross public spending. This indicates a massive development in the importance of social spending.

In terms of financing public spending, as discussed in the last two chapters, Chinese social protection funding comes from two sources: a tax-funded social welfare system and a contribution-based social insurance system. Tax-funded welfare comes from both the central government and local governments. The money can be budgeted in advance or from non-budgetary funds. Budgeted funds are used to protect various social risks such as the Minimum Living Standard Guarantee and unemployment benefits. Non-budgetary spending is mainly because of unexpected damages, such as natural disaster relief or pandemic breakout.

The contribution-based social insurance system is based on individual and/or employer contributions. Social insurance can be used to pool funds among contributors. It can either be used for protecting people against social risks that would demand large spending at a certain period of time – such as illness, childbirth, industrial accidents – or for pooling funds among people who may be in need of saving a larger amount of money over a longer period of time to even out lifetime spending such as for housing and pensions. In China, the social insurance system is not yet fully established across the country. Many people, for example farmers and rural to urban migrants in many cities, were not included in the system. This could be for several reasons. Unwillingness to join was one of the main issues; employers and individuals were reluctant to participate in the state-initiated schemes. This is partly because the potential beneficiaries did not trust the system to deliver the protection promised. At the same time, there were serious problems in the design of the system which is unable as yet to fulfil the needs of the population. For example, migrant workers cannot transfer their contribution to a different city when they have to migrate again because social insurance schemes are not transferrable between provinces. To attract people to join the schemes, the government has subsidised social insurance via taxation. For example, government subsidies play a big part in supporting rural cooperative health care. The purpose was to lower the hurdle for people to join and encourage them to be part of the schemes.

In the future, the total government expenditure on SSN will grow from 1.07 trillion yuan in 2011 to 1.94 trillion yuan in 2015 at a rate of nearly 16 per cent each year. The government spending as a proportion of real GDP will continue to grow and it will use a large part of the public finance revenue. According to the promises made by the government in the People's Congress that took place in March 2012, the idea is to increase government spending on SSN to 25 per cent of gross public spending. This will make SSN relatively more important in overall social spending. However, in the long run, expenditures made through social insurance will continue to dominate. This means more people will make contributions to the social insurance system.

Based on these changes over time, it is not difficult to see that China has been trying to establish a social protection system that would be able to take advantage of contributions from individuals, employers and the state. This system has championed minimal dependence on the state, with individuals and employers the main contributors to the system. The state is the last resort for the people suffering from extreme poverty, but the protection for the poorest has been minimal.

POLITICAL, ECONOMIC AND SOCIAL CHANGES THAT HAVE CHALLENGED THE CHINESE SOCIAL SPENDING PATTERNS

In the past decade or so, crucial social and economic changes have provided serious challenges to the existing social spending trend in China:

The first is demographic changes. The total population will continue to grow in the immediate future; however, it should then stop. The growing trend is going to reverse by 2020 if we use the low variation projection, or by 2040 if we use the high variation model developed by the United Nations Department of Economic and Social Affairs/Population Division (2011). The result is a growing number and a bigger proportion of old people (65+). The old-age dependent ratio has increased from 10 to 13 from 2000 to 2010. Starting from 2010, the growth rate of the older population will accelerate. In the next five years, the ratio will rise to almost 15. This means that a growing proportion of the population will have to be supported by a decreasing proportion of the working population. This would certainly put pressure on the sustainability of the Chinese pay-as-you-go pension system. This may also mean greater pressure on the health care and social care systems. These mean that not only will the size of the social security system grow over time, but there will also be greater demand for a changed spending structure.

Thus far, the low fertility rate has helped China to contain population growth and as a result the child dependency rate has dropped over time and it is expected to continue to drop in the near future and only start to increase from 2020, when the child dependency ratio would drop accordingly. This will partly mitigate the effect of the greater dependency ratio in the older population. However, the total dependency rate cannot escape the structural issue that the lower birth rate also means that the proportion of people who will be able to contribute to the care and support of older people is also decreasing.

The changing demographic structure also has strong implications for economic growth. As estimated by Cai (2010), during 1982 and 2000, the decline in the dependence ratio contributed 26.8 per cent to the growth of GDP per capita. However, the demographic dividend is decreasing as a result of demographic structural changes. The economy will soon reach the Lewis Turning Point. At this point the seemingly unlimited rural labour supply will dwindle and become scarce (Lewis, 1954). More pessimistic views argue that the Lewis Turning Point has already arrived (Zhang et al., 2011). In this sense, the prospect for economic growth, which is crucial for the sustainability of the social insurance-based social protection system in China, will be challenged.

The second is rural–urban migration. In 2011, there were about 253 million rural–urban migrants in cities. The largest group was migrant workers who came to cities to earn more money in urban businesses. There are about 120 million migrants of this type. As discussed by Cai (2010), China had exhausted its demographic dividend, brought about by its favourable demographic structure, but continued to enjoy the second dividend provided by rural–urban migration, which helped to bring large numbers of young labour workers from the countryside to the cities. Their presence helped to lower labour costs and made Chinese businesses competitive internationally. Another group of migrant farmers were 'passively' or even 'forcedly' urbanised because of rapid urban expansion. These farmers lost their lands and homes as city businesses or real estate developers took over their land. According to the Chinese Academy of Social Sciences (2012) about 40–50 million migrants have moved to cities as a result of land grabs since 1978. In recent years, the number has grown by three million annually. It is estimated that by 2030 the total will reach 100 million. So far, these farmers have been turned into 'semi' urban citizens who have had no record of social insurance contribution and have not all been ready to take up manual jobs, as voluntary migrant workers would do. As a result, 60 per cent of them are suffering from poverty in cities. Another type of migrant is farmers, who resettled in cities because of environmental protection (for example, eco-migration), natural disasters (for example, droughts, land inundation) or major projects (for example, Three Gorges Dam). These people lost their means of living and were usually resettled with the help of government funds to a city or suburban area of a city. The number of this type of migrant is relatively small. They have undertaken organised migration and resettlements. To name a few: Three River Source (*sanjiangyuan*) migration affected 10 000 families (50 000 people); Ningxia arid land area migration affected 12 000 households (560 000 people) by 2009; and, it is expected, another 140 000 households (490 000 people) will be affected from the Da Xinganling and Xiao Xinganling mountain areas in Northeast China, to protect forests, and Southern Shaanxi and Baiyushan Mountain migration, to help people to move out of areas that are prone to geological disasters.

The unsatisfied needs of these different types of migrants are different and have different implications for the social protection system. Migrant workers need to settle down in cities, live in affordable houses, get affordable health care, send their children to schools, receive pay that corresponds to their work and not suffer from physical abuse and social exclusion (Li, 2006). After all, when job opportunities are disappearing, they should be able to move to a different place without being trapped by their social insurance contributions. What is often forgotten is their parents and children are usually left at home. As young and middle-aged people move into cities, rural villages are left with people who would be categorised as dependents in cities. As a result, the dependency ratio in rural China is much higher than in cities and they do not really share the benefits of improved labour. Land loss farmers need to get proper compensation for their lost property so that they do not lose their lifeline as they move into cities. They also need social protection like other urban citizens. After all, they need to have a stable source of income to keep them off social benefits (He et al., 2009). The key problem faced by organised migrants is social exclusion. They are resettled in concentrated resettlement quarters of the destination cities. Even though they enjoy urban citizenship, because of cultural differences, a lack of employment opportunities in the destination and even discrimination from urban local residents, they often find it difficult to integrate (Wang et al., 2010).

The third is the political atmosphere. As shown by Li (2012), there has been a major ideology shift in China in the last few decades. The earlier stage of the reform focused on relieving businesses from the 'burden' of social protection. The more recent reforms showed a turn to the Left which highlighted the importance of protecting labour rights. For example, more types of non-contribution-based social protection were introduced to prevent people from falling below the poverty line and grant the originally excluded population the right to certain minimum levels of protection or access to services (such as minimum wage, schooling for rural children). However, this has not meant that solidarity has been enhanced as the policymakers would like it to have been. On the contrary, the split between the Leftist and the Rightist ideologies has become more obvious. As stated by Brown and Hsing (2011), ideology wise, the past 10 years in China was unclear and confusing. However, Li (2012) argues that there is consistency between welfare development and political changes and attitudes towards social protection have been openly used by different political factions to define their political images. The local models of social protection at provincial level have become a key to signal the political stances of the local leaders. This can be observed from the competing Guangdong and Chongqing Models in the recent past.

Another aspect of the political scene is that social conflicts between different interest groups began to be better defined and more articulated. These can be observed in the conflicts between urban versus rural interests in acquiring land usage rights, urban citizens versus migrants in subsidised housing and rights to urban education, migrant workers versus urban employers, urban owner occupiers versus landlords in the context of housing, and so on. These aspects would make it increasingly difficult for the governing party to use one set of principles to represent the interests of all.

These challenges all demand that the Chinese welfare system should be flexible enough to deal with the increased coverage and at the same time respond to the emergent social needs.

POSSIBLE FUTURE POLICY DEVELOPMENTS IN SOCIAL PROTECTION

Currently, the reforms can be best described in broad strokes, such as introducing new and broader coverage. The stress is on setting up the 'big framework' first. In the area of social insurance, the foci are on the number of people covered and the amount of funds collected. It is a similar story in the field of poverty reduction. This approach is often criticised for being overly ambitious, and would unavoidably cause compliance issues (Nyland et al., 2011). However, the reformers tend to stress the stage of the Chinese social and economic development which is considered not yet comparable to the 'matured' Western welfare states (The World Bank and DRC China, 2012). Following this logic, in China the priority seems not to be about how to fine-tune the system, as there is not yet a completed framework and it is important to set up a system first and then do the fine-tuning later. In this way, the reform at this stage is considered to be more 'systematic' and resembles more of a social engineering approach that tries to set the agenda rather than a piecemeal approach that tries to make patchwork corrections. In this sense, the reform is often structural and radical.

As discussed earlier, so far the reforms have been focusing on expanding the social insurance schemes to the exposed groups. Given the already high rate of participation in the national social insurance schemes, one would naturally ask what the proposed higher social spending would be on. The *China 2030* report has proposed three major changes in the social protection system that may result in a bigger role of social protection in the economy (World Bank and DRC China, 2012, pp. 298–9).

First, it proposes a social protection system which tries to offer 'flexicurity' (flexibility + security). The idea is that it is flexible enough for changing individual circumstances, such as job changes and moving between different cities, and to fit to changes in the economy. In this way, it can avoid the labour market distortion developed by past government policies to control labour and the economy and achieve greater economic efficiency. At the same time, workers would enjoy decent pay and conditions that reflect their productivity. To achieve this, the social security system should not become a barrier for workers to move between places and jobs, that is, a social security system that breaks away from the rigidity and constraints caused by the Hukou system.

Second, 'equitable and effective social services' will be developed so that the population would gain in human capital and good health. Ultimately, this will secure a productive labour force. Apart from promoting affordable childcare and free school education to senior secondary level, there will also be newly introduced social spending on early child nutrition and childhood obesity interventions. The health care system would be reformed to protect people against the shock of sudden health care needs. Service quality and cost-effectiveness will be improved and a high-quality primary care network will be set up.

The last is to set up a 'basic but secure social protection system which provides for a moderate level of security for all while respecting fiscal constraints'. The idea is to develop sustainable pension and health insurance systems for all. The system would be defragmented and reliable for all. Care services would be developed for older people and for the poor. A coherent safety net for the poor would be established which would at the same time avoid generating a poverty trap for the 'near poor'.

These three dimensions indicate that China will firmly take the path of a developmental welfare state model (The World Bank and DRC China, 2012). According to Kwon (2009, 2005), in a developmental welfare state, the state strategically uses social welfare/protection to support economic development.

The proposed improvements by the Chinese government are based on a series of assumptions about China's social and economic trends. The first is that the economy will continue to grow; thus the expansion in social protection will continue to enjoy sufficient funds in the future. The logic is that China will become a middle-income and more urbanised country in the near future and the need for improved social protection will be growing. The second is that social needs can be identified using the same approach used in the past; that is, they will continue to be centred on labour market participation. This means individuals will be helped by the state to create a healthy and productive workforce. The third is that the political climate that helps to shape the current system will continue; that is, the centre considering social protection important for legitimising the Communist Party government.

Even though China has been recognised as being a developmental state by many authors (Beeson, 2009; Lin, 2011), as commented by Cook (2012), it is different from the other East Asian countries in that it has a much lower average income per capita and greater inequality, and the central government has had a lower degree of control over the sub-national economy. Whilst the central government develops social security to maintain 'social stability as a basis for its legitimacy to govern', local governments are 'driven by the politics of accumulation and the need to maintain growth in revenues' (Cook, 2012, p. 151). The differential interests between central and local governments are, as commented by many authors, crucial barriers to the centre's control or even monitoring of local implementation. It is not difficult to see that the newly proposed reforms in *China 2030* try to promote an alignment of the central and local interests by 'selling' social protection explicitly as a means to support economic growth and hopefully to bring sub-national governments' motivation in line with the interests of the centre. As intended, this will make China more similar to other developmental welfare state regimes. However, the proposed models would have to face a whole range of challenges in the future.

KEY CHALLENGES TO THE PROPOSED REFORMS IN THE FUTURE

Despite the determination of the central government to reform social protection to make it more flexible and more inclusive, there are several important challenges in realising these changes.

The first is the technical issues that a highly unequal society would have to face. As discussed earlier, there exists a wide gap between rural and urban areas and also between richer and poorer provinces. These huge gaps made it very difficult to adopt a social protection standard or even structure that could fit all. For example, there are various proposals about how to deal with the legacies of Hukou. The ideal scenario is to remove Hukou completely and allow rural–urban migrants to move freely between rural and urban areas. However, the big gap between different localities means that a person who contributes in one place and claims the benefits at another place may not find it worthwhile to contribute more earlier and receive less in the future. The gap also means that it is particularly challenging for local authorities to agree to make social protection entitlement transferrable between different places, especially if the two places are wildly apart in terms of income, living standards and level of economic development. These factors make it very difficult to convince the highly mobile sections of the population, especially rural–urban migrants, to agree to participate (Bärnighausen et al., 2007).

The second is the constraints in the existing government structure. The Chinese government system has four layers of sub-national governments (provincial/municipal, city, county, township/village) in total. These four layers of government offer two motivations: rank-seeking and rent-seeking. Rank-seeking means that local authorities would try to prioritise what would be considered important by the higher authorities. Li and Zhou (2005) found that the promotion of provincial-level officials is significantly linked to their overall economic performance. A similar story was also found at county level (Guo, 2007). This means that the head of a local government may not be keen to support policies that would not contribute to economic growth, even if the centre may be keen to develop social protection. There was a shift from rank-seeking to rent-seeking when economic reform started (Lu, 1999). The issue of rent-seeking has been widely reported in the literature on business-government relationships. In the context of social protection, rent-seeking can be observed in the fierce competition for 'poverty county' status (Park et al., 2007).

There were some reforms to improve the governing structure and put counties directly under the control of provincial-level government. As time moved on, more provinces adopted this new system. This reform simplified the bureaucratic system and turned out to be useful in boosting local economy and partly allowing some rural counties to gain revenues to invest in local public services. In 2009, the practice was formally introduced by the central government to roll out to the whole country. Zhao (2009) showed some improvements in rural schools.

The third is the often-criticised mismatch between funding and the responsibilities imposed on the local governments. In the social protection system, the higher levels of governments define the responsibilities, and lower-level governments enforce them. This mechanism, working together with a decentralised financing system, means that even if there is not enough funding, policies have to be accepted and implemented at the local level. The result is that the local governments reinterpret the policies to suit their own means and purposes (Li and An, 2010). In practice, the central government provides a symbolic amount of funding to local governments in order to legitimise future inspections. At the same time, the local authorities also treat the central government's funding provision as a signal that the centre allows them to go ahead with what they want to do. This type of practice gradually evolves into a voluntary commitment approach in which local governments negotiate with higher authorities about what they can do and promise to deliver (Eichhorst and Bongardt, 2009). The benefit is local involvement in the decision-making process; in this way, policy packages can be more suitable to local circumstances and compliance can be improved. However, there are also some problems with this approach. Because a large part of the funding needs to be raised locally, either at the provincial or the city/county level, richer local authorities can do more than poorer ones. This can potentially increase the gap between sub-national governments and cause further difficulties for transferability between different parts of the country. In this sense, there needs to be further consideration of reforming the public finance system to allow the central government to play a bigger part in harmonising different sub-systems.

To some extent, the strategy to focus on social insurance is an easy solution. It helps to minimise the 'burdens' that city authorities have to take up in providing services and protections to 'outsiders' and has so far been an easier to achieve goal than the complete decoupling of Hukou and social welfare entitlement. This is because, in the social insurance system, employees and employers have to contribute to their own benefits. Occupation-based social insurance has been considered to be solely for the working population, that is, tax payers who have contributed to the local economy. As a result, the argument for improved coverage of migrant workers has won good support. However, offering non-contribution-based welfare turned out to be more difficult to promote. Local governments are less likely to comply. Even if there are national-level policies, local implementation appears to be weak, especially when the central government does not provide funds directly (Davies and Ramia, 2008).

Even though the central government is still cautious about abolishing the Hukou system completely, it has given local governments the power to carry out experiments and find ways to integrate rural and urban schemes locally. There are several local models so far. The first is to integrate rural and urban social insurance systems by extending urban social insurance directly to migrant workers. This has been adopted in several provinces, first in Guangdong province and later Gansu, Shanxi and Hebei. The second is an independent social insurance for migrant workers only. This model was adopted in Chengdu and in Shanghai in the early 2000s (Chan and Zhang, 2009). A third model is to have a semi-urban treatment (or a treatment that is equivalent to small-town Hukou). This system was introduced to grant rural–urban migrants the right to contribute less, in return for lower entitlement. This system was used in Shanghai and several other cities in Zhejiang province to handle the dilemma that city authorities had to face. On the one hand, migrants were unwilling to pay the high contribution rate required for urban citizens. This is because of the large gap in the income and living standards between these cities and other parts of China. If the migrants had lived in other parts of China, they would not have needed to pay so much money as contribution, and it would be quite likely that they would need to move out of these more expensive cities in the future. This means that they contribute more money earlier in these cities, but would only be able to receive less in other cities later. It was difficult to convince migrant workers to accept this deal. On the other hand, the principle of social insurance requires an equal contribution for equal entitlement. As a compromise, a middle-of-the-road treatment was introduced to allow migrant workers to contribute less than urban citizens and receive a lower level of benefits. The fourth is to encourage migrant workers to participate in rural social insurance schemes in their home villages. The assumption behind this model is that migrant workers will return to their home villages when they most need the protection.

Local variations on social protection are good for identifying best practices. However, because these practices are localised, they are only applicable to people coming from the same province. A so-called integrated system is only applicable to workers moving within their own provinces. As a result, the coexistence of multiple models makes it even more difficult for a migrant worker to transfer their entitlement to a different province, and thus further discourages their participation (Zhang and Huang, 2011).

Given the Chinese government's past record for mobilising resources to achieve a policy goal, it is very likely that the desired bigger framework can be set up. However, the longer-term challenges lie in the fact that policymakers still have to further adjust the system according to social, economic and political changes. The reality is that solutions to tackle socio-economic changes may not be accepted politically. As discussed earlier, the general public is no longer as unified as it is often perceived to be and there are clear conflicts in the interests of different social groups. People have developed a stronger sense of protecting their own interests than in the past. For example, in the early 2000s when migrant workers were first allowed to come into cities to work and live, there was little objection, and urban citizens criticised the government for generating barriers for migrants coming to cities. However, as more migrants have begun to live in cities, calls to limit migration in large cities have become louder. There are new proposals at the People's Congress by the People's Representatives to control the number of migrant workers, especially low-skilled workers in large cities like Beijing, Shanghai and Guangzhou. On the one hand, there has been serious criticism of the long-standing unequal university entrance exams taken by urban citizens and migrants (Hannum et al., 2011). On the other hand, there are open protests by urban residents to guard their own children's privilege to an urban education. Another example is the suggestion the government made to raise the retirement age to cope with the pressure faced by the pension system. The resistance was strong. Current employees consider it unfair; they argue that they have already made their contribution according to the state-proposed pension schemes and the state should stick to what they promised. At the same time, there is strong and growing doubt about the government's ability to manage pensions efficiently (Shi and Mok, 2012).

CONCLUSION

It is not difficult to see that the reform of the Chinese welfare system still has a long way to go. Reformers have to face up to social, economic and political challenges. What is more, the administration and public finance systems are too rigid to offer the true flexicurity and minimum support that the central government would like to see. After all, the reform is still focusing on building up a financial structure that can generate long-term sources of funding, but the availability of quality services to all people is only beginning to be discussed.

One key issue that has to be addressed is increasingly divided social interests. It is difficult for the single political party to address conflicting social needs at the same time. Reformers at the top level have begun to accept that they cannot 'design' the solution for the whole of China single-handedly. There needs to be some bottom-up mechanism and a system to help these groups to bargain for their interests. There are some signs of moving in this direction with the greater involvement of local authorities in policy design and the centre's willingness to engage more citizen participation in the policymaking process and service delivery (World Bank and DRC, 2012, pp. 24, 49, 343–6). However, this cannot be equivalent to decentralised funding of social services. How to strike a balance between public finance and governing structure is a serious question that needs to be addressed in the near future.

REFERENCES

Bärnighausen, T., Y. Liu, X. Zhang and R. Sauerborn (2007), 'Willingness to pay for social health insurance among informal sector workers in Wuhan, China: a contingent valuation study', *BMC Health Services Research*, **7** (1), 114.

Beeson, M. (2009), 'Developmental states in East Asia: a comparison of the Japanese and Chinese experiences', *East Asia*, **33** (2), 5–39.

Brown, K. and L. S. Hsing (2011), 'Trying to read the new "assertive" China right', Chatham House Asian Programme Paper, London: Chatham House.

Cai, F. (2010), 'Demographic transition, demographic dividend, and Lewis turning point in China', *China Economic Journal*, **3** (2), 107–19.

Chan, K. W. and L. Zhang (2009), 'The hukou system and rural-urban migration in China: processes and changes', *The China Quarterly*, **160** (6), 818–55.

Chinese Academy of Social Sciences (2012), *China Urban Development Report 2011*, Beijing: China Urban Publishing House.

Cook, S. (2012), 'Rebounding from crisis: the role and limits of social policy in China's recovery', in P. Utting, S. Razavi and R. V. Buchholz (eds), *The Global Crisis and Transformative Social Change*, Basingstoke, UK: Palgrave Macmillan, pp. 141–60.

Davies, G. and G. Ramia (2008), 'Governance reform towards "serving migrant workers": the local implementation of central government regulations', *The China Quarterly*, **193** (1), 140–9.

Eichhorst, U. and D. Bongardt (2009), 'Towards cooperative policy approaches in China – drivers for voluntary agreements on industrial energy efficiency in Nanjing', *Energy Policy*, **37** (5), 1855–65, accessed at www.sciencedirect.com/science/article/pii/S0301421509000585.

Guo, G. (2007), 'Retrospective economic accountability under authoritarianism: evidence from China', *Political Research Quarterly*, **60** (3), 378–90.

Hannum, E., X. An and H. S. Cherng (2011), 'Examinations and educational opportunity in China: mobility and bottlenecks for the rural poor', *Oxford Review of Education*, **37** (2), 267–305.

He, S., Y. Liu, C. Webster and F. Wu (2009), 'Property rights redistribution, entitlement failure and the impoverishment of landless farmers in China', *Urban Studies*, **46** (9), 1925–1949.

Kwon, H. (2005), 'Transforming the developmental welfare state in East Asia', *Development and Change*, **36** (3), 477–97.

Kwon, H. (2009), 'The reform of the developmental welfare state in East Asia', *International Journal of Social Welfare*, **18**, S12–S21.

Lewis, W. A. (1954), 'Economic development with unlimited supplies of labour', *The Manchester School*, **22** (2), 139–91.

Li, B. (2006), 'Floating population or urban citizens? Status, social provision and circumstances of rural-urban migrants in China', *Social Policy and Administration*, **40** (2), 174–95.

Li, B. (2012), 'Social welfare and protection for economic growth and social stability – china's experience', in *Centre for Governance and Leadership, A Changing China – Emerging Governance, Economic and Social Trends*, Singapore: Civil Service College, pp. 39–61.

Li, B. and X. An (2010), 'Migrants as a source of revenue in small town China', *Environment and Urbanisation*, **22** (1), 51–67.

Li, H. and L. Zhou (2005), 'Political turnover and economic performance: the incentive role of personnel control in China', *Journal of Public Economics*, **89** (9–10), 1743–1762.

Lin, Y. (2011), 'Demographic transition, developmentalism and social security in China', *Social Policy Administration*, **45** (6), 678–93.

Lu, X. (1999), 'From rank-seeking to rent-seeking: changing administrative ethos and corruption in reform China', *Crime, Law and Social Change*, **32** (4), 347–70.

Ministry of Human Resources and Social Security of PRC (2011), *2011 Annual Human Resources and Social Security Development Statistical Bulletin (2011niandu renli ziyuan he shehui baozhang shiye fazhan tongji gongbao)*, Beijing, accessed at www.mohrss.gov.cn/page.do?pa=402880202405002801240882b84702d7&guid=e578e8be726c4689a32b91e8f7882a45&og=8a81f3f133d01e170133d36bed3c04d3.

Nyland, C., S. B. Thomson and C. J. Zhu (2011), 'Employer attitudes towards social insurance compliance in Shanghai, China', *International Social Security Review*, **64**, 73–98.

Park, A., S. Wang and G. Wu (2002), 'Regional poverty targeting in China', *Journal of Public Economics*, **86**, 123–53.

Shi, S. and K. Mok (2012), 'Pension privatisation in Greater China: institutional

patterns and policy outcomes', *International Journal of Social Welfare*, **21** (s1), 30–45.
The World Bank and DRC China (2012), *China 2030: Building a Modern, Harmonious, and Creative High-Income Society*, accessed at www-wds.worldbank.org/external/default/WDSContentServer/WDSP/IB/2012/02/28/000356161_20120228001303/Rendered/PDF/671790WP0P127500China020300complete.pdf.
United Nations Department of Economic and Social Affairs/Population Division (2011), 'China', in *World Population Prospects: The 2010 Revision, Volume II: Demographic Profiles*, New York: UNPD, pp. 1–4, accessed at http://esa.un.org/unpd/wpp/country-profiles/pdf/156.pdf.
Wang, Z., K. Song and L. Hu (2010), 'China's largest scale ecological migration in the Three-River Headwater region', *Ambio*, **39** (5–6), 443–6.
Yang, J. (2011), 'At the end of 2011 the number of people joining new rural cooperative medical insurance reached 832 million (2011 niandi xinnonghe canbao renshu dadao 8.32yi)', *Health Economic News (yiliao jingibao)*, 14 June, accessed at http://info.pharmacy.hc360.com/2011/06/140840301021.shtml.
Zhang, Q. and X. Huang (2011), 'A study of which factors influence migrant workers when deciding to participate in pension insurance in Nanjing city of China', *Proceedings of the International Conference on eEducation Entertainment and eManagement*, Bali, Indonesia, 27–29 December 2011, pp. 186–9.
Zhang, X., J. Yang and S. Wang (2011), 'China has reached the Lewis turning point', *China Economic Review*, **22** (4), 542–54.
Zhao, L. (2009), 'Between local community and central state: financing basic education in China', *International Journal of Educational Development*, **29** (4), 366–73.

PART III

India

6. Historical developments and goals of social protection policies in India

Ruth Kattumuri and Manju Singh

The concept of providing for the poor and underprivileged is embedded in Indian culture and philosophy. Understanding its historical perspective is important in order to fully comprehend the nature of social protection in India. This chapter sets out a historical review of various forms of welfare that have contributed towards providing for the needs of people in the country. We attempt to present various concepts of social protection that existed in ancient India from about 3000 BC and begin with an overview of traditions and practices in ancient India spanning the Harappan civilization, the early emperors and some socio-religious institutions. We then present the reforms and the new welfare state approaches prevalent before independence. This is followed by a description of programmes and acts introduced after independence including the five-year plans. The final section discusses evolving growth trends and priorities for social protection in India.

TRADITIONS AND SYSTEMS IN ANCIENT INDIA

The Harappan Civilization

The Harappan civilization developed across the Baluchistan and Pakistan regions around 3500 BCE. These were offshoots of the Chalcolithic culture found in South Asia between 3800 and 3500 BCE who themselves had a rich history and culture (Wright, 2010). Lothal (2400 BCE) was a well-developed city in western India dating back to the beginnings of human migration for commercial pursuits during the ancient Harappan civilization. Archaeological excavations show Lothal to have had well-developed city planning, art, architecture and religious systems. It was a wealthy trading town which made pottery, beads, jewellery and metals and had a flourishing trade with the West. The changing environment and recurrent floods, combined with poor administration and a shortage of resources reduced trading opportunities with cities in the West, which led to a decline in its prosperity. The growth of human pursuits was deterred when faced with destitution caused by natural disasters and resulted in resource limitations and an increase in the poorer classes. Mulchandani (1998) describes a major flood (around 1900 BCE) in the region destroying Lothal altogether. It lacked the capacity to recover. There had been no social security measures to absorb the shocks and any survivors migrated inland. Mulchandani (1998) suggests that this initiated the state's responsibility to meet the social security needs of its poor.

When emperors ruled

The challenging experiences with natural disasters and epidemics made it necessary for kings to remain vigilant to any calamities; being equipped to provide relief for the poor and those affected became one of their main duties. It became the duty of emperors to provide for the welfare of children, women without children, widows, virgins, the helpless and prostitutes. Ways for coping with the effects of famine included public distribution of seeds and food from the royal stores at concessional rates, food-for-work programmes such as building forts or irrigation works, and commandeering private stocks of food for public distribution.

The requirement of emperors to provide for the welfare and well-being of citizens was documented in the fourth century BCE and the Emperor Chandragupta Maurya is renowned for his strong commitment to the welfare of his people. Kautilya, an advisor and minister to Chandragupta Maurya, declared social protection the state's duty in *Arthashastra* (written between the fourth century BCE and second century CE), his treatise on economic policy, statecraft and military strategy. He wrote, 'in the happiness of his subjects lies his (the king's) happiness; in their welfare, his welfare; whatever pleases himself he shall not consider as good, but whatever pleases his subjects' he shall consider as good' (Shamasastry (undated), Chapter XIX). *Arthashastra* does not include the provision of education and health among the state's responsibilities, but social protection and welfare has a wider scope, according to the treatise, that includes the maintenance of social order, increasing economic activity, protection of livelihood, protection of weaker sections of society, prevention of harassment of subjects, consumer protection, protection of children and women and the welfare of slaves and prisoners. Special protection of weaker sections of society was ensured through provisions such as shelter, food and free travel on ferries at the state's expense. Kautilya suggested provision for pensions and maintenance allowances but strongly discouraged handouts.

Shreni (guilds) offered decent work to participants during the Buddhist era (483–544 BCE) and continued over the post-Maurya era (300 CE).

Thaplyal (2001) states that the ancient Indian guild system combined the functions of democratic government, trade union, court of justice and technological institution. Thapar (2000) suggests that the extension of trade during the Maurya period (321–185 BCE) might have helped develop and stabilize the guilds, which at first were an intermediate step between a tribe and a caste. Thapar states that competition must have been an incentive for forming guilds: it was better economically to work in a body than to work individually as a corporation would provide added social status, and assistance could be sought from other members when necessary.

Ashoka (204–32 BCE), a famous Maurya emperor, was influenced by Buddhism and became a philanthropic administrator serving the needs of his people (*rajdharma*) and built universities and promoted equality of race, religion and politics. The principles of *dharma* included non-violence, tolerance to sects, obedience to parents, respect for *Brahmans* and other religious teachers, humane treatment of servants and generosity towards all. The condition of slaves was reportedly much better during the Maurya era (Thaplyal 2001).

Indian socio-political systems at this time provided training, opportunities, support and security, which included: *gurukul*, a tradition of learning, serving by living together with the teacher; *dharamshalas*, sanctuaries or rest houses for pilgrims and other needy people created as religious endowments; *devadasi*, young girls dedicated to the service of the gods/temple so that they would be provided for; giving alms to ascetics, poor and disadvantaged people became a religious obligation. Thaplyal (2001) writes that the systems that were meant to provide security were not exempt from being abused and that Buddhism and Jainism (sixth century onwards) were more egalitarian than Brahmanism.

Kannan and Pillai (2007) suggest that social security provisions during the eighth century AD included pensions and old-age benefits; maintenance allowances; sickness benefits and illness cover (servants who had worked for six years were entitled to three-quarters of their salary for a maximum of six months); and premature death benefits (family members had to be paid allowance of half the salary being earned when the servant died). *Sukraniti*, Sukracharya's exposition of labour relations and justice, dated circa tenth–sixteenth centuries, lays out guidelines for Indian princes and statesmen about how to rule as well as instructions for people on how to be law-abiding. Social protection was considered both private and a state matter (Rangarajan, 1987). Primary responsibility for maintaining the family was placed with the head of the family so that no one could become an ascetic without first providing for his wife and children. Bhattacharya (1970) states that the joint Hindu family system ensured the security of all members, and parental responsibility in the ancient Indian tradition illustrated the relationship of a patron to his clients or master to his servant.

The Mughals (early sixteenth to mid-nineteenth century) introduced *Zakat*, which was regarded as divine obligatory taxation with an aim to provide society with financial security and inculcate moral, social and spiritual values in each individual.

Thus social protection was extensively propounded as a duty of the state and the welfare of citizens has been taken care of to varying degrees by rulers and social systems since ancient times. Kautilya's *Arthashastra*, followed during the Maurya period, and the *Zakat* system, followed during Mughal rule, were forms of taxation of the rich to provide welfare for the poor and helpless. However, implementation seems to have fluctuated based on the commitment of emperors and their advisors, so there is no clear indication of systematic growth in social provision during this period.

Kannan and Pillai (2007) suggest that waves of invasions during the late Middle Ages might have resulted in declines in state-provided social security. The immediate and extended family had the main responsibility for providing for its members. Additional support was provided by religious leaders and institutions, charitable trusts, village communities and philanthropy. Traditional systems of social protection were not adequate to cope with the emergence of the modern state and market economies (Gilbert, 1976; Priyadarshee, 2011). The state had to evolve towards developing formal social protection mechanisms.

BRITISH INDIA

The concept of an enabling security for the poor and disadvantaged has existed in India since its ancient historical foundations. Cultural traditions have dictated the welfare and happiness of Indian people to be an essential and inherent role for its rulers. However, the processes were informal and depended on the largesse of rulers and patrons and were also entrenched within a hierarchical system, which generally precluded inclusion or equality.

The government of British India was conservative in its financial commitment to fulfil the welfare requirements of Indian people. This is evidenced by the extremely poor economic and social indicators when India became independent in 1947. India had among the lowest per capita incomes in the world and about a quarter of the population was living in hunger (Clark, 1972). The headcount ratio of poverty was around 50 per cent; life expectancy at birth was around 37 years, infant mortality was 146 per 1000 live births, the crude birth rate was 41 and crude death rate 25 per 1000 of the population (Radhakrishna and Panda, 2006).

The colonial state would have had to conform to international laws and was active in introducing social reforms through legislation during 1820–57. These reforms included the establishment of colleges and universities, the beginning of telegraph and railways, the raising up of a uniform administration and civil service sector, codification of civil and criminal laws and procedures, alteration of the land revenue system, benefits for factory workers and standardization of taxes. British economic policies from 1857 led to restrictions on internal trade, high inflation that increased food prices, heavy taxation of Indians, conversion of local farmland into foreign-owned plantations, and the export of staple crops to Britain (Sen, 1982). These policies, together with multiple famines (about 25), led to food shortages; as a result, 30–40 million Indians died during the second half of the nineteenth century (Kannan and Pillai, 2007). After initial apathy, recurring famines and agitations forced the British government to set up famine commissions, which led to provision of relief to the elderly and disabled, and public work opportunities in irrigation and building canals were provided for those who could work. These improvements helped reduce mortality levels. There were no major famines after 1902 until the Bengal famine of 1943, which initiated reforms in food grains trade and the development of an urban public distribution system.

Socio-political and Religious Movements

The socio-political situation during the colonial period triggered the development of various socio-religious welfare movements. Alongside the goal of achieving independence, social activists were involved in seeking to establish social legislation which purposed to eradicate harmful social practices and social inequalities, as well as making provisions for social security. These laws included: the Bengal *Sati* Regulation No. 17 of 1829 that made immolation of Hindu widows illegal, the Hindu Widow Remarriage Act of 1856, the Brahmo Marriage Act of 1872, the Hindu Inheritance (Removal of Disabilities) Act of 1928 and the Child Marriage Restraint Act of 1929 (Goel and Jain, 1988). These laws were very important even if only a limited number of people adhered to them or attained the benefits. They formed the basis for relevant welfare schemes after independence (Table 6.1).

Prominent social reformers who worked against inequality and for the provision of social security are: Raja Ram Mohan Roy, known for his efforts to abolish *sati* and who founded Brahma Sabha in 1828, which was inclusive of women; Mohandas Gandhi (1869–1948), who alongside his non-violent fight for independence was involved in the development of policies to increase economic self-reliance and reduce poverty, and led national campaigns against untouchability, worked for religious and communal unity and women's rights; Bhimrao Ambedkar (1893–1956), who undertook doctoral study at the London School of Economics and Columbia University, is the 'father' of the Indian constitution and was actively engaged in eliminating discrimination against Dalits and other underprivileged communities, including improving the status of women; Baba Amte (1914–2008), who founded three ashrams for the treatment and rehabilitation of leprosy patients, the disabled and people from marginalized backgrounds.

New Welfare State Approach

The rapid expansion of capitalist needs in the twentieth century led to the introduction of several labour laws (ILO, 1942). Post-war publications emphasized the requirement to bring all provisions under a single scheme for protection in the event of incapability to work or to obtain work, and to extend this to all employees including self-employed workers in rural and urban areas (ILO, 1944).

The need for social security provision for the working classes became evident to the government when the factory system started to expand with the establishment of cotton mills in Bombay (1851) and jute mills in Bengal (1855). Thus several landmark welfare schemes were initiated during the late nineteenth century and were amended during the early twentieth century and were further expanded after independence (Aspalter, 2003). The Apprentice Act was introduced in 1850 to improve the working conditions and working hours of children and adolescents (similar schemes were introduced by the Tata Group in 1921); this Act was improved in 1961. Under ancient Hindu law, a person converting from Hinduism to another religion became ineligible for inheriting property from their family members. The Caste Disabilities Act of 1850 allowed Indians who converted from one religion to another religion equal rights, especially in the case of inheritance. This formed the basis for the Hindu Inheritance (Removal of Disabilities) Act of 1928. The Hindu Women's Right to Property Act of 1937 amends the Hindu Law to give better property rights to women.

The first Factory Act (1881) introduced labour laws intended to improve the working conditions of the Indian labour force. This Act was applicable to all factories using mechanical power, which were employing 100 or more persons and working for more than four months in a year. This Act went through several iterative improvements. The recommendations of the Rege Committee (set up in 1943) were incorporated by the post-independence government into the Factories Act of 1948, which applies to all establishments employing 10 or more people (20 or more people in institutions not using mechanical power).

The All India Trade Union Congress was set up in 1919. The agitations by Indian reformers during 1920 led to the passing of the Workmen's Compensation Act in India in March 1923. The main objective of the act was to 'eliminate the hardship experienced under the common system, by providing prompt payment of benefits regardless of fault and with a minimum of legal formality' (Law Commission of India, 1974). The Provident Fund Act was enacted in 1925 for social security provision, but when first set up it only provided for state employees and railway workers. All government employees were paid various allowances (children's education, health care, transport and house rent for those not living in official housing) as a proportion of their basic salaries – 50 per cent of basic salary was given to employees living in the four major cities (Delhi, Mumbai, Kolkata and Chennai) and 40 per cent to all others. The Employees Provident Fund and Miscellaneous Provisions Act was introduced in 1952 to provide for the institution of provident funds, a pension fund and a deposit-linked insurance fund for employees in factories and other establishments. The Tata Group introduced a provident fund in 1920. Dearfood Allowance was introduced in Bombay and Ahmedabad in 1920. This developed into Dearness Allowance, which is a percentage of salary added on to help against inflation.

A new phase in the development of social security in colonial India began from 1942, following the global labour movement and International Labour Organisation (ILO) recommendations. The Coal Mines Labour Welfare Fund was constituted by the government in 1944 to provide organized welfare for coalmine workers. The Coal Mines Labour Welfare Fund Act of 1947 was designed to make better provision for financing measures for promoting welfare for labourers employed in the coal mining industry. It was further scaled up in 1952.

William Beveridge (who was born in 1879 in Bengal) published his 1942 report in England recommending that the government should find ways of fighting the five 'giant evils' of 'want, disease, ignorance, squalor and idleness'. The Labour Enquiry Committees would have required governments to fulfil the stipulations of the third Labour Ministers' Conferences during 1940–43. India pressed to follow the development of social security plans as in other countries; the Adarkar, Rege and Sir Joseph Bhore committees were appointed by the government of British India in 1943. The *Adarkar* Commission recommended setting up an integrated system of health, maternity and employment injury insurance; the labour investigation committee (Rege Committee) examined risks that cause insecurity and suggested appropriate welfare methods; the Joseph Bhore Health Survey and Development Committee outlined plans for medical care and health services. According to Kannan and Pillai (2007), while the three reports were comprehensive, the British government disagreed with their scope and recommendations, particularly on its financial contributions to the scheme. The value of these reports was realized in post-independence India as they formed the basis for social security projects, starting with the Employees' State Insurance (ESI) Act in 1948 to provide benefits to employees in case of sickness, maternity and lack of employment. Payment of gratuity became a legal right as stated by the Industrial Disputes Act (1947).

POST-INDEPENDENCE

Independent India followed the recommendations of the committees set up towards the end of British rule (such as Adarkar, Rege and Joseph Bhore) and introduced various government-based social protection schemes. India's development strategy was to establish a socialistic society through economic growth alongside self-reliance, social justice and poverty alleviation (Dev, 2008). The experience with the East India Company resulted in a deep mistrust of market forces and international trade. This, together with evidence of successful industrialization of the Soviet Union and the import-substituting industrialization policies of Latin America, influenced Indian nationalists to favour self-reliant national policies for economic development.

After India became a republic in 1950, a new phase of social security was initiated to tackle poverty and inequality. The Constitution of India stresses provision of socio-economic security as a fundamental right; it upholds equality of opportunity in public employment, the abolition of untouchables, states that every individual is equal by law and prohibits discrimination on grounds of religion, caste, sex and place of birth. Indian Directive Principles of State Policy promote welfare of all people through achieving state order based on justice, equality and fraternity (Constitution of the Republic of India, 1950). The provisions for state order include: right to adequate means of livelihood, distribution of ownership and control of material resources to serve the common good, prevention of concentration of wealth, equal pay for equal work for both men and women, protection of workers and children, opportunities and facilities for children to develop in a healthy manner and in conditions of freedom and dignity, organization of village *panchayats* as units of self-government, effective provision for securing the rights to work, to education, and to public assistance in cases of unemployment, old age, sickness and disability, suitable legislation to ensure a decent standard of life and full enjoyment of leisure and social and cultural opportunities to all workers, a uniform Civil Code for citizens, provision of free and compulsory education for children, and the promotion of educational economic interests for Scheduled Castes (SCs), Scheduled Tribes (STs) and other weaker sections. Articles 38, 39, 41 and 45 stipulate social, economic and political justice, namely equality, health for males and females, right to work and right to education. Article 38(1) specifies the advancement of a social order in which social, economic and political justice forms the basis of all institutions of national life. Article 38(2) stipulates that the state shall aim to minimize inequalities in status, facilities and opportunities, not only amongst individuals but also amongst groups of people who reside in different areas or engage in different vocations. Article 39(e) necessitates the state to direct its policies towards securing the health and strength of male and female workers, that children are not abused and that all citizens are not forced by economic necessity to enter vocations unsuited to their age or strength. Article 41 requires the state, within the limits of its economic capacity and development, to make effective provisions for securing the right to work, right to education and right to public assistance in cases of unemployment, old age, sickness and disablement. Article 45 persists on the introduction of free, compulsory and universal education until age 14, support of educational and economic interests of weaker sections of society, in particular of SCs and STs, and to protect them from social injustice and exploitation (Constitution of the Republic of India, 1950).

The Constitution of India clearly stipulates provision for social protection for its citizens, which is consistent with the country's traditions and culture. Additionally, various Acts had to be instituted to enable setting up formal mechanisms for welfare provision, for example the provident fund, family pension and employees state insurance. Table 6.1, compiled from various sources, provides a comprehensive summary of the evolution of key welfare schemes and Acts in India.

The average growth rate in India during the first three decades after independence remained low at 3.5 per cent and was referred to as the 'Hindu rate of growth'. The primary responsibility for family welfare has been placed with the head of the household. The Green Revolution introduced in the 1960s was important for India to attain self-sufficiency in food grains and reduce hunger. Food grains were provided through fair price shops from the rapidly accumulating stocks.

Employment opportunities for graduates were limited in both public

Table 6.1 India: evolution of labour and social welfare schemes since independence

Year	Schemes/Acts	Description
1956	School midday meals. This was introduced across all states during the 1980s and 1990s	First introduced in Madras Presidency in 1925. Revived by Tamil Nadu (TN) chief minister Kamaraj in 1956 as 'poor feeding'. Expanded by TN chief minister M. G. Ramachandran in 1982 as 'nutritious noon meal programme'. It provides free lunch to children in elementary schools on working days to enable them to attend school and improve their nutritional status. The programme was scaled up nationally through a supreme court ruling in 2001
1961	Maternity Benefits Act	Act to regulate employment of women before and after childbirth. Bihar Maternity Benefit Act in 1946. Tata Group introduced maternity benefit in 1928
1975	Integrated Child Development Services (ICDS)	To improve nutritional and health status of children aged 0–6 years; to lay the foundation for their psychological, physical and social development; to reduce the incidence of mortality, morbidity, malnutrition and school dropout; to achieve effective coordination of policy and implementation amongst the various departments to promote child development; and enhance the capability of the mother to look after the health and nutritional needs of the child through proper nutrition and health education
1977	Food for Work Programme	Creation of additional employment in rural areas, with surplus food grains available in buffer stock paid as wages
1978	Integrated Rural Development Programme (IRDP)	To raise the levels of Below Poverty Line (BPL) families in rural areas above the poverty line by giving them income-generating assets and access to credit and other inputs
1985	Indira Awass Yojana (IAY)	Provides full grants to help rural people below the poverty line belonging to Scheduled Castes (SCs), Scheduled Tribes (STs), freed bonded labourers and non-SC/STs with construction and upgrade to pucca housing. This was scaled up from 1995–96 and implemented as an independent scheme and extended to widows or the next of kin of defence personnel killed in action, ex-servicemen and retired members of the paramilitary forces

1986	Training and Employment Programme for Women	To upgrade the skills of poor and asset-less women and provide sustainable employment by mobilizing them in viable cooperative groups, strengthening marketing linkages, support services and access to credit. Rashtriya Mahila Kosh of 1993 provides micro-credit to poor women for various income-generating activities
1989	Jawahar Rozgar Yojana	To provide sustained employment by strengthening rural economic infrastructure and assets in favour of rural poor. Targeted at people below the poverty line and also for SCs and STs and freed bonded labourers. Thirty per cent of the employment opportunities are reserved for women
1995	National Family Benefit Scheme (NFBS)	Financial assistance given to the family on the death of its breadwinner (amount Rs. 10 000)
1997	Swarnajayanti Shahari Rozgar Yojana (SJSRY)	To provide employment to urban unemployed or underemployed through setting up self-employment ventures or provision of wage employment. It subsumed three earlier schemes for urban poverty alleviation – Nehru Rozgar Yojana (NRY), Urban Basic Services for the Poor (UBSP), and Prime Minister's Integrated Urban Poverty Eradication Programme (PMIUPEP)
1997	Targeted Public Distribution System	Provide essential food and cooking commodities such as wheat, rice, sugar and kerosene through state fair price shops for families below the poverty line. Developed from public distribution system introduced in the 1980s
1999	Integrated Programme for Older Persons (IPOP)	Grants in aid are given to non-governmental organizations (NGOs) for running old-age homes, day care centres and mobile medical units (MMUs). Annapurna scheme introduced in 2000 provides 10 kg of free food grains a month to senior citizens who are on their own and cannot take care of themselves and are not under the targeted public distribution system (TPDS)
1999	Swarnajayanti Gram Swarozgar Yojana	To bring assisted poor families (*Swarozgaries*) above the poverty line by ensuring an appreciable sustained level of income over a period of time, by inter alia organizing rural poor into self-help groups through the process of social mobilization, training and capacity building and provision of income-generating assets
2000	Janashree Bima Yojana (JBY)	Provides life insurance protection to people aged 18–59 years who are below the poverty line or marginally above the poverty line from 45 identified occupational groups, which include all categories below the poverty line

Table 6.1 (continued)

Year	Schemes/Acts	Description
2001	Swadhar Greh Scheme	Ministry of Women and Child Development provides financial assistance for construction of rooms/ cottages/huts for shelter and common facilities like kitchen, bathroom, training hall, recreation room, dining hall, office room, etcetera, and infrastructure facilities like water, electricity, approach road, boundary wall, etcetera
2001	Sarva Shiksha Abhiyan	Indian government programme aimed at the universalization of elementary education
2001	Valmiki Ambedkar Awas Yojana (VAMBAY)	To provide shelter or upgrade existing shelter for people living BPL in urban slums, to achieve the goal of 'Shelter for All'. The objective is also to utilize this initiative to achieve the goal of slumless cities
2005	Mahatma Gandhi National Rural Employment Guarantee Act (MGNAREGA)	An expansion of the Employment Assurance Scheme of 1993. To provide for the enhancement of livelihood security of the households in rural areas by providing at least 100 days of guaranteed wage employment in every financial year to every household whose adult members volunteer to do unskilled manual work and for matters connected therewith or incidental thereto
2007	Indira Gandhi National Old Age Pension	Rs. 200 per month per beneficiary is provided by central government to persons aged 65 years or older and belonging to BPL households
2008	Rashtriya Swasthya Bima Yojana (RSBY)	Ministry of Labour and Employment provides health insurance coverage for BPL families. Beneficiaries are entitled to hospitalization coverage up to Rs. 30 000 for most diseases that require hospitalization
2008	Unorganized Workers Social Security Act	Provides social security and welfare of unorganized workers. National Social Security Fund (NSSF) set up by the Finance Ministry in 2011 with an initial allocation of Rs. 10 000 million to support schemes for unorganized workers such as weavers, toddy tappers, rickshaw pullers and bidi workers

2009	Indira Gandhi National Widow Pension Scheme	A pension of Rs. 30 000 per month (from fiscal 2012–13) to be granted to widows aged 40–59 living BPL
2010	Rajiv Gandhi Scheme for Empowerment of Adolescent Girls	To empower adolescent girls aged 11–18 years, with specific focus on out-of-school girls through improving their nutritional and health status and upgrading various skills like home skills, life skills and vocational skills
2011	Janani Shishu Suraksha Karyakram (JSSK)	To give free entitlements to pregnant women and sick newborn babies

Source: Authors' compilation.

and private sectors even during the 1970s. The benefits offered by government employment policies made civil service and government jobs highly sought after for the status and security they provided. Private sector opportunities increased with the growth of information technology in the 1980s. Globalization opened up additional possibilities for growth. This enabled steady increases in growth during the 1980s and 1990s with the twenty-first century experiencing rapid growth. We have seen above that social protection schemes, as well as their funding, have progressively increased. However, the challenge has been in governance and implementation of established schemes.

Political Interventions

The first Prime Minister of India, Jawaharlal Nehru, was a socialist visionary committed to democracy and the new welfare state. An outline for economic planning was initiated by Subhash Chandra Bose as Congress President in 1938 and was drafted by Meghnad Saha. The British government established a planning board in 1944 and industrialists also formulated independent development plans in 1944. The Planning Commission was formally established by a government resolution in March 1950, with Prime Minister Nehru as its chairman. Its stated objective was to improve the standard of living through efficient exploitation of resources of the country, increasing production and offering opportunities to all for employment in the service of the community (Planning Commission, 1950). Nehru (1955) agonized over the scarcity of national income to provide adequately for welfare:

> there is not much to divide in India because we are a poor country. We must produce wealth, and then divide it equitably. How can we have a welfare state without wealth? Wealth need not mean gold and silver but wealth in goods and services. Our economic policy must therefore aim at plenty. Until very recently economic policies have often been based on scarcity. But the economics of scarcity has no meaning in the world of today.

Nehru envisioned Indians free from ignorance, disease and poverty and constantly strove to enable this in the country.

Indira Gandhi was her father's protégée and was able to implement some plans initiated by Nehru, including abolishing princely states with the 26th amendment to the constitution in 1971. She launched her own anti-poverty programmes, such as the successful election campaign slogan 'Garibi Hatao' (alleviate poverty) in 1971. The anti-poverty programmes created through Garibi Hatao were intended to provide the basic essentials of 'roti, kapada aur makan' (bread, clothes and house) and were funded, developed, supervised and staffed by central government in New Delhi and the Indian National Congress. They were implemented locally and were designed to enhance national support for Indira Gandhi and give the poor political worth (Kothari, 1972). According to Rath (1985), only about 4 per cent of all funds allocated for economic development went to the three main anti-poverty programmes.

The twenty-point programme (TPP), launched by Indira Gandhi in 1975, renewed the nation's commitment to eradicating poverty, raising productivity, reducing income inequalities and removing social and economic disparities. It was revised in 1982 to improve execution. It was restructured under Rajiv Gandhi in 1986 and scaled up by the Congress government in 2006. TPP covers various socio-economic aspects like poverty, employment, education, housing, health, agriculture, land reforms, irrigation, drinking water, protection and empowerment of weaker sections, consumer protection, environment and e-governance. These aspects are covered by Garibi Hatao (poverty alleviation), Kisan Mitra (support to farmers), Shramik Kalyan (labour welfare), Khadya Suraksha (food security), Subke Liye Aawas (housing for all), Jan Ka Swasthya (health for all), Sabke Liye Shiksha (education for all), Alpsankhyak evam Anya Pichhra Varg Kalyan (welfare of SCs, STs, Other Backward Classes and minorities), Mahila Kalyan (women's welfare), Bal Kalyan (child welfare), Yuva Vikas (youth development), Samajik Suraksha (social security), e-Shasan (e-governance). Sonia Gandhi has revived the Nehru-Gandhi family vision of 'unity in diversity' and 'gareeb aadmi' to 'inclusive growth' and 'inclusive social agenda' (secularism and inclusion of Muslims). Rahul Gandhi, during his election campaign in 2012, evoked the slogans of 'garibi hatao' and 'pichrapan hatao' (alleviate backwardness).

It is common among political parties to offer incentives for votes during state elections. For example, in Tamil Nadu, different parties hand out food grains, saris, sometimes even colour televisions, to the public during elections. As evidenced during elections and public demonstrations, the electorate progressively demand 'bijali, sadak aur pani' (electricity, road and water) and most recently good education policies, rural employment, health programmes and the elimination of corruption.

Five-year Plans

The Planning Commission (1950) was responsible for assessing resources, augmenting deficient resources and formulating plans for the most effective and balanced utilization of resources and determining priorities, which formed the basis of the five-year plans (FYP). Jawaharlal Nehru oversaw the setting up of FYPs, which reflect the Directive Principles of State Policy of the Constitution and emphasize the need for social security.

The First (1951–56) and Second (1956–61) FYPs discussed social security in relation to the organized sector, urban wage earners and the avoidance of industrial disputes. The provident fund and other labour welfare schemes were introduced and improved during this period. The Third FYP (1961–66) referred to the social security needs of wage earners beyond the organized sector. It proposed assistance for persons without any means of livelihood or support (such as the physically handicapped, old persons unable to work, women and children), the midday meals scheme was expanded and the Maternity Benefits Act introduced. It also stressed the need for more effective implementation and the Apprentice Act, among others, was scaled up (Table 6.1).

The Fourth FYP (1969–74) referred to the poorest section in the population (the destitute, disabled and pensioners not engaged in any economic activity) with a per capita consumption of 'roughly 35 per cent of the average in rural areas and about 28 per cent in the case of urban areas' and highlighted the need for 'special assistance'. The employees' state insurance scheme was expanded to cover medical facilities for families of insured persons and the Contract Labour Act (1970), Employee Pension Scheme (1971) and Gratuity Act (1972) were introduced. The Fifth FYP (1974–79) gave special attention to the poor in the unorganized sector and initiated schemes for their benefit wherever feasible. Several important schemes were introduced during this period: the TPP, ICDS and IRDP (Table 6.1). However, it acknowledged the inability to do much: 'since the unemployable poor run into millions, it is not possible for the country, at the present level of development, to take good care of them'. In the 1970s, following the accumulation of Green Revolution food stocks and the government-introduced Food for Work (FFW) programme in 1977, state-run fair price shops provided essential food grains, fuel, oil and vegetables at subsidized prices.

The Sixth FYP (1980–85) saw the expansion of TPP, FFW and the provident fund scheme. The family pension was extended to cover smaller establishments and rural areas. FFW was expanded into the National Rural Employment Programme (NREP) and provided a combination of food grains and cash payments. There were concerns that benefits might not be reaching the neediest landless population. Consequently, the Rural Landless Employment Guarantee Programme (RLEGP) was initiated in 1983, together with NREP. A Public Distribution System (PDS) was extended across the country during the 1980s for poverty alleviation. Wheat, rice, sugar and kerosene were provided to 330 million people who were estimated to be nutritionally at risk, through 499 000 fair price shops (Kattumuri, 2011).

The Seventh FYP (1985–90) focused on the implementation of the National Policy on Education to enable expansion of education schemes. It included: exemption from fees in elementary schools, subsidies for school feeding programmes and Operation Blackboard (which was launched in 1987 to provide minimum essential facilities for all primary schools; special efforts were stipulated to include children from SCs and STs and, to enable quality of implementation, the programme included training for teachers). This plan aimed also to achieve health for all by 2000 through the National Policy on Health (1983). NREP and RLEGP were merged in 1988 and created 490 million man-days of work a year during the Seventh FYP. The employment guarantee schemes were the most important social welfare programmes and consumed 10 per cent of the state budget in 1979–80. Some states performed better than others in implementing the employment guarantee programmes. Maharashtra implanted a successful triangular model between the dominant rural elite, the urban prosperous who were able to pay and provision for the poor, in particular the rural landless labour force. Half the taxes were raised by a special tax legislated in the state and the other half from the general revenues of Maharashtra, with a major contribution from the urban sector (60–70 per cent of the total revenue during 1975–76 to 1978–79 for the employment guarantee scheme was from taxes in Bombay; agriculture taxes contributed a maximum of 3 per cent). According to Dandekar and Sathe (1980), 58.6 million days of employment were created through the employment guarantee scheme during 1977–78, which was able to eliminate only about 22 per cent of unemployment in the state. As plans, policies and schemes for improving social welfare were being expanded, the needs were constantly growing.

Several schemes for the welfare of women and children, elderly and family benefits were introduced during the Eighth FYP (1992–97) (Table 6.1). It also expanded provision for unorganized sector workers. It acknowledged that 'workers in the unorganised sector comprised of 90 per cent of the total workforce and mostly did not have access to any benefits'. State-level initiatives such as old-age and widows' pensions were expanded. The Ninth FYP (1997–2002) proposed setting up a Department of Social Security within the Ministry of Labour. It proposed having a strong research and development unit to facilitate and accelerate the development process and to explore ways to achieve extension of social protection to all sections of the working population. The Tenth FYP (2002–07) emphasized the need to develop social security programmes, particularly pensions for the unorganized sector. The Eleventh FPY (2007–12) aimed to achieve more inclusive growth through investing more resources and political commitment to social protection. Among its priorities were: institutionalized rights-based programmes; scaling up of interventions for health care, education, social pensions, midday meals and clean drinking water; and the expansion of social protection to the unorganized sector. The Twelfth FYP (2012–17) aims for 'faster, sustainable and more inclusive' growth. It recognizes the challenge to ensure better implementation and improved accountability.

Increased growth in recent years provided access to financial resources and enabled public spending for social protection schemes in India. There has been a steady progression in the provision of welfare schemes in India, with the last decade seeing the fastest expansion in setting up or scaling up of welfare programmes (Table 6.1). The targeted public distribution system is among the largest schemes in the world. The Asian Development Bank (2007) reported the largest social protection programmes in India in terms of beneficiaries as follows:

1. Targeted Public Distribution System (TPDS) – 239 million.
2. State-funded educational assistance programmes – 86 million.
3. Medical benefit including sickness and maternity – 72 million.
4. Integrated Child Development Services (ICDS) – 39 million.
5. Public sector health insurance – 29 million.

Public sector outlays for social services show spending has steadily increased across all FYPs both in absolute terms as well as in terms of proportion of total plan outlay, as shown in Table 6.2. While overall plan outlay as a percentage of gross domestic product (GDP) has increased, so too have social services outlays, from 0.6 per cent of GDP in the First FYP to 3.3 per cent in the Eleventh FYP. The scope and depth of programmes has steadily expanded its reach to provide social protection for a wider society. At the same time it continues to evolve to ensure targeted welfare for people living in poverty with relevant schemes for those who need them the most.

The role of the states is important in implementing the programmes as well as supplementing them with additional funds for educational assistance and support to vulnerable groups such as the elderly, destitute and disabled. State governments learning from one another is also valuable within India. Tamil Nadu (TN), with a population of 72 million, has been a pioneer in implementing welfare-oriented programmes. The state had strong investments in social programmes from the 1950s, which were regularly expanded by various chief ministers, such as M. G. Ramachandran (MGR) in the 1970s. The Dravida Munnetra Kazhagam

Table 6.2 India: public sector outlays for social services

Five year plans	Years	Social services outlay	% of total Rs. (million) plan outlay	Social services outlay as % of period GDP	Total plan outlay as % of period GDP
First	1951–1956	109 960	16%	0.6	3.8
Second	1956–1961	311 160	20%	1.5	7.4
Third	1961–1966	365 790	17%	1.4	8.0
Fourth	1969–1974	217 750	8%	0.6	7.5
Fifth	1974–1979	603 290	15%	1.5	9.5
Sixth	1980–1985	959 350	14%	1.9	12.8
Seventh	1985–1990	1 351 310	16%	2.1	12.6
Eighth	1992–1997	1 687 210	18%	1.9	10.2
Ninth	1998–2002	2 388 230	21%	2.0	9.2
Tenth	2002–2007	3 948 070	23%	2.4	10.4
Eleventh	2007–2012	10 021 150	30%	3.3	11.0

Note: At constant prices, 2005 base year using GDP deflator.

Source: Authors' compilation based on five-year plans.

(DMK) government in TN expanded new initiatives in 1989 for pensions, accident relief, survivor benefits, the maternity assistance scheme and the marriage grant scheme (Dev, 2008). The TN initiative to provide cooked meals to children in government schools in Madras was initiated in 1923 and was expanded by Kamaraj in the 1960s. MGR universalized the 'midday meal scheme' for all children in government schools across the state up to Class X (tenth grade). This scheme was further expanded to cover children up to age 15. It further included pregnant women in the first four months of their pregnancy. In 1982 this scheme cost the state Rs. 1000 million and covered 12 000 000 citizens. TN has among the best administrative systems in the country. Thus it achieved strong improvements in its social indicators: literacy levels increased from 54 per cent in 1981 to 80 per cent in 2011; the poverty index (head count ratio) improved from 55 in 1974 to 21 in 2000; the human development index improved from 0.34 in 1981 (ranked seventh in India) to 0.46 in 1999 (ranked third) and 0.53 in 2001 (ranked third) (Radhakrishna and Panda, 2006). The state has been strongly committed to implementing programmes for social welfare and equality and has achieved greater inclusion of women, disabled and vulnerable people through skills training, individual assistance, bank loans, socio-economic networks such as self-help groups and Panchayat-level federations. Thus TN is a model of strong political commitment and effective implementation of social protection programmes enabling growth and inclusion.

A notable improvement in growth rate of 5 per cent occurred during the Fifth FYP (1974–79) and has been steadily growing since. A food-for-work programme was set up in 1977, which became the National Rural Employment Programme during the Sixth FYP (1980–85) and the Rural-Landless Employment Guarantee Programme was set up in 1983. Researchers have argued that social security was limited compared to the social and economic needs of developing countries and more extensive social protection was required (Kabeer, 2002; Barrientos and Shepherd, 2003). The challenge has not been about the existence of welfare schemes. As presented in Table 6.1, several schemes have existed and have been constantly expanded. The issues have largely pertained to those of limited resources and capacity, both financial and human, for efficient implementation.

INDIA FROM A COMPARATIVE PERSPECTIVE

The rationale that social protection is essential for productivity and creating capabilities and benefiting long-term social and economic development has universal acceptance (UNICEF ROSA 2008a). Design and implementation matters the most in properly shaping social protection to address issues of what, why (objectives); where, who (recipients); how and when (to implement) (Burgess and Stern, 1991). Matching fiscal and institutional capacity with required need is a major challenge. Sharing global knowledge and gaining an understanding of programmes in other countries and tailoring programmes suitable for the region that can be sustainable would be effective and efficient. Walton (2003) suggests that the difference in dynamism of the United States and Europe has more to do with the structure of institutions that incentivize innovation and the finance for those innovations rather than on safety net provisioning – the US has less provisioning for safety nets and structures incentives for innovation in its institutions, which seems to enable more dynamic growth; Europe has lots of safety net provisioning and appears to have slower growth. Walton also gives the example of Finland to counter the above argument in that it has high levels of provisioning and is, on average, as highly competitive as the US. As India continues to develop its social protection policies it can both learn from what works from the West's experience and avoid the mistakes and policies that are no longer relevant. The country will also have to explore and evolve its own strategy for social security commensurate with its circumstances, available resources and development goals.

The *World Social Security Report 2011/12* (ILO, 2010) states that more than half of all people lack any type of protection at all and the number of people in South Asia with access to even the most basic protection is estimated to be less than 10 per cent. The overall spending on social programmes in South Asia of around 8 per cent of GDP is the lowest of all regions. This includes all forms of social assistance, social insurance, education programmes and health programmes.

India spent 4 per cent of its GDP (1129 billion INR or 25 billion USD) on social protection (SP) programmes in 2004–05 and is on par or above the Asian average and is higher than the average of other South Asian countries on all four Social Protection Summary Indicators of expenditure, coverage, distribution and impact (Asian Development Bank, 2007). The distribution of total expenditure in India is as follows: 45 per cent for social security and welfare, 24 per cent for education, 23 per cent for housing and community affairs programmes and 8 per cent for health (UNICEF ROSA, 2008b). All poor people receive some social assistance through Targeted Public Distribution Systems, which provide basic food at subsidized costs. All children are covered through educational assistance programmes wherein elementary education is free and includes free nutritious midday meal schemes. All people are eligible for free primary health care.

CONCLUSION

The growth rate in India in the last decade has been very high by traditional standards and mostly ranged between 8 and 10 per cent. Absolute poverty continues to decline – India's head count ratio, based on the aggregate of rural and urban population BPL, fell from 37 per cent in 2004 to 30 per cent in 2009–10 (World Bank, 2011). The opportunities available in a growing Indian economy are enabling prosperity for some sections of the population while some other sections of the population are being left behind, resulting in growing inequality – the Gini coefficient is 36.8 (UNDP, 2007). This has necessitated a renewed commitment to systematically enhance social protection programmes to enable growth and inclusion.

Half of India's population is below 25 years of age; 65 per cent is below 35 years of age; and 320 million will be of working age by 2020. Investing in its demographic dividend is essential for sustaining development, and enabling people to achieve their full potential is crucial for the well-being of every society. It is extremely important to enhance policies to educate and skill India's young population, make them employable and provide employment opportunities. The Right to Education Bill is an important step in this direction and good implementation and regular monitoring are necessary to achieve its objectives. Public attitudes and perceptions need to be managed through information, education and communication. For example, some parents educating their children in private schools have expressed discomfort with their children being educated alongside children from disadvantaged backgrounds who secure admission through the right to education scheme. Knowledge sharing would help enable understanding and informed judgements and would avoid stigma and discrimination and enhance inclusion.

Higher growth in recent years has expanded fiscal capability and provided an impetus to enhance social security programmes, including for the unorganized sector. The cost of social security for organized sector workers living below the poverty line (consisting of an old-age pension, a maternity benefit, health insurance and death/disability benefit) was estimated to be 0.33 per cent of GDP in 2007, which is lower than the total costs of the National Rural Employment Guarantee Act (0.39 per cent of GDP), total health costs (1.39 per cent of GDP) and total education costs (2.87 per cent of GDP) (UNICEF ROSA, 2008a). Financing social security is additionally through levies in the form of a surcharge on income taxes, finding resources from existing tax revenues and/or using earmarked product group/trade-based taxes. As the schemes are extended to various sectors and workers move above the poverty line, it is intended that beneficiaries will contribute to services as they move up the income ladder.

Integrated models for implementing social protection programmes which involve multiple stakeholders – including government, family, religious, social and private institutions, civil society organizations and NGOs and community participation – should ensure better performance of the programmes. Technology (such and the unique identification scheme) will be beneficial for authentication and improve governance and impede leakages. Regular monitoring and evaluation of programmes will not only help to improve performance but will also provide feedback regarding the feasibility, accountability and sustainability of the programmes commensurate with the country's fiscal capability.

India has had a long tradition of providing welfare for its people, dating back to ancient India. Social protection under the British was limited with only sporadic concern. Several interventions were introduced post-independence but implementation was inefficient and poverty remained widespread. Rapid economic growth in recent years has enabled the expansion of social protection programmes and provides various possibilities for the future. Challenges of governance and implementation remain and greater attempts are being made to address them.

REFERENCES

Asian Development Bank (2007), *Scaling Up of the Social Protection Index for Committed Poverty Reduction. Volume 9: India Country Report*, Manila: ADB.

Aspalter, C. (2003), 'The state and the making of the welfare system in India', *Journal of National Development*, **3** (1), 149–79, accessed at http://ssrn.com/abstract=1725132.

Barrientos, A. and A. Shepherd (2003), 'Chronic poverty and social protection', paper prepared for the International Conference on Staying Poor: Chronic Poverty and Development Policy, University of Manchester, 7–9 April.

Bhattacharya, V. R. (1970), *Some Aspects of Social Security Measures in India*, Delhi: Metropolitan Book Co. Pvt. Ltd.

Burgess, R. and N. Stern (1991), 'Social security in developing countries: what, why, who, and how?', in E. Ahmad, J. Drèze, J. Hills and A. K. Sen (eds), *Social Security in Developing Countries*, Oxford: Clarendon Press, pp. 41–80.

Clark, C. (1972), 'Extent of hunger in India', *Economic and Political Weekly*, **7**, 2019–27.

Constitution of the Republic of India (1950), accessed at http://indiacode.nic.in/coiweb/welcome.html.

Dandekar, K. and M. Sathe (1980), 'Employment guarantee scheme and food for work programme', *Economic and Political Weekly*, **25** (15), 707–13.

Dev, M. S. (2008), *Inclusive Growth in India: Agriculture, Poverty and Human Development*, New Delhi: Oxford University Press.

Gilbert, N. (1976), 'Alternative forms of social protection for developing countries', *Social Service Review*, **50** (3), 363–87.
Goel, S. L. and R. K. Jain (1988), *Social Welfare Administration: Volume 2, Organisation and Working*, New Delhi: Deep and Deep.
International Labour Organisation (ILO) (1942), 'Approaches to social security: an international survey', Studies and Reports Series M No. 18, Montreal: ILO.
ILO (1944), 'Social security: principles and problems arising out of the war', Reports/International Labour Conference, 26th Session, Montreal: ILO.
ILO (2010), *World Social Security Report 2010/11: Providing Coverage in Times of Crisis and Beyond*, Geneva: International Labour Office.
Kabeer, N. (2002), 'Safety nets and opportunity ladders: addressing vulnerability and enhancing productivity in South Asia', Working Paper 159, Brighton: University of Sussex, Institute of Development Studies.
Kannan, K. P. and V. N. Pillai (2007), *Social Security in India: The Long Lane Treaded and the Longer Road Ahead Towards Universalization*, Munich, Germany: University Library of Munich.
Kattumuri, R. (2011), 'Food security and the targeted public distribution system in India', Asia Research Centre WP 38, accessed at www2.lse.ac.uk/asiaResearchCentre/_files/ARCWP38-Kattumuri.pdf.
Kothari, R. (1972), 'Political economy of Garibi Hatao', *Economic and Political Weekly*, **VII** (32–33), special.
Law Commission of India (1974), *Sixty-second Report on the Workmen's Compensation Act, 1923*, accessed at http://lawcommissionofindia.nic.in/51-100/Report62.pdf.
Mulchandani, A. (1998), 'The Indus valley civilization at Lothal', accessed at www.harappa.com/lothal/text.html.
Nehru, J. (1955), 'An address to the Indian National Congress', Avadi, Madras, 22 January, accessed at www.mainstreamweekly.net/article3133.html.
Planning Commission (1950), *History of Planning Commission*, Government of India, accessed 9 March 2012 at http://planningcommission.nic.in/aboutus/history/index.php?about=aboutbdy.htm.
Priyadarshee, A. (2011), 'Evolution of social protection', *The India Economy Review*, accessed at www.theindiaeconomyreview.org/Article.aspx?aid=101&mid=5.
Radhakrishna, R. and M. Panda (2006), *Macroeconomics of Poverty Reduction: India Case Study*, Mumbai: Indira Gandhi Institute of Development Research, accessed at www.igidr.ac.in/pdf/publication/PP-057.pdf.
Rangarajan, L. N. (trans.) (1987), *The Arthasastra of Kautilya*. New Delhi: Penguin.
Rath, N. (1985), 'Garibi Hatao: can IRDP do it?' *Economic and Political Weekly*, **20** (6), 238–46.
Sen, A. K. (1982), *Poverty and Famines: An Essay on Entitlements and Deprivation*, Oxford: Clarendon Press.
Shamasastry, R. (trans.) (undated), *Kautilya's Arthashastra*, accessed at https://docs.google.com/file/d/1DxCC4BhnRmuqKGmhybMM3OkxEu7PsWG3vNY7stAwy5FCnhV4iAf6kdTkwjc7/edit?hl=en&pli=1.
Thapar, R. (2000), *Ashoka and the Decline of the Mauryas*, Delhi: Oxford.
Thaplyal, K. K. (2001), 'Guilds in ancient India (antiquity and various stages in the development of guilds up to AD 300)', in G. C. Pande (ed.), *Life Thoughts and Culture in India*, Delhi: Munshiram Manoharlal Publishers Pvt. Ltd, pp. 995–1006.

UNDP (2007), *Human Development Report 2007/8: Fighting Climate Change; Human Solidarity in a Divided World*, Hampshire and New York: Palgrave Macmillan.
UNICEF ROSA (2008a), *Regional Policy Makers' Symposium on Social Protection in South Asia. Dhaka, April 2008*, Kathmandu: UNICEF.
UNICEF ROSA (2008b), *South Asia – Some Key Facts on Poverty and Inequality*, accessed at www.unicef.org/socialpolicy/files/key_initiatives.ppt.
Walton, M. (2003), *The Role of Safety Nets in Social Policy: Roundtable Discussion*, Transcript of Remarks, World Bank Social Safety Nets Primer Launch, 1 December, accessed at http://siteresources.worldbank.org/SAFETYNETSANDTRANSFERS/Resources/PrimerLaunchScript_Walton.pdf.
World Bank (2011), *Social Protection for a Changing India: Main Report*, accessed at https://openknowledge.worldbank.org/handle/10986/2745.
Wright, R. P. (2010), *The Ancient Indus: Urbanism, Economy, and Society*, Cambridge and New Delhi: Cambridge University Press.

7. Social protection in India: current approaches and issues

Rohit Mutatkar

India is one of the most plural societies in the world, with people belonging to different religions, ethnic groups, language groups and living in regions with diverse cultures. But it has also been a historically hierarchical society, which is reflected in a complex social structure and social inequalities. India is the largest democracy in the world in terms of its population and in recent years it has emerged as one of the largest and fastest growing economies in the world. However, it also has one of the largest numbers of people in poverty in the world and contemporary Indian society is characterized by the presence of vast socio-economic disparities. Current issues of social protection in India may need to be understood in this wider context of development.

This chapter seeks to provide an overview of the current issues and approaches relating to social protection in India and is organized as follows. Section 2 outlines a brief profile of economic growth, poverty and inequality in India, which provides the context for understanding issues of social protection. Section 3 discusses the key features and issues relating to legislation for the right to work and the right to food in India. Section 4 focuses on social protection issues of informal workers and old-age social security in India. Section 5 concludes the chapter.

ECONOMIC GROWTH, POVERTY AND INEQUALITY IN INDIA

Elimination of mass poverty has been one of the major objectives of development planning in India since independence in 1947. India has sought to achieve this through the process of economic growth, as well as through direct poverty alleviation interventions. After liberalization of the economy was initiated in 1991, the Indian economy registered high growth rates and it has emerged as the second fastest growing economy in the world. However, endemic deprivation coexists in India alongside these

Table 7.1 India: selected socio-economic indicators

(a) Demographic	
Total population (billion) (2011)	1.21
Rural population (%) (2011)	68.84
(b) Economic	
GDP average annual growth rate (%) (2007–12)	8.0
GNI per capita (PPP$) (2010)	3550
Contribution of agriculture to GDP (%) (2009–10)	14.62
Contribution of industry to GDP (%) (2009–10)	20.16
Contribution of services to GDP (%) (2009–10)	65.22
(c) Literacy and gender gap	
Literacy rate (%) (2011)	74.04
Male literacy rate (%) (2011)	82.14
Female literacy rate (%) (2011)	65.46
(d) Health and nutrition	
Life expectancy at birth (in years) (2011)	65.4
Proportion of underweight children under 5 years of age (%) (2004–09)	43.5
Maternal mortality ratio (per 100 000 live births) (2007–09)	212
Infant mortality rate (per 1000 live births) (2009)	50
(e) Poverty and inequality	
Proportion in poverty (headcount ratio, %) (2009–10)	29.8
Proportion in poverty – rural (headcount ratio, %) (2009–10)	33.8
Proportion in poverty – urban (headcount ratio, %) (2009–10)	20.9
Total number of poor (in millions) (2009–10)	354.68
Gini coefficient (2004–05)	0.33

Source: UNDP (2012), Government of India (2012), World Bank (2011).

macroeconomic achievements and large sections of the population continue to remain socially, educationally and economically deprived. This is reflected in various indicators such as poverty, illiteracy, infant mortality and undernutrition among children, as shown in Table 7.1. The relative magnitude of these deprivations is reflected in socio-economic disparities, namely inter-group disparities, (caste, tribe, religion), regional disparities (inter-state, intra-state, rural–urban), and gender disparities.

The nature of the policy paradigm in India appears to be biased towards achieving faster economic growth, with not much emphasis given to progress on social indicators, which are important in addressing the multi-dimensional nature of human development. While policymakers in India routinely make announcements regarding closely monitored economic growth targets, the magnitude of undernutrition in children does not receive similar attention. As a result, India has the dubious distinction of more than 40 per cent of children in the zero–five age group being undernourished, which is one of the highest levels of child undernutrition in the world. This statistic has declined very slowly in spite of high rates of economic growth. According to the *Global Hunger Index Report 2011* (IFPRI, 2011) India is in the category of nations where hunger is 'alarming', and it is one among only three developing countries where the hunger index between 1996 and 2011 worsened. The neglect of human development is also reflected in India's rank of 134 out of 187 countries in the United Nations Human Development Index (UNDP, 2011). Additionally, India's rank on various social indicators (except per capita national income) has worsened even within the South Asian region in the past two decades (Dreze and Sen, 2011).

The growth process itself, particularly after liberalization of the economy and the consequent processes of globalization, appears to be skewed in favour of certain sections and sectors of the economy and dominated by corporate interests, thereby accentuating the already existing socio-economic disparities. Thus, while economic reforms introduced in the country in the early 1990s helped to create greater opportunities for those with education, skills, resources, infrastructure, and those with power and influence, they failed to address the most deprived sections of society and those living in backward regions. The economic reform policies led to more opportunities for growth in the corporate sector, but did not address the needs of the agricultural sector. A greater role for the private sector in the post-liberalization period meant a decrease in public investment in infrastructure, agriculture and the social sectors. A reduced priority for the agricultural sector, in which 60 per cent of the workforce is concentrated, has resulted in agrarian distress and the phenomenon of farmers' suicides in some parts of the country. There has also been a gradual urbanization of poverty, as people from rural areas have been migrating to urban areas in search of livelihoods; about 23 per cent of the urban population of the country now lives in slums. Regional and social group disparities in India have also been accompanied by development-induced displacement, particularly in tribal regions, which is related to the process of economic globalization in recent decades. This has contributed to conflicts and violent protests against the state in many such regions across the country.

As a result of these processes, though the Indian economy in the aggregate grew much faster after liberalization, the most disadvantaged sections of society could not participate in this growth, thus further widening the disparities in society (Rao, 2009). Consequently, the country is now represented by two contrasting images: the image of a globalizing India with one of the world's fastest growing economies, on the verge of entering the first world; and the contrasting image of an India where millions of people still struggle for food and their day-to-day survival concerns. These disparities have been accepted, at least in principle, in policymaking, and the approach paper of the Eleventh Five Year Plan (2007–12) therefore had as its objective not only 'faster growth', but also 'inclusive growth', which is being continued as an objective in the Twelfth Five Year Plan (2012–17) as well (Government of India, 2006, 2011).

Addressing the multiple dimensions of deprivation faced by large sections of India's population and promoting inclusion in the economy and society is therefore the key challenge for development policy and implementation in India. This provides the context for understanding the current approaches and issues relating to social protection in India.

RIGHT TO WORK AND RIGHT TO FOOD

India has had a long history of social protection programmes and policies. The magnitude of deprivation that exists even after more than six decades of development planning, however, seems to indicate that these may have had only a limited impact in addressing the structural causes of poverty and deprivation. These programmes and policies have suffered from many weaknesses, such as being largely top-down and with weak systems of accountability and a lack of transparency, resulting in the poor being the principle victims of large-scale corruption and lack of implementation of schemes and programmes intended for them.

In recent decades, social protection policies have also been characterized by the approach of targeting the 'poor'. Thus, while the people identified as 'poor' or 'below the poverty line' (BPL) are eligible for assistance through a range of government programmes and schemes with respect to food subsidies, housing, credit and various anti-poverty programmes, those who are classified in the category of 'above the poverty line' (APL) are not eligible for any of these. There has been much debate on how the poor should be identified for the purpose of targeting. The means-testing surveys carried out have led to large exclusion errors, due to problems in the methodology and the administrative difficulties inherent in such an exercise. Thus, many poor and vulnerable households have been considered ineligible for government assistance.

Recent years have seen the emergence of landmark rights-based legislation in India, including the right to information, right to work, right to education, forest rights for tribal people and an ongoing struggle for a right to food. These mark a paradigm shift from the service delivery or provider-beneficiary approach of earlier government schemes and have important implications for social protection. An important feature of this legislation is that it has been achieved through pressure on the government by civil society campaigns and people's movements. This received institutional support in the form of a National Advisory Council, consisting of prominent social activists who played a crucial role in drafting much of this legislation and pressurizing the government to enact it despite adverse propaganda. The higher judiciary in India has also played an important role in interpreting some of the economic and social rights in the Directive Principles of State Policy as linked to the right to life, which is a fundamental right under the Indian constitution.

The Right to Information (RTI) Campaign is important in the context of social protection, as it linked the right to information to the right to life and was based on the recognition that real change in society can come about only if people can hold the government and public servants accountable, so that they are forced to respond to the needs of the poorest citizens. But accountability cannot come about without information regarding government decisions and functioning. The RTI Act (2005) empowers people to secure access to this information, which is available through public authorities (Roy et al., 2008).

Another piece of legislation which has been equally historic in its significance is the National Rural Employment Guarantee Act (NREGA) 2005. The NREGA entitles anyone in rural areas, who is willing to do unskilled manual labour at the statutory minimum wage, to be employed on public works within 15 days of applying. If employment is not provided, an unemployment allowance has to be paid. The work guarantee in the NREGA is subject to an initial limit of 100 days per household per year and only one person per household in any work at a time. However, it marks a big departure from earlier public works programmes, such as the food-for-work programme, which were not founded on a rights-based approach, and is the first step towards realizing the right to work in India.

Permissible work under the NREGA includes minor irrigation, water conservation, drought proofing, desilting of tanks, flood control, land development, rural roads and any other work notified by central government in consultation with state government. There are supposed to be mandatory worksite facilities such as drinking water, shade, medical aid, and a crèche if more than five children below the age of six are present. There are gender-related provisions such as equal wages for women and men, prohibiting gender discrimination of any kind and a provision that at least 33 per cent of labourers in any work should be women. Private contractors are banned from implementing the NREGA. To ensure the primacy of labour-intensive work, there is a provision that the wage-material ratio should not be less than 60:40 and the wages of skilled and semi-skilled labourers are to be included in material costs. The central government is supposed to pay for wage costs, 75 per cent of material costs and some administrative costs, while the state governments pay for the unemployment allowance, 25 per cent of material costs and other administrative costs. There are also transparency guidelines in the Act, such as the mechanism of social audit to prevent corruption, and the implementation of the Act is sought to be participatory through the involvement of democratic institutions at the local level (Right to Food Campaign, 2007).

The NREGA is a self-targeting scheme and therefore avoids the exclusion and inclusion errors inherent in the BPL targeting approach adopted in many other social protection programmes in India. The NREGA was initially implemented in 200 'backward' districts of India, but has now been extended to the whole of rural India. Expenditure on the NREGA is estimated to be about 0.5 per cent of gross domestic product (GDP). There have been various studies carried out regarding its performance, which include government data in this regard as well as studies carried out by researchers and civil society organizations. These indicate that those participating in the NREGA largely belong to the poorest households and a majority also belong to the Scheduled Caste and Scheduled Tribe communities, meaning the NREGA has been able to reach out to the most deprived sections of the population. On average, the participation of women in the programme has been found to be higher than the stipulated minimum requirement of 33 per cent, but there have been wide regional variations in this regard (NCEUS, 2009).

Surveys of workers in the programme and especially women workers have indicated various positive benefits, including dignified employment, greater ability to incur expenses on food, health and education, repaying of loans, reduction in distress migration, economic empowerment and asset creation at the village level. However, these surveys have also indicated various operational deficiencies, which continue to exist in the implementation of the scheme. For example, a large proportion of rural workers are still not aware of their entitlements and other provisions under the scheme or are not yet empowered to utilize them. Being a demand-based scheme, this has been one of the factors resulting in a large proportion of rural households not being able to benefit from the 100 days of employment guaranteed by the scheme. Additionally, there have been very few instances of the unemployment allowance being paid. The sustainability and productivity of assets created under the scheme have also not yet been focused upon. Since the NREGA is implemented through the respective state governments, there has been wide variation in the performance of the scheme across different states. Thus, though the NREGA has been a historic piece of legislation in India in the context of social protection, the challenge now is ensuring its effective implementation and addressing the operational deficiencies, especially in the poorer-performing states (NCEUS, 2009).

The Right to Information, Right to Work and Right to Food Campaigns in India have been interlinked and have drawn on each other. The demand for the right to work arose as part of the Right to Food Campaign in India in 2001, in the context of a public interest litigation filed by the People's Union for Civil Liberties (PUCL) in the Supreme Court of India, which demanded that the right to food be recognized as a legal right of every person in the country. This was against the backdrop of prevalent hunger in drought-affected areas of the country coexisting with millions of tonnes of food grain stocks being held by the Food Corporation of India. The central government and some state governments responded to the Supreme Court that they were already implementing a range of food, livelihood and social security schemes, which adequately secured the right to food to all people. However, the petitioners in reply provided evidence regarding the grave problems in the coverage and implementation of these schemes (Mander, 2012). Since then, Supreme Court hearings on the 'right to food case' (*PUCL* vs *Union of India*, Civil Writ Petition 196 of 2001), which is still under litigation, have continued to be held at regular intervals and have led to various Supreme Court 'interim orders' on the right to food. In one of its first such orders the Supreme Court converted some of the existing government schemes vital for food security into legal entitlements and also ordered an expansion of some of the schemes (Mander, 2012). This included, for example, the Supreme Court directing all state governments to introduce cooked midday meals in government and government-assisted schools within six months, and a similar order calling for the provision of functional '*anganwadis*' (childcare centres under the Integrated Child Development Services Scheme (ICDS)) in every habitation (Dreze, 2004; Right to Food Campaign, 2008). The Supreme Court has also appointed its own independent commissioners to monitor compliance with the court orders in the right to food case and to track hunger and the performance of related government programmes across the country (Mander, 2012).

In 2011, the government introduced a National Food Security Bill, which was yet to be enacted as of 2012. The bill is expected to cover approximately 70 per cent of all Indian households, which is the largest proportion of households covered by such a programme anywhere in the world (Haddad et al., 2012). The bill has proposed entitlements for various groups under various schemes, including extended coverage of targeted households eligible to receive subsidized foodgrain under the

Public Distribution System (PDS), children's entitlements, entitlements of pregnant and lactating women, entitlements of special groups like the destitute, persons living in starvation, migrants, and those in an emergency or a disaster. Other provisions include reforms in the targeted PDS, which include introducing schemes such as cash transfers to the targeted beneficiaries in lieu of their foodgrain entitlements. However, the bill has been critiqued on several fronts by the Right to Food Campaign. These include: the proposed continuation of a targeted PDS instead of a universal system as demanded; the proposed move towards cash transfers in place of food subsidies; inadequate provisions relating to agriculture; and the bill not being a 'food security act' as intended, but only a 'food entitlements act', with weak provisions and implementation mechanisms (Khera, 2009; Right to Food Campaign, 2012).

One of the issues of debate that has been raised in this regard is the proposed use of direct cash transfers to the poor instead of food subsidies through the PDS. The PDS is the largest safety net programme in India and provides essential commodities such as foodgrains, sugar and fuel (kerosene) to the poor at subsidized rates through a network of fair price shops throughout the country. It has been subject to significant policy changes over the past two decades, moving from a universal scheme to a geographically targeted scheme and then to a targeted scheme for BPL households. Expenditure on the PDS is estimated to be almost 1 per cent of GDP. However, the PDS has been critiqued as suffering from systemic flaws in its design and leading to corruption and leakages in its implementation. It has therefore been argued that there should be fundamental reforms in the PDS, which should allow households the option of a cash transfer instead of a food transfer (World Bank, 2011). However, those opposed to cash transfers argue that there would be an even stronger incentive for corruption and leakages in a cash transfer scheme. Furthermore, a cash transfer may not be able to protect the poor in the situation of a price rise (Ghosh, 2011). It has been argued that large-scale substitution of the PDS by direct cash transfers may not be feasible in the absence of institutional conditions such as a strong banking structure, but could be piloted in a few poor areas in metropolitan cities. It is also argued that there have been state-wise variations in the performance of the PDS and some states such as Chattisgarh have also undertaken successful state-level PDS reforms by extending coverage, improving delivery and increasing transparency. This could provide directions for reforms in the PDS in the National Food Security Bill (Saxena, 2012).

Another important issue of debate has regarded targeted versus universal provisions in various government programmes and schemes. The approach of targeting the 'poor' for social protection programmes such as the PDS and a watertight categorization of households into BPL/APL has been leading to large exclusion errors. It also views poverty in a static sense, not recognizing the possible mobility of households into and out of poverty. Many people, such as the homeless and destitute, are unable to benefit from social protection programmes such as the PDS because they do not have any address or proof of identity. Seasonal migrants are not eligible to access social protection schemes at their migration destination. One of the measures being adopted by the government to address such issues is to provide all citizens with a unique (and biometrically based) identification number, in the proposed unique identification (UID) card scheme. However, critics have pointed out that UID would at best be only a determinant of identity and cannot solve the problems of determining the beneficiaries in the government's targeting approach. For example, the National Food Security Bill proposes the categories of 'priority', 'general' and 'excluded' households for the purpose of targeting under the PDS, but does not provide any clear criteria for their identification.

Besides the PDS, two other important social protection programmes for food security have been the Midday Meal Programme and the ICDS. Both programmes, which focus on children, witnessed a substantial expansion in terms of coverage and outlay after the Supreme Court orders on the right to food. The Midday Meal Programme is supposed to provide a cooked midday meal to all primary and upper-primary school children in government and government-aided schools. There are nutrition norms in terms of calories, proteins and micronutrients to be provided in the meal. Data indicate that there has been varied implementation across states and lower coverage in urban areas. Studies on the impact of the programme have found a positive impact in increased enrolments, but its impact on other educational outcomes and on child nutrition need to be understood better. There has also been a concern that in the functioning of many schools, provision of midday meals tends to be prioritized over the quality of education (World Bank, 2011).

Saxena (2012) makes the important observation that food alone will not address the problem of underweight children, since this would require multi-sectoral interventions in areas such as health, hygiene, quality of water and a change in cultural practices related to child rearing. The ICDS is supposed to provide supplementary nutrition, health care and pre-school education to children under six through '*anganwadi*' centres and also provide services to adolescent girls and pregnant and lactating mothers. Saxena (2012) points out that the ICDS has not been successful in having a significant impact on reducing child malnutrition, since it has placed a priority on food supplementation rather than on other nutrition and health education interventions and has largely focused on children older than three, by which time malnutrition has already set in. The ICDS has also been operating very poorly in urban slum areas and faces implementation problems such as a lack of accountability and an irresponsible reporting system with a tendency to under-report the extent of malnutrition. Thus, a recent comprehensive evaluation of the ICDS by the Planning Commission showed that the outcomes have been disappointing in spite of a significant increase in its outlay. The National Food Security Bill would thus have to take into account a range of multi-sectoral issues and linkages to comprehensively address the concerns of food security in India, and especially among children.

SOCIAL SECURITY FOR INFORMAL WORKERS

A key issue regarding the current structure of social protection in India is that the vast majority of workers are employed in the unorganized (informal) sector with no job security, unfavourable working conditions and no social security benefits such as health, maternity and old-age security. In recognition of these concerns, the government of India set up a National Commission for Enterprises in the Unorganized Sector (NCEUS) in 2004. The mandate of the commission was to examine the problems faced by enterprises and workers in the informal sector and suggest appropriate remedial measures. The commission recognized that informal workers exist both in the informal sector and the formal sector and gave clear definitions of these terms. On the basis of these definitions, it estimated that 93 per cent of the workforce in India could be categorized as informal workers. This includes agriculture, which is largely informal (NCEUS, 2008; Kannan and Papola, 2009).

NCEUS prepared a number of reports to highlight various aspects of the informal economy and workers employed in it. It found that 77 per cent of the Indian population in 2004–05 was living on a per capita expenditure of less than 20 rupees per day (approximately $2 in terms of purchasing power parity) (Kannan and Papola, 2009). These were categorized as 'poor and vulnerable', with the remaining 23 per cent being middle class and higher income groups. The 'poor and vulnerable' category included 88 per cent of the Scheduled Caste and Scheduled Tribe population, 80 per cent of the 'Other Backward Classes' population and 85 per cent of the Muslim population. About 94 per cent of workers in this category were informal workers. Most of the population of this category were also either illiterate or without primary education. The commission observed that these groups thus emerge as a coalition of the socially, educationally and economically deprived.

NCEUS reports document that informal workers in India are a vast and heterogeneous category. A large part of the informal workforce is accounted for by the agricultural sector, which is largely peasant-based. Agricultural labourers in rural areas and casual labourers in urban areas have the highest incidence of poverty among all occupational groups. Health, maternity and old-age security are the major social security concerns of informal workers. Only 6 per cent of informal workers in the country are covered by some form of social security from the government and another 2 per cent through coverage by non-governmental organizations and organizations of informal workers. Kerala is the leading state in this regard with more than half of its informal workers covered by public social security.

In its documentation of the working conditions of informal workers, NCEUS found that 85 per cent of informal wage workers in rural India, and 57 per cent of such workers in urban India, were receiving wages below the nationally recommended minimum. The reports document bad working conditions, especially for those working in non-agricultural establishments. These include long working hours, unhygienic conditions, delayed wage payments, absence of safety equipment and lack of sanitation provision. The reports also discuss issues of child labour, women workers and migrant workers in India, and of specific occupational categories such as domestic workers and street vendors (NCEUS, 2008; Kannan and Papola, 2009).

The commission observed that faster economic growth in India in the period from 1993–94 to 2004–05 was associated with a decline in the growth of employment and average earnings in comparison to the previous decade. It also observed that there was very little growth of formal employment in this period, and whatever growth in employment took place seemed to be almost entirely of informal employment of workers. The growth rate of employment among the poor and vulnerable groups was much lower than the middle and higher-income groups. Thus, in terms of both quantity and quality of employment, the poor and vulnerable groups lagged behind the other groups during the period of rapid economic growth. The benefits of growth seem to have bypassed them (NCEUS, 2009).

NCEUS submitted three sets of proposals to the government: (a) a national minimum social security scheme for all informal workers, (b) minimum conditions of work for wage workers in the informal sector, and (c) promotional measures to reduce poverty and enhance livelihood opportunities for all workers in the informal sector.

It recommended that a national scheme of minimum social security for all informal workers should be introduced on a statutory basis in order to address their core needs with regard to health, death or disability and old age. This includes: health benefits for all family members to cover expenses for hospitalization, maternity benefits for female workers or the spouse of the main worker, life insurance cover to provide survivor benefits in the event of natural or accidental death of the registered worker and old-age security consisting of a state pension for workers belonging to BPL households and a contributory provident fund for workers belonging to APL households.

It was recommended that the social security scheme should be based on an insurance model with contributions from workers, employers and the government at the rate of one rupee each day. In case of self-employed workers or where there are no directly identifiable employers, the government would pay the contribution of employers and would also pay the contribution of workers, if they are from BPL households. NCEUS suggested a dedicated organizational setup to implement the social security scheme through national and state-level security funds and boards and through local-level workers' facilitation centres. It recommended linking with the vast network of post offices in the country to implement the scheme. While maintaining that there should be a national minimum social security for all informal workers across the country, it suggested that it may be left to state governments to add on or provide additional benefits (Kannan, 2006).

On minimum conditions of work for informal workers, NCEUS recommended additional national legislation to prescribe a set of minimum standards, including: an eight-hour working day with at least a half-hour break; one paid day of rest per week; a statutory national minimum wage for all wage workers and home workers; penal interest on delayed payment of wages; no deductions from wages in payment of fines; the right to organize; non-discrimination on the basis of sex, caste, religion, HIV/AIDS status and place of origin; adequate safety equipment at the workplace and compensation for accidents; protection from sexual harassment; provision of childcare; and provision of basic amenities at the workplace (Kannan and Papola, 2009).

To reduce poverty and increase opportunities for livelihoods, an action plan was recommended to cover workers and microenterprises in both the agricultural and non-agricultural sectors. For wage workers who are mostly casual labourers, NCEUS suggested strengthening public employment programmes like the NREGA in both rural and urban areas, while for self-employed workers it suggested a series of measures for accessing credit, technology, marketing and raw materials to improve their productivity and thereby their earnings (NCEUS, 2008; 2009). It should be mentioned that there have been major self-employment programmes in India in the past decade, by provision of credit by the government through the formation of self-help groups (SHGs) for poor women. More than three million SHGs have been formed across India, most notably in Kerala and Andhra Pradesh. However, it has been found that these programmes have only been successful where credit has been accompanied by adequate infrastructural and institutional support such as extension and marketing. The government has sought to strengthen this approach through the establishment in 2010 of a National Rural Livelihoods Mission, which aims to ensure greater coverage among rural poor households and, in addition to self-employment, would also promote wage employment for youth through a placement scheme.

The contrast between the formal and informal sector in the provision of social security benefits also extends to old-age social security. Thus, while in the formal sector most workers have been eligible to receive benefits of a pension or provident fund after retirement, such old-age social security benefits have been almost non-existent for those who worked in the informal sector. The proportion of the population aged 60 years and above in India was 7 per cent in 2009 (approximately 88 million people), with an increasing dependency ratio. This is projected to increase further, both in terms of the number of old people and their proportion to the younger population. An important demographic feature is the feminization of the elderly, with the gender ratio among the elderly showing an increasing trend from 94 women per 100 men in 1991 to 105 per 100 in 2011. The 2001 census showed that about half of all elderly women were widowed while only 15 per cent of elderly men were widowers (Subaiya and Bansod, 2011).

A National Social Assistance Programme (NSAP) was initiated by the government in 1995 and continues to be in operation, comprising the following schemes: (a) pension for persons aged 65 years or older who belong to a BPL household, (b) pension for widows aged 40–64 years, (c) pension to severely disabled persons, (d) financial assistance in case of death of the primary family breadwinner (18–64 years of age), and (e) free foodgrain rations for senior citizens who, though eligible, remain uncovered under the pension scheme.

However, the provision under these schemes remains minimal. For example, in the pension scheme the central government provides an assistance of 200 rupees per month and the state government is supposed to provide at least a matching contribution. The coverage of these schemes is also still limited to a very small proportion of potential beneficiaries, which may be due to many people not being aware of these schemes as well as due to the strict and often dubious eligibility conditions and the resulting problems in implementation.

The issue of old-age social security was also a major concern of the

NCEUS recommendations to the government. These recommendations proposed to extend a minimum social security including old-age security to every worker in the country within five years and at a cost estimated to be not more than 0.5 per cent of GDP (Kannan, 2006). Against the backdrop of the NCEUS reports, the government enacted an Unorganised Workers Social Security Act in 2008. However, this has been critiqued as a watered down version of the NCEUS recommendations, with no dedicated fund or empowered authority for its implementation. Thus, most of the NCEUS recommendations were yet to be acted upon by the government as of 2012.

CONCLUSION

This chapter has sought to provide an overview of some of the current issues and approaches relating to social protection in India. The present development context in India is characterized by the country continuing to have some of the worst indicators of human development in the world, despite being one of the fastest growing economies. Dreze and Sen (2011) state that, in this context, 'there is probably no other example in the history of world development of an economy growing so fast for so long with such limited results in terms of broad-based social progress'. The government's neoliberal policy has prioritized the objective of economic growth, but the nature of the growth has further widened socio-economic disparities, which, in turn, has led to the policy objective of 'inclusive growth'.

A combination of civil society campaigns and judicial activism has resulted in important rights-based legislation in India regarding, for example, the right to information, the right to work in the form of a national rural employment guarantee scheme, and an ongoing struggle for the right to food which would address the major concern of undernourished children. Recent years have also seen important policy recommendations made to the government with respect to providing social security to informal workers, which would include old-age social security and improving the quantity and quality of employment. The future prospects of social protection in India will depend on how these policy and implementation issues develop.

REFERENCES

Dreze, J. (2004), 'Democracy and right to food', *Economic and Political Weekly*, **39** (17), 1723–31.

Dreze, J. and S. Sen (2011), 'Putting growth in its place', *Outlook*, 14 November, accessed at www.outlookindia.com/article.aspx?278843.
Ghosh, J. (2011), 'Cash transfers as the silver bullet for poverty reduction: a sceptical note', *Economic and Political Weekly*, **46** (21), 67–71.
Government of India (2006), *Towards Faster and More Inclusive Growth: An Approach to the 11th Five Year Plan*, New Delhi: Planning Commission.
Government of India (2011), *Faster, Sustainable and More Inclusive Growth: An Approach to the Twelfth Five Year Plan*, New Delhi: Planning Commission.
Government of India (2012), *Press Note on Poverty Estimates, 2009–10*, New Delhi: Planning Commission.
Haddad, L., C. P. Chandrasekhar and B. Swain (2012), 'Overview – standing on the threshold: food justice in India', *IDS Bulletin*, **43** (special issue, July), 1–7.
International Food Policy Research Institute (IFPRI) (2011), *2011 Global Hunger Index*, Washington, DC: IFPRI.
Kannan, K. P. (2006), 'Feasible and affordable', *Seminar*, December, accessed at www.india-seminar.com/2006/568/568_k_p_kannan.htm.
Kannan, K. P. and T. S. Papola (2009), 'Workers in the informal sector: initiatives by India's National Commission for Enterprises in the Unorganized Sector', *International Labour Review*, **146** (3–4), 321–9.
Khera, R. (2009), 'Right to food act: beyond cheap promises', *Economic and Political Weekly*, **44** (29), 40–4.
Mander, H. (2012), 'Food from the courts: the Indian experience', *IDS Bulletin*, **43** (special issue, July), 15–24.
National Commission for Enterprises in the Unorganised Sector (NCEUS) (2008), *Report on Conditions of Work and Promotion of Livelihoods in the Unorganised Sector*, New Delhi: Academic Foundation.
NCEUS (2009), *The Challenge of Employment in India: An Informal Economy Perspective*, New Delhi: NCEUS, Government of India.
Rao, Hanumantha, C. H. (2009), 'Inclusive growth: recent experience and challenges ahead', *Economic and Political Weekly*, **44** (13), 16–21.
Right to Food Campaign (2007), *Employment Guarantee Act: A Primer*, Delhi: Right to Food Campaign.
Right to Food Campaign (2008), *Supreme Court Orders on the Right to Food: A Tool for Action*, Delhi: Right to Food Campaign.
Right to Food Campaign (2012), *Right to Food Campaign's Critique of the National Food Security Bill 2011*, Delhi: Right to Food Campaign.
Roy, A., D. Nikhil and P. Suchi (2008), 'The Right to Information Act 2005: a social development perspective', *India Social Development Report 2008*, New Delhi: Oxford University Press.
Saxena, N. C. (2012), 'Hunger and malnutrition in India', *IDS Bulletin*, **43** (special issue, July), 8–14.
Subaiya L. and D. Bansod (2011), 'Demographics of population ageing in India', Working Paper Series on Ageing, UNFPA supported project on Population Ageing in India.
United Nations Development Programme (UNDP) (2011), *Human Development Report 2011*, New York: UNDP.
UNDP (2012), *Data on Key Economic and Human Development Indicators*, India: UNDP.
World Bank (2011), *Social Protection for a Changing India*, Washington, DC: World Bank.

8. Future prospects of social protection in India

Rohit Mutatkar

The chapter on current approaches and issues of social protection in India indicated the existing situation of social protection in India with respect to some of the key issues and some of the recent policy concerns and initiatives that have emerged. In continuity with this discussion, this chapter seeks to highlight some of the major policy challenges and the political and administrative factors that may be expected to determine the direction of social protection policies and their implementation. The chapter concludes with a statement on the opposing forces which are likely to influence the future scenario of social protection in India.

SOCIAL PROTECTION CHALLENGES IN INDIA

According to the 2011 census, India has a population of 1.21 billion people, which accounts for 17.5 per cent of the world's population. It is projected that by 2025, India will have a population of more than 1.4 billion and will overtake China as the most populous country in the world. Though there is no consensus on the estimates of poverty in India, even according to the most conservative official estimates the absolute number of poor in India consists of at least 300 million people. This is larger than the population of most countries in the world. India's biggest states are comparable to some of the largest countries in the world in terms of their populations. The demographic dimension also extends to the functioning of current social protection programmes such as the National Rural Employment Guarantee Act (NREGA), Public Distribution System (PDS), Mid-Day Meal Programme and Integrated Child Development Services (ICDS), which are some of the largest programmes in the world in terms of population covered. For example, the midday meal programme benefits 140 million school children daily, making this possibly the largest school feeding programme in the world (Mander, 2012). However, possibly because of the scale of the population involved and the persistence of mass deprivations in India, the deficiencies in the functioning of the programmes tend to be highlighted more than the successes. Thus, India may be expected to face a huge demographic challenge to provide social protection to its citizens in its multiple dimensions, such as food-security, employment, old-age social security, housing and health care.

A key feature of development policy in India over the past two decades has been its focus on faster economic growth as the major policy objective. However, as discussed in the chapter on the current situation of social protection in India, the economic growth process has not led to the desired improvement in social indicators, such as with respect to child undernutrition. The growth process has also not addressed the priority concerns of the most deprived sections of the population, which is reflected in socio-economic disparities in India in various dimensions. While the government has adopted the policy objective of 'inclusive growth', there is no clarity on what the specific approaches or policies that an objective of inclusive growth involve are and in what way these are different from those adopted previously. Thus, social protection policies in the future will have to face the continuing challenge of social inclusion and human development of the most deprived sections of the population such as with respect to social group, region and gender.

The Scheduled Castes (SCs) and Scheduled Tribes (STs), who together comprise about a quarter of India's total population, are known to be the most deprived social group categories in India across a range of socio-economic indicators. Contemporary Indian society is characterized by a notable feature of a hierarchy among social group categories in development outcomes, with STs and SCs at the bottom, followed by Other Backward Classes (OBCs) and then the category of higher caste groups at the top. India has a long history of affirmative action policies for SCs and STs based on constitutional provisions. Seats are reserved in legislative bodies at the state and central governments, in appointments to public sector jobs and in admissions to government educational institutions. In addition, virtually every ministry at the central and state levels has a vast number of provisions for the welfare of these groups, which include separate budgetary provisions. In recent decades, some of these policies have also been extended for the OBC category. Together, these policies have been described as the largest attempt ever made by any country to integrate historically marginalized groups of people into the development mainstream (Galanter, 1991).

However, while affirmative action policies for historically disadvantaged social group categories based on constitutional provisions may have led to upward mobility among certain sections of these groups, they have not addressed the structural causes of poverty and deprivation. Thus, poverty and inequality in India continue to be group-level phenomena. The practice of 'untouchability' has reduced, but it continues to exist in spite of being banned by law, and caste-based discrimination is still observed. There has been very little attempt to empower the historically disadvantaged groups such as tribal people by reaching out to them, making them aware of the provisions for their welfare and increasing their capacity to access these provisions. Reservation policies have also led to divisive identity politics, thus diluting their intended potential as a tool for social justice.

The tribal people in particular have also been politically marginalized and have been the worst victims of the process of economic globalization by way of displacement due to large-scale development projects in tribal areas. While in the period prior to the liberalization of the economy this took place largely due to projects such as construction of dams in tribal areas, in the post-liberalization period this is also taking place due to mining projects in tribal areas – which are usually rich in natural and mineral resources – and through the creation of special economic zones by which other rural areas have also been affected. The 'development-induced displacement' in tribal areas is symptomatic of the increasing demand for land and land-based products in the current economic environment and there have been controversies over land being taken away from farmers for the purpose of industrialization. This has led to ongoing debates on a 'Land Acquisition, Rehabilitation and Resettlement Bill'. Some of the tribal regions in the country have also become areas of left-wing extremism against the state and this has resulted in much violence in these regions. The left-wing extremists have taken advantage of the marginalization of tribal people to try and draw on their support. Thus, issues of tribal development are emerging as being politically important as the presence of left-wing extremism in tribal regions is being viewed as a major internal security threat.

In recent years, the issue of poverty and deprivation among Muslims in India has also come into the limelight, raising further issues of group-level poverty and deprivation in addition to caste and tribe. Muslims comprise about 13 per cent of India's population and in absolute numbers India has the second highest population of Muslims in the world. A committee appointed by the government to look into the social, economic and educational status of Muslims in India found that their levels of poverty, and especially that of the lower-caste Muslims, are next only to that of Scheduled Castes and Scheduled Tribes. The committee has made several recommendations for their socio-economic development. The most deprived social groups in India also include the 'denotified and nomadic tribes', who have historically emerged as among the most socially excluded groups and are denied most citizenship rights. Here, too, a committee appointed by the government has made recommendations towards including these groups in mainstream development. Implementing the recommendations of these committees would have an important bearing on the welfare of these communities in the coming years.

There are gender disparities in India similar to many other developing countries. However, a progressive feature in India in recent years has been the provision of reserved seats for women, with the objective of their political empowerment. Thus, one half of the elected seats in India at the local rural and urban council level and sub-district and district level are reserved for women; this provision is in the process of being extended to both the state and central legislative bodies. It may be expected that the increasing political empowerment of women would lead to social protection initiatives becoming increasingly sensitive to women's concerns and also lead to their economic empowerment. Social protection programmes will have to face the challenge of reaching out to the most 'backward' sections of society. Thus, a disabled girl child belonging to one of the lowest castes and living in one of the most backward regions of the country would exemplify the most deprived section of society and be most in need of social assistance for her survival.

An important issue in this regard is that of targeting vis-à-vis universal provisions in various government programmes and schemes. The current approach of using the below poverty line/above poverty line (BPL/APL) categorization for targeting the 'poor' has been leading to large exclusion errors. A common eligibility criterion of BPL across a range of programmes and schemes also does not recognize that multiple dimensions of deprivation need not necessarily overlap. For example, a cultivator household may not be chronically food insecure, since it produces enough for its household foodgrain requirements, but it may still be in need of monetary assistance to construct or repair a house. In the current approach of BPL targeting, the very survival of a most deprived household is threatened if it is wrongly categorized as APL. Thus, methodological and administrative issues relating to targeting would need to be resolved for social protection programmes to reach the deprived people. There are also no proper targeting mechanisms in place yet for the urban poor. With some of the worst human development indicators in the world, it may be important for the government to adopt the principle of universalization with regard to the basic needs of the people. In this regard, it would also be important to strengthen schemes such as the NREGA, which are self-targeting schemes, due to the manual labour involved in its work.

The targeting issue is not confined only to the BPL/APL distinction, but also extends to social group categories and backward regions. The SC and ST categories comprise within them more than 400 caste and tribal groups respectively, and there are known to be variations in living standards across ethnic groups within these categories. Thus, it would be important to reach out to the most deprived ethnic groups even within these categories. While the district is commonly identified as a unit of action for public policy with regard to backward regions, it would be important to identify more disaggregated pockets of deprivation, which may extend from being blocks within a district to urban slum ward areas. The most backward regions and areas are also found to be strongly correlated with the composition of their populations, which largely comprise those from the most deprived social groups.

Classifying a household in a BPL category, or identifying a particular ethnic group or region as being backward, will by itself not be enough to help the most deprived people to come out of poverty. What the poor require by way of interventions are relief interventions that will take care of their immediate survival concerns and sustainable livelihood interventions that will help them to come out of poverty and lead to a reduced dependence on relief interventions. Thus, it would also be important to address the structural causes of poverty. This may also involve various redistributive measures, such as land reforms. However, in the current Indian context, while poverty alleviation appears high on the agenda in the policy rhetoric, there is not much mention of redistributive measures to achieve this goal.

According to the 2011 census, the urban population comprises 31.2 per cent of the total population of India. This is expected to exceed 40 per cent by 2030. Most poverty alleviation schemes in India have been largely focused on rural areas. Current social protection programmes such as the NREGA are rural programmes; and programmes such as ICDS are weak in their coverage in urban areas. However, with increasing urbanization and the spillover of rural poverty into urban areas, it would be important to address issues of social protection in urban areas, which would include low-cost housing as a major concern. In this regard, the National Commission for Enterprises in the Unorganised Sector (NCEUS) has recommended the extension of the NREGA into urban areas. It states in one of its reports:

> The Commission is of the view that there should be an urban counterpart to the NREGA. The principles and framework of such an urban employment programme could be the same but with due diligence to the characteristics of the urban labour market as well as the nature of urban context. The Commission is of the view that there exists considerable scope for such a programme. It could be an ideal instrumentality for: (1) construction of publicly funded low cost

> housing that would, first and foremost, target the slum dwellers (2) provide electrification, water supply and sanitation facilities to such housing areas (3) introduce slum improvement programmes wherever feasible (4) undertake projects for greening urban areas to alleviate pollution. (NCEUS, 2009, pp. 214–15)

A strategy of 'growth-mediated development' is expected to lead to an increase in employment opportunities and is also expected to lead to an increase in government revenues, which may then be used to finance various social protection programmes. With regard to employment, the NCEUS reports have documented that economic growth in India has bypassed the 'poor and vulnerable' sections of the population and has led to neither an increase in the quantity nor the quality of their employment. In this context, the NCEUS has stated that 'the most important conclusion that follows from the findings of the Commission is that all these efforts to improve the quantity and quality of employment in the unorganised sector would require a new approach to economic planning in India. The objective of our planning process from now should be maximising employment, in terms of quantity and quality and social development' (NCEUS, 2009, p. v). However, the suggested new approach is in sharp contrast to the current rhetoric of 'inclusive growth' which tends to view inclusion as the end product of sustained rates of high growth, rather than being concomitant with the growth process (Breman, 2010). In spite of the NCEUS recommendations with regard to improving the conditions of work, livelihoods and social security of unorganized workers, most are yet to be acted upon with any urgency (Breman, 2010).

While economic growth has led to an increase in government revenues in India, the tax to gross domestic product (GDP) ratio continues to be less than 20 per cent. The proportion of public expenditure on the social sector also remains low even when compared to other developing countries. For example, the proportion of public expenditure on health is only about 1.4 per cent of GDP. A key debate regarding public expenditures on social protection schemes in India is regarding subsidies vis-à-vis cash transfers. It has been argued that subsidy schemes may not be the best way of improving the welfare of the poor, due to corruption and leakages in various schemes. Instead, cash transfers to the poor are advocated. The expenditures proposed to be covered by way of cash transfers include food and fuel subsidies through the PDS, fertilizer subsidies, rural housing and self-employment programmes. However, the main argument against cash transfers in the Indian context has been that cash transfers cannot and should not replace the public provision of essential goods and services, but rather supplement them (Ghosh, 2011). Notwithstanding such arguments, the government of India appears to have decided on a policy for a gradual introduction of cash transfers, starting with kerosene and fertilizers. Thus, the finance minister in his budget speech of 2011–12 announced that 'to ensure greater efficiency, cost effectiveness and better delivery for both kerosene and fertilisers, the government will move towards direct transfer of cash subsidy to people living below the poverty line in a phased manner' (Ghosh, 2011, p. 69). The prime minister of India recently set up a 'National Committee on Direct Cash Transfers' under his chairmanship, as a 'mechanism to coordinate action for the introduction of direct cash transfers to individuals under the various government schemes and programmes' (Government of India, 2012). The unique identification (UID) card is to be used as one of the important instruments for the introduction of direct cash transfers.

Most social protection programmes in India have been financed from general budgetary provisions. However, some of the programmes such as the midday meal have also been financed through a special tax levied for the purpose. The nature of the financing of social protection programmes may be expected to be an important policy issue for the government in the years to come and also in the context of the demographic challenge. Innovative social insurance experiments which have been tried out in various states of the country and also recommended by the NCEUS may provide a model for extending social insurance programmes on a larger scale throughout the country.

A major concern of social protection policies in India is that despite the large expenditure incurred on various programmes and schemes, they have not had the desired impact. There has been corruption and leakages in the implementation process at various levels. There has also been a multiplicity of programmes and schemes at both the central and state government levels, leading to various overlaps and confusion amongst the administration and the general population, with many of the intended beneficiaries not even being aware of the various schemes or how to access them. The division of responsibility and coordination between the central and state governments has also not been clear, which has contributed to the lack of a coherent and integrated approach to social protection. There have hardly been any administrative reforms that have taken place to deal with the contemporary challenges of development administration. The 73rd and 74th amendments to the Constitution sought to decentralize powers to the rural and urban local bodies, which would lead to people's participation in the development process and greater accountability at the local level, but most state governments in India have not fully implemented the required devolution of powers. Thus, most programmes and schemes remain centralized in their planning and implementation. Schemes such as the NREGA have given an important role to 'panchayati raj institutions'. But, this would also require capacity building of the local bodies and efforts in this regard are still lacking in most states.

However, it is important to note here that there have been state-wide variations in the performance of these programmes and schemes, which is due both to the history of social policy initiatives in particular states and to recent social policies. Thus, Dreze and Sen (2011) note that in at least three Indian states – namely Kerala, Tamil Nadu and Himachal Pradesh – universal provision of essential services has now become an accepted norm. They note that early universalization of elementary education along with land reforms and decentralization are some of the major factors which have led to Kerala's well-known social achievements. Tamil Nadu was the first state in India to introduce free and universal midday meals in primary schools, which later became a model for such a scheme at the country-wide level. The ICDS and the NREGA in Tamil Nadu have been functioning well and the state also has a universal PDS both in rural and urban areas. Himachal Pradesh is an example of a state with recent initiatives in social policy, especially in elementary education, and it has now adopted universalistic policies in the provision of various essential social services. Thus, as noted by Dreze and Sen (2011), it is not an accident that these three states have the best social indicators among Indian states. For example, a simple index of children's education, health and nutrition achievements clearly places these three states at the top (Dreze and Sen, 2011). Other states in India, as well as the central government, can draw lessons from the comparative experiences of social policy and implementation within India itself, besides looking at international comparative experiences.

The World Bank (2011) in its review of social protection in India commissioned by the government of India, proposed that central social protection programmes in India should aim over time for a '3+Block' strategy. This would consist of:

1. A major social assistance programme, by way of a significantly reformed PDS, merged for specific groups with existing social pension programmes, and in reform of PDS, a preference for a predominantly cash transfer approach.
2. A public works programme, for which the NREGA would be the building block, as well as piloting expansion in urban areas.
3. A basic social security package for those outside the formal sector, which would consist of the core types of social security, which the government aims to expand, such as life, disability, old-age pension and health.

The World Bank review recommends that beyond the three 'pillars' or blocks, states could receive an additional transfer and implement state-specific social protection interventions. It states that a common core national social protection system under the three blocks could promote portability of basic entitlements, and would allow more flexibility to states or districts in deciding their social protection expenditure priorities, while still maintaining a common national core social protection system. The review recommends making a transition from the current programme-driven approach to social protection towards an overarching social protection system, which would lead to a more coherent social protection strategy.

The future prospects of social protection in India, however, would depend not only on a coherent social protection strategy and on effective administrative implementation, but on the political will to follow a strategy of human development rather than a focus only on economic growth. Kohli (2012) argues that there has been a pro-business tilt in the Indian state that is responsible both for the progressive dynamism at the apex of the Indian economy and the failure to include India's numerous excluded groups at the bottom of the economy. He argues that economic growth in India has led to new power relations and the power and influence of Indian business has grown significantly in recent decades; these groups have used their influence to mould state behaviour and public opinion through various means, such as electoral finance, corruption and control over the media. Driven by a close alliance with business interests, the major objective of the state is now focused on faster economic growth, while earlier redistributive commitments such as land reforms are no longer considered feasible policy options. The poor, by contrast, are large in number and participate actively in the electoral sphere, but their impact on policies that affect their lives remains limited. Identity politics of caste, religion and regional identity continues to dominate over developmental politics and there is only a rhetorical commitment to the poor, driven by short-term electoral considerations.

Thus, with the initiation of economic liberalization in India, there has also been pressure on the state to withdraw from social services, which would lead to a privatization of these services, and there has also been a much greater corporate influence on policymaking. For example, Dreze and Sen (2011) report the attempt of biscuit manufacturers to introduce their products by way of 'nutritionally fortified biscuits' into the midday meal programme and the supplementary meals provided in the ICDS. The term 'reforms', commonly used in policy discourse in India, has become closely associated with privatization and pro-business policies. The proposed move by the government to implement a policy of direct cash transfers in place of subsidies may also be interpreted as the withdrawal of the state from public provision of essential goods and services and leading to their privatization.

However, the past two decades have also seen people's movements and civil society campaigns which have resulted in various rights-based legislations and contributed towards an ongoing shift in the development discourse in India towards a rights-based approach. For example, civil society activists have now also taken up the issue of the old-age pension as a right and are drafting a set of recommendations to the government in this regard. Dreze (2004) makes the important point that various economic and social rights such as the right to food, right to work, right to information, right to education and right to health should not be viewed in isolation, since they complement each other and together hold the promise of reviving the directive principles of state policy as given in the Constitution of India. There are also ongoing nationwide civil society campaigns in India to reduce corruption and move towards a more participatory democracy, in contrast to the existing representative democracy.

The sustainability of the influence of civil society campaigns on social protection policies and their future implementation would, however, depend on a number of factors. While the National Advisory Council, consisting of prominent social activists, has played an important institutional role in influencing government legislation on social policy, this is not a constitutional body but only an advisory body set up by the existing coalition government for an interface with civil society. Therefore its continuation in the future is likely to depend upon electoral outcomes and other political circumstances. Rights-based legislation will not be effective in and of itself unless the most deprived people are empowered to realize these rights; civil society organizations would have a key role to play in this regard, especially since legislation such as the NREGA and RTI (right to information) is still in the early stages of implementation. The experiences in enacting these pieces of legislation indicate that it is the details of the legislation that are important and civil society organizations need to play a continuing watchdog role to ensure that key provisions are not diluted. The long-term sustainability of civil society interventions would also depend on how far they are able to strengthen democratic institutions at the lowest level, which would give the most deprived sections of society an institutional mechanism to be involved in social protection policies and their implementation.

The higher judiciary in India has played a very important role in both the enactment of rights-based legislation and monitoring its implementation. Mander (2012) points out one example of judicial intervention where, in 2009, in compliance with Supreme Court directions, the Delhi government opened more winter shelters for the homeless in two nights than it had done in 60 years post-independence. Such 'judicial activism' has also been critiqued in the context of the judiciary playing the role of the executive. However, a continuing active role for the higher judiciary in the future will be crucial in pushing the state towards fulfilling its constitutional obligations.

CONCLUSION

The role of the state will be critical in addressing the various challenges for social protection in India and determining its future prospects. In the existing situation, there is pressure on the state to withdraw from social services and give a greater role to market forces and the private sector as is consistent with the neoliberal policy framework and its focus on economic growth; at the same time, there is pressure from civil society campaigns and the higher judiciary for the state to fulfil its constitutional obligations as given in the directive principles of state policy. This also involves striving for a more participatory democracy and developmental politics in India, in contrast to the existing representative democracy which is largely based on identity politics. The outcomes of this transformation within the democratic process would play an important role in influencing the future prospects of social protection in India.

REFERENCES

Breman, J. (2010), 'India's social question in a state of denial', *Economic and Political Weekly*, **45** (23), 42–6.

Dreze, J. (2004), 'Democracy and right to food', *Economic and Political Weekly*, **39** (17), 1723–31.

Dreze, J. and A. Sen (2011), 'Putting growth in its place', *Outlook*, 14 November, accessed at www.outlookindia.com/article.aspx?278843.

Galanter, M. (1991), *Competing Equalities: Law and the Backward Classes in India*, New Delhi: Oxford University Press.

Ghosh, J. (2011), 'Cash transfers as the silver bullet for poverty reduction: a sceptical note', *Economic and Political Weekly*, **46** (21), 67–71.

Government of India (2012), 'PM constitutes national committee on direct cash transfers', Press Information Bureau, accessed at http://pib.nic.in/newsite/erelease.aspx?relid=88620.

Kohli, A. (2012), *Poverty Amid Plenty in the New India*, New Delhi: Cambridge University Press.

Mander, H. (2012), 'Food from the courts: the Indian experience', *IDS Bulletin*, **43** (special issue, July), 15–24.

National Commission for Enterprises in the Unorganised Sector (NCEUS) (2009), *The Challenge of Employment in India: An Informal Economy Perspective*, New Delhi: NCEUS, Government of India.
World Bank (2011), *Social Protection for a Changing India*, Washington, DC: World Bank.

PART IV

Brazil

9. The Brazilian social protection system: history and present configuration

Maria Paula Gomes dos Santos

The aim of this chapter is to describe briefly the evolution of the Brazilian social protection system. Taking into consideration that social protection policies in any country determine and are determined by economic structures and political conflicts (Esping-Andersen, 1990), this chapter will emphasize the country's main economic and political inflections that shaped policy decisions on social protection throughout the last century. It will also comment on the outcomes generated by these decisions on the country's current social conditions, and on the challenges it still faces.

As in many Latin-American countries, Brazil first instituted a Bismarkian model of social security in the 1920s, along with the country's industrialization and urbanization. From a collection of private pension schemes, covering only a few categories of urban workers, the system was expanded and nationalized in the 1930s, though still restricted to the labour force in urban economic activities. Throughout the twentieth century, coverage continued to grow, especially in the 1970s during the military regime when the country experienced an 'economic miracle' and the number of formal jobs escalated.

But it was only after the 1988 Constitution that social protection acquired a broader framework, becoming a 'social right' for every citizen. Since then, income security schemes have been enlarged, in order to cover citizens with reduced contributory capacity; and national systems of social services – such as health care, education and social work – have been improved, amplifying significantly the scope of the state's responsibilities in social protection, as well as in social promotion. These movements have required involvement of the three federative government levels (the nation, the federal states and municipalities), demanding a formidable fiscal effort from all of them.

Despite the big challenges still faced by these systems – particularly as regards the quality of service delivery – such effort has seemed worthwhile:

Brazilian poverty rates, as well as inequality indexes, have dropped considerably in the last 10 years. Unequivocally, economic growth has played an important role in this process since the mid-2000s, as well as the measures to control inflation and promote monetary stabilization taken in 1994.

In order to provide a comprehensive picture of these developments, this chapter contains four sections besides this introduction. In section I, the origins and evolution of Brazilian social protection institutions will be outlined. These correspond to the years between the 1920s and the 1980s, when social protection basically meant *social insurance*, that is, the provision of pensions and health care for urban workers on a contributory basis. Section II tells how the struggles for democratization in the late 1980s led to the writing of the 'Welfare State Constitution', inspired by a Beveridgean conception of social protection. It also analyses the delays in implementation of the demands of the new Constitution, favoured by the neoliberal environment of the 1990s. The third section approaches the further developments of the social protection systems from 2003 on, when economic growth was resumed and a political coalition of social democratic tendency took office in the national government. The chapter ends with some final remarks.

ORIGINS: SOCIAL SECURITY FOR MODERNIZATION, 1923–88

As in most Western countries, social protection as a public concern emerged in Brazil along with the country's industrialization and urbanization. Scholars such as Oliveira and Teixeira (1986) largely converge in affirming 1923 as its founding year, when a parliamentary decree, known as the Eloy Chaves Law, proclaimed every railway worker entitled to a fully funded pension scheme. This decree ordered every company in this business to organize such schemes, which would be funded by contributions from employers, employees and railway users. According to the decree, the only role assigned to the state in those schemes was mediation of occasional conflicts among parties. Three years later (1926), this policy was also applied to workers in docks and ships, while other urban workers would become entitled in the years to come. As mentioned, these social security schemes were privately funded and managed, in line with the liberal convictions held by government in those times.

The Brazilian economy was then mostly rural, based on coffee plantations and exports. Railway, dock and ship workers were the main salaried workers engaged in these activities: carrying the coffee from the hinterland to the docks and from the docks to the consumer markets abroad. This is probably the main reason for the privilege of these workers in being the first ones granted social security. The country then had an emerging industry, which employed mostly foreign workers (Italians, Spaniards and Portuguese). But their claims for social rights were ignored at that time, if not criminalized (see Santos, 1979; Fausto, 1976).

In the 1930s, Brazilian social security entered a new phase, initiated by the first term of the Getúlio Vargas government (1930–45). Supported by a coalition of pro-industry actors (workers and entrepreneurs), Vargas took power through a *coup d'état* – known as the 1930 Revolution – and pursued industrial development as a central goal of his government. Indeed, despite its totalitarian nature, the Vargas regime managed to change the face of the economy, transforming it from an agro-exporter economy into an industrial one, while spurring its urbanization and modernization.

The industrialization process initiated at this time took place under strong state command. Multiple roles were played by the state through planning, advising, funding and regulating economic activities, as well as in the provision of infrastructure, such as roads, ports, power generation plants, communication services and basic industry (mining, oil, steel, metallurgy, electricity). Foreign and private capital also engaged in the process as they were offered advantageous conditions. This process evolved over the following 35 years, under different political regimes, entailing a long cycle of industrialization and growth (between 1930 and 1980, the gross domestic product (GDP) grew at an average rate of 6.5 per cent each year), which favoured employment creation and a steady rise in social security coverage.

Regarding the accomplishment of the industrial development project, the state's role in controlling the social order in the 1930s and 1940s was as important as its intervention in the economic process. For that, Vargas instituted a corporatist state inspired by Mussolini's fascism (see Schmitter, 1974), in which parliament was shut and business and work representatives became part of the state's structure through 'syndicates' which represented workers and employers. These, in turn, were totally submitted to the control of the state, which legislated about their Constitution, the nomination of their officers, as well as their functioning rules (Santos, 1979). Additionally, distribution of power between workers' and capitalists' associations was made absolutely asymmetric: while capitalists directly took part in the state's economic decisions by holding permanent seats in the state's economic agencies (Diniz, 1978; Santos, 1979; Werneck Vianna, 1998), workers were expected to guarantee a 'peaceful' environment for industrial prosperity.

In order to achieve this, Vargas designed a comprehensive system of 'labour rights' which was implemented throughout the 1930s and 1940s; these comprised: regulated working hours (including rules for women and a minimum working age), employment registration, paid vacations, a minimum wage and social security. As a result, multiple social security institutes were progressively created in those years, along with the various professional syndicates (trade unions), to provide benefits such as pensions and health care. These institutes operated only for workers in the urban economy, and had their managers and bureaucrats directly nominated by the state, through the Ministry of Labour. Social security schemes were then financed by employers, employees and the state, each paying for one-third of the expenses. At first, these were fully funded schemes, but due to financial imbalances throughout the years, a pay-as-you-go system replaced the capitalized one during the 1940s.

Financial imbalances were mostly caused by the system's escalating costs, generated by the clientelistic pattern that marked social policymaking at that time. As a general rule, each institute was concerned with specific 'baskets' of benefits and services. The 'generosity' and scope of these baskets, in turn, depended on the degree of loyalty shown by each union to the government. Therefore, the closest and most compliant unions were gifted with more and the most generous benefits, while the others lagged behind. As a result, a political competition was installed among occupational groups due to differentiated benefits, which were, in turn, granted regardless of any financial considerations (Santos, 1979; Werneck Vianna, 1998). Besides its economic pitfalls, this practice also generated, in the long run, a very heterogeneous and stratified social protection system that led to huge inequalities among workers. Considering that rural workers were not allowed to set up either trade unions or a social security institution, they were totally excluded from social protection. In 1940, according to the national census, these workers represented 35 per cent of the country's adult labour force. In fact, during this decade, it can be calculated that social security was restricted to only 14 per cent of Brazilian workers. This picture prevailed until the 1960s, with effects on the country's social stratification that would be felt for many years ahead, and still persist today.

As can be easily concluded, such an arrangement allowed the state at once to forge an industrial working class and to control its demands. Under such 'political management', social security institutions became crucial not only for the industrialization project, but for the stability of the regime (Santos, 1979). On the other hand, the system's fragmentation along occupational categories, with their differentiated social rights, accounts for the deep social inequalities that have continued to pervade Brazilian society.

Regarding social assistance, the Vargas Era enacted the first policy in the field in 1938, when the National Social Service Council (*Conselho Nacional de Serviço Social*, CNSS) was instituted. This council laid the foundations for the organization of social assistance services that prevailed in the country for the next 50 years. The task of assisting the 'less fortunate' was assigned to charity organizations, while the state had a role only in financing the services provided by them, by means of subsidies, tax exemptions and transfers. Therefore, until 1988 social assistance was a minor policy in Brazil. Its goals were unclear, its beneficiaries unknown, and its providers fragmented (IPEA, 2009). Organized under the principle of moral duty, social assistance was exempt from any regulatory principle, planning or demand estimates, while it was subject to parsimonious and discontinued funding (Sposati, 1989). As a result, the field evolved on a philanthropic basis and became subject to political bargaining between the state and private institutions.

After the deposition of Vargas in 1945, Brazil experienced a 'mild' democratic regime, until the start of the military regime in 1964. In this period, in spite of the full functioning of parliament, left-wing parties were still outlawed, and trade unions remained under very repressive policies (Santos, 1979, p. 80). Partisan politics remained irrelevant, and policy decisions about social security continued to be made through clientelistic bargains. As a result, public social spending increased even more, causing discrepancies among occupational groups to escalate, and financial imbalances to deepen (Santos, 1979; Teixeira and Oliveira, 1986).

This began to change in 1960, when the National Congress approved the Organic Law of Social Security (LOPS), which finally equalized social security benefits and contributions. But social security institutes had not yet been unified, and provision of services and benefits remained segmented. Nevertheless, this law represented the demise of clientelistic and particularized bargaining in the social security system.

The unification of the social security institutes took place in 1966, two years after the installation of the military regime. An exception was made for the civil servants' social security institute, which remained active until the end of the 1970s. The objectives of the new government were then twofold: on the one hand, it aimed to rationalize the system, as suggested by specialists on many occasions since the Vargas government; on the other, the decision was also intended to disempower trade unions and their leadership, who in fact controlled the institutes and had been important supporters of the deposed regime.

Therefore, a new institution – the National Social Security Institute (INPS) – was created to unify and centralize the provision of benefits and services. Different from the previous institutes, this one was to be ruled only by government and employer representatives, without the participation of workers. Benefits remained the same, comprising pensions (for the retired and survivors), insurance against work accidents, paid leave in case of illnesses (related or unrelated to jobs), and health care services.

Health services were to be provided either by professionals employed in the institute itself, or by outsourced (private) organizations and personnel. The outsourcing of medical care and hospital services had been, in fact, a central strategy of the military government to expand the private supply of health services at the time, and became increasingly prevalent during the 1970s. Such expansion ultimately led to the emergence of a politically influential private health care sector in the country. As a result, when the national universal health system – Sistema Único de Saúde (SUS) – began to be built, the use of veto powers by the private health care industry surged, thus creating difficulties for the implementation of the SUS (see Werneck Vianna, 1998).

By launching a new accumulation phase, the military regime carried out massive investments and efforts to develop a base industry. These ended up promoting a radical change in industry in the following decade, and the years between 1964 and 1980 were marked by an 'economic miracle' in which high real growth rates were registered: in 1973, GDP growth achieved the rate of 13.9 per cent.

In such an environment, social security entitlement was extended to other professional groups, such as domestic, rural and autonomous workers. However, eligibility for benefits remained conditional on payment of contributions, and benefits paid to peasants and rural workers were lower than those received by urban employees. Workers with no contributory capacity remained unprotected, although a social assistance benefit was started in 1974 – the 'Lifetime Monthly Income' – for those aged 70 or above who had made a minimum of 12 contributions to the social security system. It is also noteworthy that the operational capacity of the social security system in the 1970s and 1980s was not expanded along with the increase of its beneficiaries in the period, which undermined its efficacy in providing good services and benefits.

This situation became even worse during the recession of the 1980s, when the system was pushed into a deep crisis. With the end of a long period of economic growth, another phase began, marked by 25 years of economic stagnation with high inflationary pressures and growing external debt. In the political field, this period was marked by transition to democracy, in which a new foundation was laid for the country's economic and social development.

THE 1988 WELFARE STATE CONSTITUTION IN A NEOLIBERAL ENVIRONMENT

By the mid-1980s, movements towards political redemocratization gained momentum. At the same time, economic recession contributed to the deterioration of living conditions, particularly for the poorest. The streets were occupied by social movements and politicians who demanded restoration of the democratic rule of law, as well as a new social pact which would change the country's structure of opportunities.

The democratic transition – performed at a 'slow and gradual pace', as defined by the military – involved two main steps: the first consisted of an indirect election of a civilian president, in 1985, intended to run the country until a new federal Constitution was settled when a new president would be directly elected. The second was the writing of this new Constitution by a National Constituent Assembly, which was directly elected in 1986 and worked from 1987 to 1988.

Besides removing the 'authoritarian refuse' from the national institutions, the Constitution welcomed the demands for a new social pact, bringing to the forefront a number of principles and commands that contributed to important changes in the country's social protection framework. Among these changes, one of the most significant was the recognition of the state's responsibility in providing social welfare for all, regardless of contributions or payments. To achieve this, the new constitutional text broadened the scope of 'social security' beyond its historical meaning of 'social insurance'. As stated in its 194th Article: 'Social security includes an integrated set of initiatives by public authorities and society, to ensure the rights to health, welfare and social assistance.'

'Social security' then began to mean the new social pact convened by society, in substitution of the old one held since the Vargas Era. According to Werneck Vianna:

> The choice of the term 'Social Security' by the Brazilian Constitution of 1988 represents a concerted decision to expand social protection beyond its original meaning of 'social insurance' [. . .] It means a compromise among different political groups in favor of the ILO definition, in which social security accounts for a safety net for all who need it, regardless of any contributory status. It also extends the concept of social risk beyond circumstances of the loss of working capacity – due to old age, sickness, disability, maternity, accident at work – to include others like, for example, insufficient income. (Werneck Vianna, 2003, p. 2)

This new conception would unfold in new provisions for social protection, while old ones would be reframed. Social assistance cash benefits, so far insignificant in the Brazilian income security matrix, were granted to old people (aged 65 and above) and persons with disabilities in poverty. Social security for rural workers, peasants, fishermen and collectors was enhanced through the equalization of their benefits (in value and type) to those provided to urban employees. Unemployment insurance, which was created in 1986, acquired a new design and a new funding strategy.

In addition – and of great importance to the effectiveness of these benefits – there was the Constitution's demand that no benefits should be lower than the minimum wage. Altogether, these provisions entailed a more comprehensive income security matrix, which would be still improved in the years after 2000, as will be seen in the next section.

The social protection framework given by the 1988 Constitution also declared the state responsible for providing essential services for all, such as education, health care and social work. Therefore, from then on, social assistance – both benefits and services – was no longer a matter of charity or benevolence, but of social right.

Other responsibilities – concerning housing, sanitation, labour and employment – were also assigned to the state, which was supposed to accomplish them through partnership with the private sector.

The framework of social policies stipulated by the 1988 federal Constitution allowed for social protection and social promotion. Social protection comprised social security – including unemployment insurance, the Old Age and Disability Grant and Bolsa Família (family allowance) – and some social services – including universal health care. Social promotion comprised some social services – including secondary education and employment services – and state-provided infrastructure for housing, sanitation and rural development.

In fact, the new Constitution laid the institutional basis of a complex system of social policies, made up of a wide network of public institutions and resources. It also determined that this system should be funded and operated by the three federative levels of the state: the federal government, the member states and the municipalities. Policy decentralization had been another important issue debated during the Constitution discussion, since there was a widespread perception that inefficiency and corruption that had plagued social policies up to this point were due to extreme policy centralization and the government's lack of accountability.

However, in the five years that followed the Constitution's enactment, implementation of the new constitutional provisions was systematically delayed. This was due on the one hand to economic constraints caused by a deep recession and escalating inflation, which reached the rate of 1500 per cent in 1990. On the other hand, the delay was greatly influenced by the neoliberal environment that prevailed at this time, both nationally and internationally.

On the domestic front, the democratic environment allowed for an extensive reconfiguration of the political arena, in which political parties and interest groups were reorganized along new divisions. In line with the neoliberal paradigm that dominated international economic thinking, many national economists and policymakers began to propose a revision of the newly granted social rights on the basis of their fiscal costs, which, according to them, would undermine Brazilian competitiveness. In turn, international institutions like the International Monetary Fund (IMF), the World Bank and the Inter-American Development Bank largely conditioned their financial support to indebted countries on the adoption, by these countries, of their structural adjustment agenda, which meant, among other things, severe retrenchment of the states' social spending.

The election of President Fernando Collor de Mello in 1989 – the first direct presidential election to take place since the beginning of the military regime and after the new Constitution's enactment – epitomizes this political moment, marked by a conservative reaction conducive to an alignment of the Brazilian state to the Washington Consensus.

During the three years of Collor's mandate, except for the regulation of unemployment insurance, the making of legislation required for implementing the new social rights was systematically postponed, while social policies remained underfunded. This was part of the strategy to achieve fiscal adjustment and to control inflation, which were pursued since the very first day of his administration.

Collor was impeached by parliament in 1992 on corruption charges. But, underneath this impeachment there was also great dissatisfaction with his disastrous stabilization plan, as well as with the abrupt way he implemented international trade liberalization.

Itamar Franco, the elected vice-president who completed Collor's mandate, took office in 1992 in the midst of severe economic constraints and persistent inflation. Despite that, he finally initiated the regulation of the new social rights, as commanded by the 1988 Constitution.

However, as established in the Constitution's Temporary Provisions Act (3rd Article), a revision of the Charter was supposed to take place in 1993. Taking advantage of the occasion, representatives of the 'conservative reaction' tried to propose a reform of the social security system, with the aim of cutting costs, especially regarding pensions and social assistance benefits. In a situation where the Chilean pensions reform of the 1980s was actively recommended by international financial institutions (see World Bank, 1994), leading economists and politicians suggested the adoption of a similar model in Brazil. The idea was faced with strong resistance, however, both in parliament and within the state bureaucracy itself, which estimated the transition costs of such reform as about two and a half times the country's GDP. In view of that, the project of a structural reform of Brazilian social security was temporarily suspended.

By the end of his mandate (in 1994), President Franco achieved the most valuable of the goals ever set by any Brazilian government since the 1980s: the control of the rampant price inflation. The *Real* Plan, headed by Fernando Henrique Cardoso, who was then the minister of economy, finally succeeded in promoting monetary stabilization, bringing hope to the nation of better economic prospects.

At the end of that year, Cardoso was elected to the presidency for the period 1995–98. In fact, he ended up serving two presidential terms, since he was re-elected in 1997 for the term 1998–2002. His first mandate took place in quite an optimistic environment. Monetary stabilization had immediately increased people's purchasing power and promoted growth in consumption, in tax revenues and in the GDP itself, which allowed for social spending to expand.

However, as put by Amitrano and Petrelli (2012), 'public spending had only a moderate expansion in the period' due to 'the government's attempt to use fiscal policy as an anchor for the stabilization policy'. In fact, expansion of social spending from 1995 to 1998 was largely driven by the implementation of the social rights set by the Constitution of 1988. Insofar as the social security and social assistance benefits were implemented, more individuals were incorporated into the social protection system.

On the other hand, this increased the number of benefits paid on a monthly basis, which led to increasing preoccupation with the short-term fiscal costs of the system, as well as with its long-term trends. Therefore, the new social rights remained under fire and in 1995 President Cardoso submitted a proposal to parliament for a constitutional amendment intended to reshape the national pensions system.

After three years of parliamentary negotiations, a constitutional amendment was approved, although the changes made had a more restricted scope than initially planned. The most significant of these was the introduction of actuarial elements into the pensions formula for private sector employees. This new formula – named 'the pensions factor' – was basically intended to prevent the early retirement of those employees. According to data from the Ministry of Social Security, the average retirement age was, at that time, around the age of 54. Indeed, the reform reduced the pensions value of prospective retirees if they planned to retire before the age of 60 (women) or 65 (men) and if their prospective benefits were to be higher than the floor value (one minimum wage).

The reform also hit the civil servants' pensions system, by setting an age of retirement (60/65) and by suppressing a few 'privileges' previously granted to these workers. Nevertheless, only in 2012 did a more structural reform take place – one that introduced a ceiling for civil servants' benefits, as well a complementary pillar of defined contribution in their pension regime.

When Cardoso's second term began (1998), very different macroeconomic conditions were in place. As a result of two agreements signed with the IMF – one in 1998 and another in 2002 – tough targets for a fiscal surplus had been set, which significantly shrank resources available for investments and current expenditure. Besides that, in early 1999 the national currency suffered a new crisis, due to its artificial overvaluation which had been used by the Central Bank as a strategy to control inflation. So, in line with the neoliberal agenda, new social investments were gradually redirected to poverty alleviation policies, among which were the conditional cash transfer programmes (Cardoso Jr. and Jaccoud, 2003).

The introduction of cash transfers into the Brazilian social protection system had already been put on the agenda at the beginning of that decade. The issue was first debated in 1990, when a bill was submitted to parliament in order to allow for the creation of a negative income tax for adults (over 25) in poverty. Although this bill had not passed, the perception that the state should provide some kind of monetary protection for families and children in poverty began to be disseminated in political and academic circles. By the mid-1990s, the idea was put into practice by a few local administrations (municipalities, state governments, as well as the Federal District Brasília), which initiated cash transfer programmes, most of them conditioned to families' investment in children's education: school enrolment and attendance. As described by Britto and Soares (2011, p. 1), this kind of condition was seen 'as a means of tying a short-term offset policy (the income transfer per se) with long-term structural objectives (breaking the vicious cycle of intergenerational poverty by increasing the human capital of future generations)'.

Given the success of such local initiatives, the national government started its own Conditional Cash Transfer (CCT) programme in 1996, designed to combat child labour; and began to co-finance local programmes in 1997. In 2001, other programmes were launched: the Bolsa Escola (school allowance) and the Bolsa Alimentação (food allowance), both of them to a national target audience. New programmes designed to meet specific needs continued to be created, and by the end of 2002 there were seven CCT programmes in operation, each one managed by a different state agency based on different information systems and with different objectives, criteria and rules (see Cotta and Paiva, 2010; Soares and Satyro, 2010). In fact, these programmes were seen by that time as having a transitional character, since welfare provisions were conceived so far as related to job positions. But, contrary to expectations, they happened to open a new era for the Brazilian social protection system, for they laid the foundations from which the Bolsa Família would evolve, from 2003.

Attempts to reduce or abolish the social security rights set by the 1988 Constitution did not succeed during Cardoso's mandate, except for the 'mild' reform made to the pensions system in 1998. Social spending showed a growth trend in this period, both in current prices and as a share of GDP. Total federal social spending increased 32 per cent (real values) between 1995 and 2002 and rose from 11 to nearly 13 per cent of gross national product (GNP). Social assistance spending, in particular, showed a total growth of about six times, from 0.1 to 0.6 per cent of GDP.

SOCIAL PROTECTION UNDER LABOUR POLITICS

The election of President Lula in 2002 marked an important turning point in the country's political history. It was the first time that a Labour party rooted in trade unions had won the competition for national government, under the leadership of a blue-collar worker.

It was not a smooth beginning, however. By the end of 2002 and the beginning of 2003, the Brazilian currency was hit hard by a speculative shock, due to market suspicions that the new Labour government would not honour the country's international debts. As a result, 2003 was a bad year for the Brazilian economy, with the Real deeply depreciated against the dollar and economic activity depressed.

Nevertheless, contrary to market expectations, the new government enhanced the fiscal adjustment initiated by its predecessor, setting targets for a primary surplus that ranked above those agreed with the IMF. Additionally, a new pensions reform was submitted to parliament in 2003, concerning the civil servants' regime, which was considered very costly in fiscal terms, and regressive from a distributional perspective. These decisions helped to calm the markets and helped government to recover international credibility.

On the other hand, international restrictions began to soften in mid-2003 due to the expansion of international trade, especially for primary commodities for which Brazil has always had a clear comparative advantage. Consequently, exports boomed, with an average growth rate of 10 per cent between 2003 and 2006. By the end of 2004, GDP growth had already resumed, keeping an upward trend until the end of 2010.

In this situation, the Labour government had the conditions to start fulfilling its main campaign promises, the main one being to end hunger in Brazil. In October 2003, the Bolsa Família Programme was launched as the most prominent policy in this regard. Created through the merging of the previous CCT programmes, Bolsa Família reached 6.5 million families in 2004, and double this number by the end of 2012.

When it comes to fighting poverty and inequality, Bolsa Família has undoubtedly had a major impact, especially if one considers that it costs only 0.4 per cent of GDP. But its enactment also has political importance, since it is the first cash transfer targeted at families that have members at working age. In this sense, the creation of Bolsa Família represents a significant breakthrough in the Brazilian social policy tradition, according to which poverty and vulnerability were understood as resulting exclusively from joblessness or non-performance of work. In line with this, solutions were expected to come from economic growth, formal job creation and the consequent inclusion of vulnerable groups in the contributory social security system. Even when growth alone proved to be insufficient to create decent jobs, and the persistence of poverty and inequality became evident, the introduction of large-scale non-contributory cash transfers to working-age adults faced strong political resistance in the country. This reflected the traditional meritocratic convictions that had historically prevailed in Brazilian society, and the widespread thinking that these transfers create disincentives to labour market participation. However, such resistance has softened since the start of Bolsa Família, for it became clear that its target audience consists of poor and extremely poor households whose adult members *do* participate in the labour market, although this does not guarantee them sufficient income for a dignified survival.

During President Lula's second mandate (2006–10), credit and investments also expanded, leading to job creation, wage increases and greater household consumption. For the period between 2003 and 2010, the average GDP growth rate achieved the rate of 4.4 per cent per year. As a consequence, more room was opened for social spending. On the other hand, according to Amitrano and Petrelli (2012), household consumption growth in this period 'was undoubtedly associated with the consolidation and expansion of income transfer programs through the Bolsa Família program, as well as real increases in the minimum wage, (which had an) impact on social security benefits'.

In fact, the association of GDP growth and the expansion of cash transfers has had a two-way effect: while GDP growth allowed for more social transfers, these also played an important role in spurring it, in a kind of virtuous cycle. Since 2004, and particularly from 2007, transfers to families have become much more significant, due to the constitutional indexation of the social benefits (unemployment insurance, pensions, Old Age and Disability Grant) to the minimum wage, which, as will be shown, had important increases in the period.

There is no doubt that recovery of the real value of the minimum wage has been essential to strengthen the income safety net entailed by the 1988 Constitution. This recovery process started in 1994, along with the implementation of the monetary stabilization plan (the *Real* Plan); but its impacts increased even more from 2007, when an agreement was made between the national government and the trade unions, in which the minimum wage adjustment began to follow the national prices index *plus* the GDP growth rate of the preceding two years. This rule is still in place.

As a result of this policy, the minimum wage had a total increase of 50 per cent between 2003 and 2010, which represents an average annual growth of 8.3 per cent. Besides its direct effects on the labour market, this growth has had very positive effects on social protection benefits like social security, unemployment insurance and the Old Age and Disability Grant. It is significant that Bolsa Família benefits are not indexed to the minimum wage, being adjusted by specific decisions of the president of the republic.

When it comes to analysing the evolution of federal social expenditure between 1995 and 2010 its steady increase in the whole period becomes very clear. The expenditure starts from a threshold of R$234 billion in 1995, reaching R$638.5 billion in 2010 – meaning a real growth rate of 172 per cent in 16 years. This evolution represents an increase in federal social spending of 4.3 percentage points of GDP in the period. If population growth in the same period is considered, federal social spending per capita had more than doubled in real terms, from 1995 (R$1471.46) to 2010 (R$3324.84).

Social assistance, which had grown to 0.6 per cent of GNP by 2002, continued to grow to 1.1 per cent of GDP by 2010; this was mostly due to increases in the take-up rates of the Old Age and Disability Grant and of Bolsa Família, as well as the rise in the value of the benefits during the period.

On the other hand, in the social security branch (mostly pensions) a less rapid growth took place, rising from 5 per cent of GDP in 1995 to 6 per cent in 2002 to just over 7 per cent in 2010; this can be explained by the pension reforms made in 1998 and 2003, which set more restrictive rules for retirement, for both private sector employees and civil servants.

As far as partisan politics can explain differentials in social spending, the presence of a Labour-influenced coalition in the Brazilian federal government is correlated to a social spending pattern that seems higher than that observed in the previous period (1995–2002) when governing parties espoused neoliberal convictions. On the other hand, it cannot be forgotten that each of the governing coalitions faced very different domestic and international economic environments; the first was marked by severe external restrictions, while the second met more favourable conditions.

Nevertheless, it is beyond dispute that, apart from any short-term political and economic determinants, the main factor to explain social expenditure growth since 1995 – along with the expansion of social protection – is the new social protection framework inscribed in the 1988 Constitution. Since its inception – or more properly, since the development and regulation of its commands – social policies and social protection have become more institutionalized, and acquired a more comprehensive configuration, for which more public resources were needed.

In the next and final section of this chapter, a more detailed examination is made of the different benefits that assure income security to the Brazilian working population, which can be seen as a national income security matrix.

THE INCOME SECURITY MATRIX: INSTITUTIONAL CONFIGURATION, COVERAGE, BENEFITS AND THEIR SHARE IN THE SOCIAL SPENDING

In 2010, more than half of the Brazilian population received monetary benefits from the country's social protection system. These transfers, both contributory and non-contributory, represented expenditure of more than R$300 billion (or US$150 billion) from the public fund, as shown in Table 9.1.

Each of these benefits meets different risks and circumstances which vary from job loss to insufficient family income. This broad profile had made the system quite effective in fighting poverty and inequality (as will be shown in the next chapter of this book). In the following lines, a brief description of the existing monetary benefits of the Brazilian income

Table 9.1 Brazil: income security matrix

Benefits, number of beneficiaries and total spending – 2010		
Benefits	Beneficiaries (million)	Total spending (Reias million)
Social security	26 000	246 000
Unemployment insurance	8 000	19 200
Old Age and Disability Grant	3 400	22 000
Bolsa Família	67 500	13 500
Total	104 900	300 700

Source: Ministry of Social Security, Ministry of Labor and Ministry for Social Development administrative data, 2010.

security matrix is given, covering dimensions such as: the kinds of benefit provided; the population groups addressed; the eligibility criteria for the beneficiaries; and their expenditure.

Social Security (Pensions and Aids)

After 90 years, this is certainly the strongest and most traditional instrument for income protection in the country. In spite of not reaching all the population, social security mobilizes the greatest share of federal social spending.

Its institutional configuration represents a two-pillar system: the first is public and mandatory, totally managed by the state (through the Social Security National Institute), while the second is represented by the complementary pillar, of voluntary schemes run by private agents.

The mandatory pillar is organized on a pay-as-you-go model. It is mostly funded by contributions of employers and employees, though the state is supposed to cover any deficits derived from a mismatch between payments and revenues.

This pillar comprises two branches: the so-called 'General Regime' (RGPS), which applies to workers in the private sector of the economy; and the branch of the 'Special Regimes' (RPPS), which covers public servants in all levels of government. Both assure a variety of benefits, such as pensions for retirees and survivors and temporary aids that assist insured workers in case of sickness, maternity/paternity, accidents and imprisonment (paid to the family of the insured sentenced person).

The complementary pillar, in turn, consists of pension schemes provided by private firms, and can be organized through two different arrangements: pension funds and pension insurances. Pension funds are mutual schemes, sponsored by employers and employees of public and private organizations. Pension insurance is purchased on an individual basis, by banks and insurance companies.

The General Regime

Laws 8.212 and 8.213 of 1991 provide the conditions under which workers have access to benefits of the General Regime, as well as the minimum and the maximum value of benefits. Defined by the 1988 Constitution, the minimum value for benefits equals the minimum wage, while the maximum value is periodically established by parliament. In 2012, the highest value for social security benefits amounted to almost R$4000, approximately US$2000.

All workers in the formal labour market are compulsorily affiliated to the system, and pay contributions that amount to 11 per cent of their wages, while employers pay 22 per cent of their total payroll. In spite of the system's Bismarkian principle, rural workers (peasants) as well as fishermen and collectors are entitled to a special contributory regime, as mentioned earlier in this chapter. Instead of paying a share of their salaries (in many cases, non-existent), their contributions are paid by the buyers of the goods produced by them, as a share of the values traded.

Indeed, workers in this group benefited most from the changes made by the 1988 Constitution, since they became entitled to the same rights held by urban workers. Their benefits were raised from 50 per cent to 100 per cent of the minimum wage. Additionally, until the enactment of the Constitution, it was not possible for a single rural household to apply for more than one pension benefit, no matter how many individuals in it worked. Since then, benefits have been based not on the household production unit, but on individual workers. All peasants, fishermen and collectors aged 16 and above and working in household production were then included as 'special insured' workers, not only the head of the family. This led to a great expansion of social protection for workers in this group. From 1990 to 1992, the number of special insured workers jumped from 2.5 million to about eight million. This number has fallen in the following years, to about 6.5 million, due to a decrease in the rural population (IPEA, 2009).

Retirement pensions are provided on two different bases, the first being the worker's contribution time (minimum of 35 years for men and 30 years for women), and the second being the worker's age (65 for men and 60 for women). Retirement on the basis of age is granted for those who, having achieved the reference age, have contributed to the system for at least 15 years. For those whose benefits values rank above the minimum wage, and who retire after the full contributory period (30 or 35 years), a deflator rate is applied to their pensions according to their age.

Since 1996, but more intensively after 2006, a number of policy initiatives have been implemented in order to improve coverage of informal urban workers. These initiatives focus on workers with low contributory capacity, who work in individual jobs or small firms, and consist of reductions in contributions to a very basic level (in some cases, to 5 per cent of the minimum salary) while ensuring access to all kinds of benefits; retirement cannot be before the age of 65/60.

Unemployment Insurance

First created in 1986, unemployment insurance had limited coverage until 1990, due to the absence of specific funding sources, as well as very restrictive access criteria. The 1988 Constitution included it among the workers' rights and designed a new funding mechanism; it was no longer attached to current revenues of the public budget, but supported by a specific fund that could be capitalized in order to pay for the rise of disbursements in times of extensive unemployment. This fund is made up of resources that come from specific contributions paid by enterprises to the national treasury.

During 1989, negotiations involving parliament and the executive branch of the government resulted in a new law, which broadened the social insurance coverage and raised the value of its benefits, as well as the amount of resources made available for their payment. Aside from this, the law allowed for the new fund to finance other employment services, such as labour intermediation and professional training. Altogether, these changes laid the basis for the creation of a public employment system in Brazil, which is now operative.

At present, the value of the benefit corresponds to the average of the wages received by the worker in the last three months before his/her dismissal. This value cannot be lower than the minimum wage.

Social Assistance

Until the 1990s, social assistance cash benefits values in Brazil were not defined, while their distribution was made under unclear criteria. Payments were often discontinued, the number of beneficiaries was very low and funding resources were scarce.

As mentioned before, the 1988 Constitution commanded the integration of social assistance to the national social security framework, discontinuing the legacy of the Vargas Era of contributory-based social protection. This change expressed, on the one hand, the new national commitment to address situations of insufficient income and deprivation, historically neglected in the country. On the other hand, it signified the state's recognition that social support, rather than a charitable action, is a right of vulnerable citizens.

Thus, social assistance policies since comprise of two kinds of provision: cash transfers and social work with families and individuals in vulnerable conditions.

Regarding cash transfers, two kinds of benefits compound the general income security matrix: the Old Age and Disability Grant (*Benefício de Prestação Continuada* – BPC) and the Bolsa Família Programme (PBF). Each will be presented in more detail in the following paragraphs.

The Old Age and Disability Grant (BPC)

With its origin in the Constitution, the Old Age and Disability Grant provides a monthly income to elderly citizens aged 65 or older and to disabled people of any age, with no conditions to work or to make an independent living. In both cases, applicants must be considered to be in 'extreme poverty', which means living with a family per capita income up to one-quarter of the minimum wage (approximately US$77.50). Given the indexation of this benefit to the minimum wage, the poverty line it identifies undergoes automatic correction when the minimum wage increases. In turn, this can generate automatic increases in the number of eligible beneficiaries.

The benefit is means-tested and its value equal to the minimum wage. Three and a half million people received the benefit every month in 2010: 1 600 000 of which were persons with disabilities and 1 400 000 were elderly.

Together with contributory social security pensions (especially those applying to rural workers, peasants, fishermen and collectors), the Old Age and Disability Grant has been of great importance for fighting poverty among old people in Brazil. In 2010, less than 8 per cent of people aged 65 or older were below the poverty line.

Due to the significant coverage of rural old people by contributory social security, the Old Age and Disability Grant is mostly an urban benefit, which has been extremely valuable to those segments of urban workers with no employment history, or whose careers were marked by instability and low wages which prevented access to social insurance.

The Bolsa Família (Family Grant Programme)

Bolsa Família provides a monthly cash transfer to families in poverty and extreme poverty. Two poverty lines are considered, though both are different from the one used for the Old Age and Disability Grant. The first (extreme poverty) corresponds to a monthly per capita income up to U$35; the second (poverty), a monthly per capita income between U$35.01 and U$70.

Being a conditional cash transfer programme, there are some elements which condition the receipt of benefits by families. These include: (i) Education: school attendance of at least 85 per cent of the annual school days for children and adolescents aged 6–15 years and a minimum of 75 per cent for adolescents aged 16–17 years; (ii) Health: compliance with the national immunization schedule for children, as well as submission to the monitoring of their growth and development by the state, through the national health system (SUS). Pregnant women and nursing mothers aged 14–44 years also have to undergo official monitoring.

The programme is funded and coordinated by the federal government, but municipalities take the responsibility for the enrolment of beneficiaries (including the active search for potential beneficiaries) and monitoring the families' compliance with the conditions of cash transfer. These tasks are performed by the social work branch of social assistance. Despite challenges in coordination, decentralized management has resulted in successful gains in the programme's implementation and management.

Several states and municipalities have their own cash transfer programmes. In these cases, agreements are convened with the federal government, which enable their integration with the national framework.

When Bolsa Família was first launched in 2003, it covered 3.6 million families, but by 2004 it covered nine million households. In 2010, there were 12.7 million families receiving benefits.

When President Dilma Rousseff (of the Labour Party) took office in 2011, eradication of extreme poverty became a government priority, as despite the significant reductions in poverty and inequality observed in the years before he took office, data from the 2010 national census showed 16 million people were still living in extreme poverty. This can be explained, among other reasons, by difficulties faced by the state in reaching those who live in distant parts of the country, or in segregated areas of large cities.

To tackle this, the government launched the programme *Brasil Sem Miséria*, which comprises three strategic lines of action: monetary transfers, access to public services (education, health care, social assistance, sanitation and electricity) and inclusion in production (professional qualification and job creation). A number of initiatives along these lines have been developed since June 2011, through partnerships among public and private actors.

Regarding monetary transfers, a benefit complementary to Bolsa Família has been paid to families in extreme poverty with children aged from zero to six, since this is the most represented age group among the country's poorest. With this, the federal government expects to reduce the incidence of extreme poverty in this group by 62 per cent. So far, this has been seen as a transitional benefit, with *Brasil Sem Miséria* expected to conclude in 2014.

CONCLUSION

The Brazilian social protection system began to be built in the 1920s, alongside the development of companies which provided economic infrastructure, namely railways, ports and shipping, for the international trade of coffee. It consisted of multiple privately funded pension schemes, organized by each firm for its workers and financed by contributions of employers and employees.

From the 1930s to the 1940s, while industrialization gained momentum, national social security institutes were created by the federal government to provide pensions and health care for urban workers. These institutes were organized on an occupational basis, in line with their trade unions, which were then totally controlled by the state – a corporatist state, in the mould of Italian fascism.

At that time, benefit and contribution plans were distinct and unequal between occupational categories, although all were financed by employers, employees and the state. In its origins, therefore, Brazilian social protection had a clear Bismarkian configuration, which lasted until the 1960s, when the multiple institutes were unified along with their benefit and contribution plans.

In the 1970s, entitlement to social security was extended to rural, domestic and individual workers, and a social assistance benefit was created for the elderly from the age of 75. This allowed for a significant expansion of social protection, but was accompanied by reductions in the monetary value of the benefits in the coming years, during a long period of rampant inflation and economic stagnation, which ended only in the mid-1990s.

On the institutional front, however, great changes were made in the system by the 1988 Constitution, which affirmed the state's responsibility in assuring social security, not only on a contributory basis, but also through non-contributory monetary transfers. Additionally, it commanded the indexation of minimum benefits to the minimum wage, with the aim of preventing great losses in their purchasing power. In spite of the long lag until the effective implementation of the Constitution's command regarding social rights, the new social protection framework began to show its positive impacts from 1995, and more intensively from 2004, when a new wave of growth and prosperity reached the country.

At present, social protection in Brazil has extensive coverage, especially when it comes to monetary benefits, which are regularly paid to almost half of the country's population. In the last 17 years, this has led to a reduction in poverty and inequality, expansion in consumption and a reasonable protection against external economic shocks.

On the other hand, this has involved a significant fiscal effort, as well as a high tax burden, of about 30 per cent of the GDP. While it can be argued that this pattern will not be sustainable in the long run, undoubtedly, in the long run, the country will continue to transform.

REFERENCES

Amitrano, C. R. and V. Petrelli (2012), 'Financial globalization and market-state relationship: a comparative study on growth regimes in developing countries', unpublished manuscript.

Britto, T. and F. Soares (2011), 'Conditional cash transfers and the basic income grant in Brazil: will they ever merge?', IPC One Pager, No. 124, Brazil: International Policy Centre for Inclusive Growth, accessed at www.ipc-undp.org/pub/IPCOnePager124.pdf.

Cardoso Jr., J. C. and L. Jaccoud (2003), 'Políticas Sociais No Brasil: Organização, Abrangência E Tensões Da Ação Estatal', in *Questão Social e Políticas Sociais no Brasil Contemporâneo*, Brasília: IPEA, pp. 181–260.

Cotta, T. C. and L. H. Paiva (2010), 'O Programa Bolsa Família e a Proteção Social no Brasil', in *Bolsa Família 2003–2010: Avanços e Desafios*, Vol. 1, Brasília: IPEA, pp. 57–101.

Diniz, Eli (1978), *Empresario, Estado e Capitalismo No Brasil: 1930/1945*, Rio de Janiero: Paz e Terra.

Esping-Andersen, G. (1990), *The Three Worlds of Welfare Capitalism*, Princeton, NJ: Princeton University Press.

Fausto, B. (1976), *Trabalho Urbano e Conflito Social*, São Paulo: DIFEL.

IPEA (2009), *Politicas Sociais: Acompanhamento e Análise. N. 17: Vinte Anos da Constituição Federal*, Ch. 4, Brasilia: IPEA.

Oliveira, J. and S. F. Teixeira (1986), *Previdência Social: 60 anos de história da Previdência no Brasil*, Rio de Janeiro: Vozes.

Santos, W. G. (1979), *Cidadania e Justiça*, Rio de Janeiro: Campus.

Schmitter, Philippe C. (1974), 'Still the century of corporatism?', *The Review of Politics*, **36**, 85–131.

Soares, S. and N. Satyro (2010), 'O Programa Bolsa Família: Desenho Institucional, Impactose Possibilidades Futuras', IPEA Discussion Text Series, No.1424, Brazilia: IPEA, accessed at www.ipea.gov.br/sites/000/2/publicacoes/tds/td_1424.pdf.

Sposati, A. (1989), 'A assistência social e a trivialização dos padrões de reprodução social', in A. Sposati, M. C. Falcao, S. M. T. Fleury (eds), *Os Direitos (dos desassistidos) sociais*, São Paulo: Cortez, pp. 5–30.

Werneck Vianna, M. L. T. (1998), *A Americanização (perversa) da Seguridade Social no Brasil*, Rio de Janeiro, Revan.

Werneck Vianna, M. L. T. (2003), *A Nova Política Social No Brasil: Uma Prática Acima De Qualquer Suspeita Teórica?*, accessed at www.igpp.com.br/pos/images/stories/cienc.pol.4/CP%2058.pdf.

World Bank (1994), *Averting the Old Age Crisis: Policies to Protect the Old and Promote Growth*, Washington, DC: Oxford University Press.

10. The efficiency and effectiveness of social protection against poverty and inequality in Brazil

Sergei Soares

The previous chapter in this book has made it clear that, albeit through sometimes arduous means, in 2012 Brazil has a social protection system that offers protection against the main vulnerabilities that afflict individuals and families. Leaving aside the provision of health, education and social services and concentrating only on income transfers, Brazil still has a system that is reasonably comprehensive. Social insurance provides generous protection to formal workers and their families against a lack of income due to old age, serious disease, disability or the death of a family breadwinner. Social assistance provides less generous protection to those in poverty who are suffering income deprivation due to old age or disability and it offers even less to those simply living in poverty.

The objective of this chapter is to measure the impact of this protection on poverty and inequality. Of course, fighting poverty and inequality is not the sole objective of the Brazilian social protection system – if it were, it would be difficult to justify generous social insurance pensions to individuals in families well above the poverty line, let alone excuse pensions that increase rather than decrease inequality.

Given Brazil's large income gaps and persistent poverty, however, the fight against inequality and destitution must be one of the most important yardsticks to measure the success of social policy.

The chapter begins with an outline of the types of income transfer, their size and their distribution among the population. It continues by measuring the effectiveness of social protection in combating poverty. The 1994 and 1999 survey microdata are used and counterfactual poverty rates are calculated as if the social protection system did not exist; these counterfactual rates are then compared with those rates which do exist. These calculations are undertaken for poverty and extreme poverty in general and also for important demographics, by age, gender, race, region and area of residence (urban or rural).

The final part of this chapter measures the effectiveness of social protection in combating inequality. A standard Gini decomposition by factor components is used. This consists of dividing the contribution of any income source to inequality into two components: the first measures how progressive (pro-poor) or regressive (pro-rich) each income source is and is called the concentration coefficient; the second is the weight of each income source in total income.

SIZE OF TRANSFERS AND THEIR DISTRIBUTION

In order to have an indication of the size of the different types of transfer, we can use two criteria: the number of beneficiaries and the budget relative to gross domestic product (GDP). Note that beneficiaries are not the same in all cases: in legal terms the beneficiary of a social security benefit is one individual, but the beneficiary of a Bolsa Família benefit is the whole family.

Table 10.1 shows both beneficiaries and the budget for the three transfers that will be analysed below, as well as unemployment insurance (although it is not possible to undertake distributive analysis for this due to data limitations).

Table 10.1 shows that pensions tower over all other benefits. At 5.5 per cent of GDP, social security pensions are the top expenditure item. If you add public employee pensions, it accounts for almost 8 per cent of GDP. With almost 22 million benefits, social security pensions are also the largest type of transfer by this criterion, followed by Bolsa Família at 12 million.

Table 10.1 Brazil: size of each type of transfer, 2009

Type of transfer	Beneficiaries (million)	(as % of population)	Expenditure (% of GDP)
Pensions	21.7	11.3%	5.5
Temporary social security benefits	2.1	1.1%	0.5
BPC	3.5	1.8%	0.6
Bolsa Família	12.4	6.5%	0.4
Unemployment insurance	7.4	3.9%	0.6
Public employee pensions	3.2	1.7%	2.1

Source: Central Bank of Brazil, Ministério de Desenvolvimento Social, Boletim de Políticas Sociais, AEPS Infologo.

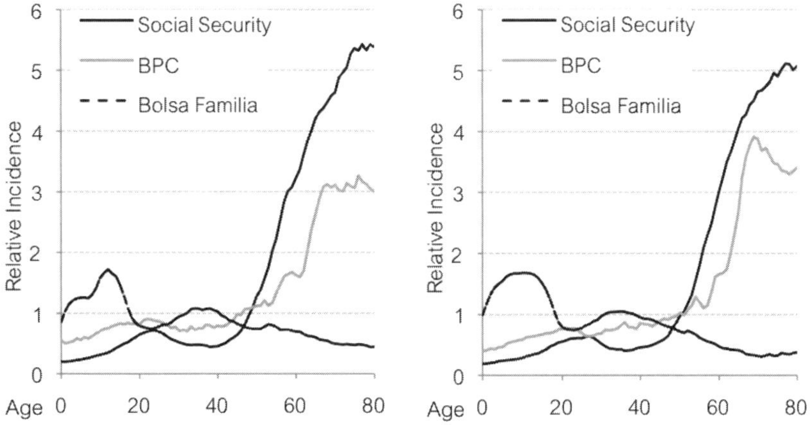

Source: Author's computations based on PNAD (*Pesquisa Nacional por Amostragem de Domicílios* (National Household Sample Survey)) household survey microdata.

Figure 10.1 Brazil: distribution of benefits by age

Social security, to a certain extent, mirrors the unequal regional income distribution, handing out more generous payments per capita in the wealthier south and south-west than in the poorer north and north-east. This is not surprising since social security is largely a contributory policy from which what you receive is roughly equal to what you paid in. On the other hand, the relative incidence of both the Continuous Cash Benefit (BPC) and Bolsa Família, particularly the latter, is higher in poorer regions.

As shown in Figure 10.1, social security payments are, not unsurprisingly, overwhelmingly concentrated among the elderly, although there is a small peak at around age 30 that corresponds to young widows. BPC payments are also concentrated in an older demographic, but less so than social security since the BPC is also paid out to handicapped people of all ages.

Finally, Bolsa Família is heavily concentrated among children, as should be expected given its design, and sparsely concentrated among the elderly since they have the lowest poverty rates, by age.

With regard to gender, Bolsa Família and BPC are almost exactly equally distributed between men and women. For Bolsa Família, this is to be expected given that families will on average have as many males as females. The gender balance is slightly surprising for BPC, however, since women qualify for the old-age benefit five years before men and also live longer.

Men receive, on average, less from social security than women. While the contributory nature of social security means that those men who receive benefits receive higher benefits than their female counterparts (the 'individual benefit effect'), women begin to receive benefits five years before men and live a few years longer on average (the 'age effect'). Ultimately, the 'age effect' dominates the 'individual benefit effect'.

The relative incidence by race or ethnicity mirrors the relative incidence by region. (Here a terminology is used that only approximates to the Brazilian chromatic classification.) Those who are classified as of European or East Asian origin have higher lifetime earnings and thus receive more in social security benefits in old age; the reverse is true for those ethnic groups with lower lifetime earnings.

With the income-targeted BPC and Bolsa Família, however, those ethnic groups receiving lower social security benefits receive, on average, more.

The distribution of benefits by type of area (urban/rural) follows the same pattern as region or skin colour. Those in urban areas receive more generous social security payments and rural dwellers receive higher BPC and, particularly, Bolsa Família benefits.

POVERTY

As explained in the introduction, this section will create counterfactual poverty rates by removing the various components of the social protection system and then putting them back together again to see the effect of individual benefit programmes. It is important to state that these counterfactuals are not what would happen if social protection happened to vanish overnight; people would react and change their behaviour, thus changing the whole income distribution in ways we can only guess at. Rather, the counterfactuals presented here are for the purpose of showing the size and impact of the system as it is today.

To begin with, if we remove all government transfers from the household survey, 27.7 per cent of the Brazilian population would suffer with incomes beneath our nearly official poverty line of R$140 (close to US$2 per day by purchasing power parity). Adding social insurance (basically pensions) would reduce this to 17.3 per cent. Adding the BPC disability and old-age social assistance benefit would further reduce this to 16.5 per cent. Finally, adding Bolsa Família income – which is also counted as social assistance – would bring it down to 14.5 per cent, which is the actual observed poverty rate. This means that social protection lifts 13.2 per cent of the Brazilian population out of poverty.

In 2004 the numbers were as follows: 36.8 per cent would have been poor without social protection, 26.2 per cent with only social insurance, 25.7 per cent with the addition of the BPC, and 24.8 per cent with Bolsa Família finally added in. Not only has poverty fallen considerably, but the effectiveness of social protection has also increased from 12.0 percentage points in 2004 to 13.2 in 2009.

Comparing regions, the counterfactual poverty that would be observed considering per capita household income from all sources excluding government transfers in 2004 was close to one-quarter of the population in the three wealthy regions – south, south-east and centre-west – but was much higher in the north and particularly in the north-east, where it topped 60 per cent. Five years later it was down to 17–18 per cent in the three most developed regions and to almost half of the population in the north-east. When we add social insurance to this income, we see that poverty rates dive dramatically. They fall in 2009 to close to 11 per cent or less in the richer areas and about one-third of the population in the north-east. When the BPC Social Assistance Transfer is added to this, the poverty rate changes very little, but does fall. Finally, when the Bolsa Família income is added we get the actual observed poverty numbers, which fall by one to four percentage points when compared to the previous scenario.

Comparing age groups, there are far too many numbers to report in detail, but the results can be summarized.

First, the effect of social insurance on poverty for those aged 60 or over is much greater than the effect of any other transfer for any other age group. It brings poverty rates from over 60 per cent to less than 5 per cent. This is to be expected; these are people receiving back what they paid in over time, and many elderly households have few sources of income aside from their social security. Second, the effects of social insurance on other age groups is much smaller but still relevant, reducing poverty rates by about five percentage points. Some of this is due to survivor pensions but for the most part it is due to younger people living in households with retired people – remember that poverty is defined by household per capita income. Third, the BPC grant is totally irrelevant for all but the elderly. This is perhaps something of a surprise – there are almost no children in families with elderly poor people. A fourth result is that Bolsa Família is effective in reducing poverty, mostly among children and those aged 25–40 (their parents, presumably), by three to four percentage points. This is not very much for a programme as renowned as Bolsa Família. The reason, of course, is that while Bolsa Família has many beneficiaries, the benefits themselves are relatively modest.

The final result is also the most disheartening: poverty among children remains unsatisfactorily high in Brazil. While the general poverty rate in Brazil is close to 15 per cent, among those aged 15 years or under it is between 20 per cent and 30 per cent. That the most vulnerable should also be the least protected is completely unacceptable.

Comparing men and women, there are quite small differences in poverty by gender, or in the effects of adding benefits, as is to be expected given that it is defined by per capita income.

There are, however, very large differences in poverty rates for different ethnic groups, both before and after social protection. While in 2004 pre-social protection poverty rates were close to 45 per cent for most minority ethnic groups, about one-quarter of those of European origin were in pre-social protection poverty and less than one-fifth of those of East Asian origin (mostly descendants of Japanese immigrants). Five years later, most minority groups were still above 30 per cent, with European origin down to 20 per cent and East Asian origin unchanged. As with other population demographics, pensions make major inroads on pre-social protection poverty, bringing down poverty rates for all races to below 25 per cent. BPC and Bolsa Família bring them down a little more.

Finally, when we look at differences between urban and rural localities, the differences are also striking. In 2009, rural pre-social protection poverty rates were almost 30 percentage points above urban rates. After all social protection is added in, the difference falls to about 20 percentage points.

From all of the information above, the following conclusions can be drawn:

First, social protection significantly reduces (counterfactual) poverty in Brazil. About 30 million people who are not in poverty would fall beneath the poverty line if social protection were to disappear overnight and nothing else changed.

Second, social protection protects the more vulnerable against poverty better than the less vulnerable. The fall in poverty from pre-social protection to post-social protection levels is higher in the north and north-east than elsewhere; it is higher among most minority ethnic groups than among those of European origin; it is 10 points higher in rural than in urban areas.

The notable exception is age. If we consider that children and the elderly are the two vulnerable groups by age, the social protection system does a very good job in protecting the elderly but a very poor one indeed in protecting children. The one benefit aimed at children is also by far the most modest in size.

Thus, the social protection system is quite good at protecting against poverty, but fails when it comes to children.

INEQUALITY

Two of the most relevant incidents in recent Brazilian economic history are the unprecedented fall in inequality and a considerable increase in the tax burden. Social protection is the link between the two. Figure 10.2 has two vertical axes. The left axis shows the Gini coefficients from 1995–2009; the right axis shows the evolution of cash transfers to individuals as a percentage of GDP over the same period.

Two things stand out. The first is that transfers increased from roughly 12 per cent of GDP in the mid-1990s to almost 16 per cent of GDP in 2009 – more than many Latin-American countries collect in taxes for all expenditures. One should not forget that social protection has to be paid for; this is one of the reasons that the total tax burden has risen from about 27 per cent to 34 per cent of GDP.

The second is that as transfers have risen, inequality has fallen.

One way to look at changes in inequality is a decomposition by factor components of the Gini coefficient. Families do not draw all their income from a single source. They may have labour income, capital income

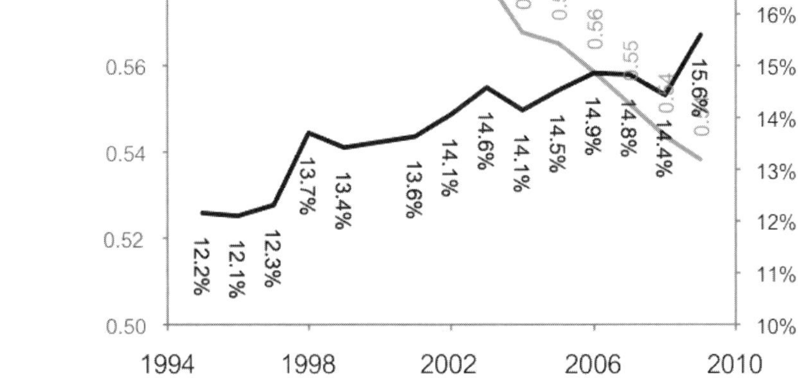

Source: Author's computations based on PNAD household survey microdata and national accounts.

Figure 10.2 Brazil: inequality and transfers, 1995–2009

and – what interests us here – social protection income. Even if all their income comes from one of these traditional categories, it should still be possible to subdivide it. For example, labour income can be subdivided into minimum wage labour income and other labour income, or government transfers can be subdivided into retirement pensions and conditional cash transfers.

It is possible to define the contribution to equality, also called progressivity, of a given income source. We call this the concentration coefficient, which can be calculated much in the same way as a Gini coefficient, except that individuals are ordered differently (Soares et al., 2006; Hoffmann, 2007). For the objectives of this chapter, it suffices to say that the concentration coefficient is on a scale from +1, which indicates a totally regressive income source which is all in the hands of the wealthiest individual, to –1, which indicates a totally progressive income source which is all in the hands of the poorest individual.

One way to classify transfers as progressive and regressive is to compare their concentration coefficients to the general Gini coefficient. The transfers which have a concentration coefficient greater than the Gini coefficient will lead to more inequality if their income share grows; they are thus classified as regressive. If the concentration coefficients are less than the Gini coefficient, it will lead to reductions in inequality if their income share grows; these can be classified as progressive.

Figure 10.3 shows that the composition of transfers is divided into the clearly progressive and the clearly regressive. The remainder of social protection (mostly pensions for private sector employees not indexed to the minimum wage) consists of transfers where the concentration coefficients are very close to the Gini coefficient and can thus be neither classified as progressive nor as regressive.

While regressive transfers fell from 36 per cent of total transfers in 2001 to 29 per cent in 2009, progressive transfers almost doubled as a percentage of total transfers from 1997 to 2010. This means that over the last 15 years, not only have transfers as a percentage of GDP increased by more than three percentage points, but their composition has become far more progressive, with the progressive share almost doubling in relative size.

The effect of transfers on income inequality has been extensively studied. Soares (2006), Hoffmann (2010), Soares et al. (2006, 2010), de Barros et al. (2007), have all quantified the effects of Bolsa Família on inequality (this relatively small programme has exceptional appeal for researchers) and most of them also quantify the effects of BPC. Hoffmann (2007, 2009, 2010), de Barros et al. (2007), Ferreira and de Souza (2008) and Silveira (2010) quantify the impacts of pensions on inequality. It would not be too ambitious to say that new research will only fill in small

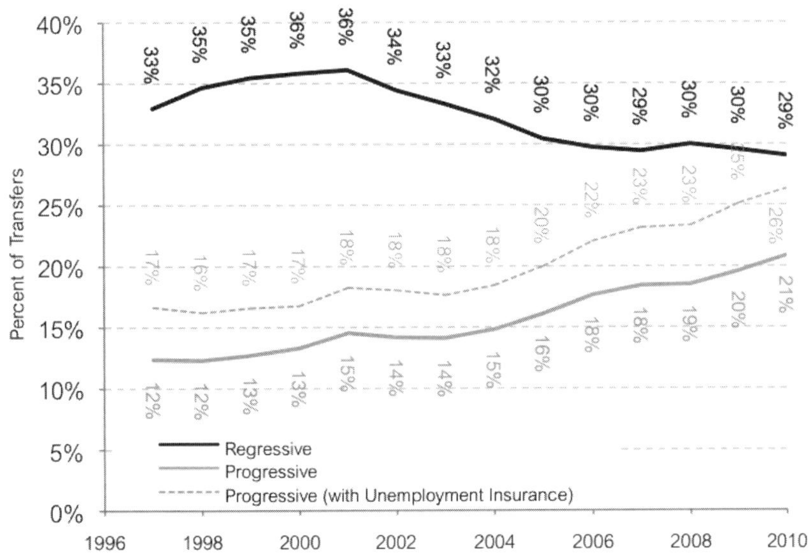

Source: Author's computations from PNAD household survey microdata.

Figure 10.3 Brazil: composition of transfers, 1997–2010

details. The general conclusion is that transfers contributed substantively to the reduction in inequality, but in different ways. All studies have this same general conclusion, although the numbers vary quite a bit according to the decomposition methodology and income identification strategy. This chapter will neither go into the technical details of each study nor present a catalogue of findings and comments on their minor differences. Instead it will use the concepts – concentration coefficients – which have been used thus far to calculate the effect of social protection on the fall in inequality.

One of the most interesting results in the calculus of inequality is that the Gini coefficient of an income distribution is nothing more than the weighted sum of the concentration coefficients of its constituent factor components where the weights are their income shares:

$$G = \sum_k C_k \mu_k \quad (1)$$

where G represents the Gini coefficient, μ_k the income share of component k in total income, and C_k its concentration coefficient.

This static equation can be easily differenced to provide a dynamic result:

$$\Delta G = \sum_k [\bar{\mu}_k \Delta C_k + (\bar{C}_k - \bar{G})\Delta \mu_k] \tag{2}$$

where the ΔG symbol represents the difference between one period and the next and the bar over a given variable represents the average between the two periods.

Equation (2) allows us to map changes in inequality according to what happens to each income source. Both an increase in the income share (μ_k) of an income source less concentrated than the Gini coefficient and the diminution of the concentration (C_k) of any income source will lower inequality. Conversely, if an income source more concentrated than the Gini coefficient becomes more important or if any income source becomes more concentrated, inequality will increase.

To return to the fall in Brazilian inequality, Table 10.2 shows a Gini decomposition by factor shares according to equation (2). The income division used is analogous to that used in the section on poverty: original income denotes all income but social protection income and social protection income is divided into social insurance, BPC and Bolsa Família.

The second entry in each line in Table 10.2 shows the accumulated fall in inequality from 1995: the first line shows that inequality fell 0.43 Gini points from 1995 to 1999 and the last line that it fell 5.8 points from 1995 to 2009. The third column shows how much of this variation was due to changes in all income sources except social protection and the last four columns show the impact of social protection on inequality.

The first panel shows the absolute changes and the second shows the changes due to each income source as a percentage of the total change in the Gini coefficient. The second panel is more informative. The most important results seem to be as follows:

The first is that social protection, although important, has not been the major driving force in the fall of inequality. Social protection can claim credit for about one-quarter of the fall in inequality from 1995 to 2009, leaving three-quarters in the hands of the labour market. This is not a negative result, but it does show that there are limits to what social protection can do.

The second is that social insurance at first hindered the fall in inequality, but subsequently began to help. The positive numbers on the first panel and negative ones on the second panel show that until 2001 social insurance was undoing much of the reduction in inequality coming from the labour market. This was mostly because of pensions for state employees, which the 1988 Constitution packed full of privileges which have since

Table 10.2 Brazil: inequality decomposition by factor components

From 1995 to	Δ Gini	Original income	Social protection			
			Total	Social insurance	BPC	Bolsa Família
In total Gini points						
1999	−0.559	−0.790	0.231	0.290	−0.060	0.000
2001	−0.429	−0.509	0.080	0.278	−0.043	−0.155
2003	−1.678	−1.490	−0.188	0.174	−0.072	−0.290
2005	−3.145	−2.407	−0.739	0.010	−0.266	−0.483
2007	−4.553	−3.238	−1.315	−0.405	−0.312	−0.598
2009	−5.840	−4.345	−1.495	−0.343	−0.355	−0.796
As a percentage of total inequality reduction						
1999	100%	141%	−41%	−52%	11%	0%
2001	100%	119%	−19%	−65%	10%	36%
2003	100%	89%	11%	−10%	4%	17%
2005	100%	77%	23%	0%	8%	15%
2007	100%	71%	29%	9%	7%	13%
2009	100%	74%	26%	6%	6%	14%

Source: Author's computations.

been drastically curtailed. By 2005 the accumulated impact of social insurance was about zero and by 2009 it had turned strongly positive.

The third is that the BPC has helped to reduce inequality, but its contribution has been modest.

The final and perhaps most interesting finding is the impressive impact of Bolsa Família on inequality. Considering that its benefits hover around 0.4 per cent of GDP, that Bolsa Família is responsible for 14 per cent of the fall in inequality is quite impressive.

CONCLUSION

The objectives of this chapter have been to quantify the impacts of social protection on poverty and inequality. Evidently, reducing poverty and inequality are not the only, and perhaps not even the most important, reasons behind social protection. Nevertheless, in a country plagued by both high poverty and high inequality, spending almost 16 per cent of GDP on transfers that do little against either poverty or inequality would be unwarranted.

By luck or design, or a mix of both, the Brazilian social protection system has strong positive impacts on both poverty and inequality.

As regards poverty, we see that social insurance has an impressive role in combating poverty, particularly – as would be expected – among the elderly. Another positive fact is that the reductions in poverty due to social insurance are higher among the most vulnerable: those who live in the north or north-east, those who live in rural areas, and most minority ethnic groups. The same occurs with social assistance. Both the BPC and Bolsa Família reduce poverty more among those that are most afflicted by it.

However, not everything is positive in the social protection system. One of the groups most vulnerable to poverty – children – is also among the least assisted. Children suffer the highest post-social protection poverty rates in Brazil. This is because the benefits provided by the main child-centred programme, Bolsa Família, are not very high.

Against inequality, the most impressive finding is that Bolsa Família has a strong impact. It has reduced the Gini coefficient by 0.8 of a point and this is 14 per cent of the fall in inequality between 1995 and 2009. An obvious question is how this programme can be so ineffective against poverty but so effective against inequality. The answer is that most of the Brazilian poor have incomes that lie far below the poverty line. This means that while Bolsa Família considerably improves their lives, they are still beneath the poverty line. This is a considerable improvement in poor people's lives, however, and is measured by the Gini coefficient. Bolsa Família, therefore, has a strong impact on inequality but is rather weak against poverty.

REFERENCES

de Barros, R. P., M. de Carvalho and S. Franco (2007), 'O Papel das Transferências Públicas na Queda Recente da Desigualdade de Renda Brasileira', in R. P. de Barros, M. N. Foguel and G. Ulyssea (eds), *Desigualdade de Renda no Brasil: Uma Análise da Queda Recente, Vol. 2*, Brazil: IPEA, pp. 41–86, accessed at www.ipea.gov.br/sites/000/2/livros/desigualdaderendanobrasilv2/Cap16.pdf.

Ferreira, C. R. and S. C. I. de Souza (2008), 'Aposentadorias e Pensões e desigualdade da renda: uma análise para o Brasil no periodo 1998–2003', *Revista de Economia Contemporânea*, **12** (1), 41–66, accessed at http://dx.doi.org/10.1590/S1415-98482008000100002.

Hoffmann, R. (2007), 'Transferências de Renda e Redução da Desigualdade no Brasil e em Cinco Regiões, entre 1997 e 2005', in R. P. de Barros, M. N. Foguel and G. Ulyssea (eds), *Desigualdade de Renda no Brasil: Uma Análise da Queda Recente, Vol. 2*, pp. 17–40, Brazil: IPEA, accessed at www.ipea.gov.br/sites/000/2/livros/desigualdaderendanobrasilv2/Cap15.pdf.

Hoffmann, R. (2009), 'Desigualdade da distribuição da renda no Brasil: a contribuição de aposentadorias e pensões e de outras parcelas do rendimento domiciliar per capita', *Economia e Sociedade* (UNICAMP), **18**, 213–31.

Hoffmann, R. (2010), 'The evolution of income distribution in Brazil: what promotes and what restricts the decline in inequality', conference paper presented at A Comparative Analysis of Growth And Development: Argentina and Brazil, University of Illinois, 22–23 April.

Silveira, F. G. (2010), *Tributação, Previdência e Assistência Sociais: Impactos Distributivos*, Mimeo.

Soares, F. V., S. Soares, M. Medeiros and R. G. Osório (2006), *Programas de transferência de renda no Brasil: impactos sobre a desigualdade*, Brazil: IPEA.

Soares, S. (2006), 'Análise de Bem-Estar e Decomposição por Fatores na Queda da Desigualdade entre 1995 e 2004', *Econômica*, **8** (1), 83–115.

Soares, S., R. P. Ribas and F. V. Soares (2010), 'Targeting and coverage of the Bolsa Família programme: why knowing what you measure is important in choosing the numbers', IPC Working Paper No. 71, Brazil: IPC, accessed at www.ipc-undp.org/pub/IPCWorkingPaper71.pdf.

Soares, S., P. H. G. F. Souza, R. G. Osório and F. G. Silveira (2007), 'Os Impactos do Benefício do Programa Bolsa Família Sobre a Desigualdade e Pobreza', in J. A. de Castro and L. Modesto (eds), *Bolsa Família 2003–2010: Avanços e Desafios – Volume 2*, Brazil: IPEA, pp. 27–52.

11. Political dimensions of social protection in Brazil

Anthony Hall

Much attention has recently been focused on the relative success of Brazil's social protection policies in addressing acute poverty. Chapters by Sergei Soares (Chapter 10), and by Bastagli and Soares (Chapter 12), in this volume, bear ample witness to their positive impact on levels of poverty and inequality in Brazil since the 1990s. However, while the spotlight has been shone on their technical efficiency and effective, municipalised implementation procedures, for example, the key political drivers that underpin and sustain 'social assistance' in Brazil should not be ignored or downplayed – especially in the case of the high-profile Bolsa Família (BF). In this and other such protection programmes, political factors have been instrumental in the birth and evolution of these policies, and will continue to be so into the foreseeable future.

In Chapter 2, Midgley observes that social protection programmes simultaneously serve several goals: welfare, economic and political. Brazil is no exception, and a number of complementary political factors have driven forward Brazil's social assistance agenda. These are evident in terms of: (i) the historical origins of social protection in Brazil, (ii) re-democratisation and the acquisition of more universal social rights under the 1988 Constitution as a mark of citizenship, (iii) the subsequent use of BF cash transfers for electoral purposes, (iv) path dependence and policy lock-in across the political spectrum generated by the extreme popularity of conditional cash transfer (CCT) programmes such as BF, (v) the opportunity costs of foregone investment into basic social infrastructure and the emergence of a new social policy paradigm, and (vi) 'soft' foreign policy influence as Brazil's expertise in the social assistance field is exported to Africa and elsewhere.

EARLY POLITICAL ROOTS OF SOCIAL PROTECTION IN BRAZIL

Social provision in Brazil originated in the 1920s as a corporatist, Bismarckian-style formal employment-based contributory welfare system for a relatively privileged urban minority. Contributory 'social insurance' schemes were designed to foster workers' social and political integration under state corporatism during the period of industrial modernisation under the Vargas *Estado Novo* (Lewis and Lloyd-Sherlock, 2009; Gomes dos Santos, Chapter 9, in this volume).

'Social assistance', designed for the poorest, dates to 1938 with the establishment of the National Social Service Council (*Conselho Nacional de Serviço Social* – CNSS), aimed at providing financial subsidies to private sector charities and the Catholic Church, with limited direct state participation. Very much a residual model, non-monetary benefits were selectively provided to the poor and destitute based on moral, philanthropic, personal, populist and clientelistic interests (Jaccoud et al., 2010).

This corporatist-statist model of social policy remained largely unchallenged during military rule (1964–85). Furthermore, in the 1970s, military administrations strengthened social insurance as a mechanism of forced savings to promote rapid growth and low inflation. During these economic 'miracle' years, 'social rights' had to be earned and were awarded by the military regime to compliant groups who did not clamour for political rights (Lewis and Lloyd-Sherlock, 2009). As pressures for re-democratisation mounted, however, the social insurance and philanthropic approaches were exposed as inappropriate and self-evidently incapable of providing more universal coverage. The increasing scale of the labour market, both formal and non-formal, as well as the country's rapidly growing poor population, left far too many people vulnerable.

In Brazil, during the closing stages of military rule and the phase of political 'opening' (*abertura*), the demand for social justice and 'paying the social debt' formed an important part of the re-democratisation process (Guimarães de Castro, 1993, p. 80). During the formulation of Brazil's new Constitution, there was wide-ranging debate about social policy reform that exerted pressure within the Constituent Assembly to shift provision towards a more institutional-redistributive or social democratic model. Stakeholders included traditional unions and, more significantly, new grass-roots social movements, as well as the expanding middle class and liberal professions.

Four innovations stand out in the new Constitution: (i) the inclusion of social assistance as a form of social security; (ii) ensuring care for all those in need regardless of contributions or employment status; (iii) the introduction of non-contributory benefits for the disabled and elderly in poverty; and (iv) decentralisation in programme implementation. In addition, the central role of the family as the focal point of social protection and the continuing importance of volunteer work were emphasised (Brazil, 1988; Jaccoud et al., 2010).

The importance of political drivers in pushing forward social policy innovation in Brazil became clear during the country's period of economic hardship following the 'miracle' years of the 1970s. Between 1985 and 2004, Brazil's economic performance was considered mediocre, with low growth and a poor record of poverty reduction. Macroeconomic stabilization policies introduced by then Finance Minister (later President) Fernando Henrique Cardoso in 1994 (the *Real* Plan) ended two decades of hyperinflation and set the scene for greater fiscal stability and enhanced public sector spending. However, the conscious political decision to counter poverty through extending social protection, mandated under the 1988 Constitution, in addition to successful macroeconomic stabilisation policies, is considered to have been a key factor in reducing poverty during the 1990s. Economic recovery alone does not account for this social awakening (Ferreira et al., 2010).

CITIZENSHIP AND SOCIAL RIGHTS

The 1980s marked a fundamental turning point in the direction of social policy in Brazil, underpinned and catalysed by the new Constitution of 1988. Influenced by T. H. Marshall's principle of 'social citizenship' and by Beveridge's welfare state ideals, albeit indirectly and in a very different context, the Constitution broadened the concept of social rights and recognised the government's central responsibility for protecting its citizens (Brazil, 1988). In the wake of numerous Latin American military dictatorships during which civil liberties were severely repressed, 'Social policy "rights" emerged as a badge of citizenship before full political rights were enjoyed by many individuals'. At the same time, 'social goods are explicitly presented as an unconditional right of citizenship' and the notion of 'citizenship as consumption enhances the position of the state as a supplier of public goods' (Abel and Lewis, 2002, p. 13).

Brazil's Constitution of 1988 thus marked a watershed in social policy. It introduced the notion of welfare rights that went far beyond contribution-based entitlements within the formal, urban industrial and civil service sectors. Yet although these groups continue to absorb the bulk of social spending, especially on generous pensions for the civil service, from then on social policy acquired a much broader remit. In the wake of two decades of military rule (1964–85), it was time to bring on board the rest of the population.

Pressure from civil society during negotiations in the Constituent Assembly widened the social franchise, recognising the need to afford social protection to formerly excluded groups. Rescuing the 'social debt' was not only an integral part of the opposition discourse against the military regime. It became a cornerstone of the political campaign mounted by the main opposition party, the PMDB (Party of the Brazilian Democratic Opposition Movement). The intellectual community further endorsed the introduction of a strong social agenda, in the belief that inclusion of the poor would be a major prerequisite for the consolidation of democracy.

Citizenship was now expressed at least in part through access to more widespread social rights independently of the ability to contribute financially. This principle rapidly established itself as a *sine qua non* of Brazil's progressive new democracy. Furthermore, the new Constitution significantly strengthened the executive arm of government and its ability to enact legislation, thus facilitating the introduction of new policy instruments. In the words of one analysis, 'The constitutional delegates' main concern was to prevent decisional paralysis derived from Congress's veto or incapacity' (Figueiredo and Limongi, 2003, p. 62). New forms of political participation were also introduced, such as people's right to introduce legislation, the popular referendum and participation in policy implementation, along with greater fiscal and administrative autonomy at state and municipal levels.

This new ethos of social citizenship gave rise during the early 1990s to a number of policy innovations. These included the non-contributory continuing cash benefit (BPC) social assistance programme for the poor, elderly and disabled, which currently benefits 3.5 million people. The even wider-ranging and more expensive rural pension programme (PSR) was also introduced during this period and now pays a monthly minimum salary to 8.3 million informal workers.

In addition, from the mid-1990s, several municipal governments introduced innovative conditional cash transfer schemes such as Bolsa Escola (to boost primary school attendance), anti-child labour provision (PETI) and food supplements (Bolsa Alimentação). These three cash transfer schemes soon acquired national coverage and, along with others, were loosely amalgamated under President Lula's 'Zero Hunger' initiative, only to be formally integrated from 2004 as *Bolsa Família* under a unified administration within the Ministry of Social Development (Hall, 2006, 2008).

ELECTORAL CAPITAL AND POLITICAL CONTROL

From the beginning of President Lula's first term in January 2003 his public anti-poverty commitment was unequivocal. In his inaugural address, he famously declared that, 'If by the end of my term of office every Brazilian has enough food to eat three times day, I shall have fulfilled my mission in life' (BBC News, 2003). Despite a faltering start to 'Zero Hunger', Bolsa Família was soon established to restructure and streamline the CCT element of social assistance. The sheer force of Lula's charismatic personality and his ability to communicate with poorer working classes via the media, due in some measure to his history as a trade union leader, had enabled him to gain popularity and remain untainted by numerous corruption scandals associated with leading members of his Workers' Party, the PT (Bourne, 2008).

Most analysts also believe that the success of Bolsa Família in reaching previously excluded groups was an additional factor in Lula's high rate of public approval and subsequent re-election in 2006. The fact that Lula took pains to identify himself with the programme, alongside government and PT efforts to portray BF as the president's personal gift to the nation, certainly did nothing to harm his electoral prospects. Research into voting trends in Brazil offers strong evidence that BF reaped major political gains for President Lula, his successor Dilma Rousseff and the PT more generally. Furthermore, as discussed below, the consolidation of BF seems likely to have created a path dependence in policymaking towards social assistance that nowadays transcends ideological or partisan differences.

The potential electoral advantage conveyed by BF to government is facilitated by the fact that the programme is controlled by the executive and has not required complex political negotiations to be enacted. In Brazil's highly fragmented, multi-party system, the governing party has no absolute majority in Congress. In order to pass legislation, the PT must normally enter into long-winded negotiations with other parties. These usually involve much horse-trading to build appropriate coalitions for measures to be approved, pork barrel politics, shady dealings and much-publicised allegations of corruption. The implementation of BF has, by and large, been largely free of such shenanigans, aside from some examples of questionable practices coming to light at municipal level where local politicians have used the programme to their personal advantage and where some ineligible groups have benefited. By and large, however, the record of BF is remarkably clean in this respect. President Lula's personal endorsement of BF also strengthened its legitimacy.

Finally gaining power in 2002 after four attempts at the presidency,

Lula and the PT relied heavily on the support of urban-based working and middle-class voters. Yet his humble origins in the rural north-east, together with his record as a staunch, anti-military industrial trade unionist in São Paulo, appeared at that time to cut little ice with voters. On the contrary, in order to discredit and humiliate him openly, political opponents exploited these aspects of his background to cast doubt over his suitability to be president (Bourne, 2008). During his first term of office, however, Lula confounded his critics by achieving a high level of popularity. While this was due partly to his personal charisma, a complementary factor was, arguably, the rapid expansion of BF from 2004 to 2006, especially in the months immediately preceding the election.

Important light has been shed on the key role played by Bolsa Familia in the re-election of President Lula in 2006. There was a marked switch of support for Lula from the more prosperous south towards the poorer north and north-east of the country. In the words of Hunter and Power (2007, p. 3), there was 'a groundswell of support among Brazilians in the lowest categories of income and educational achievement' during the 2006 re-election campaign. In the north and north-east regions Lula received 60–85 per cent of the votes. In part this reflected the appeal of Lula personally rather than support for his Workers' Party (PT), which had become tainted by various corruption scandals, but which Lula had managed to bypass. However, there is clear evidence that BF certainly reinforced Lula's electoral following.

Prior to the October 2006 elections there was a major BF recruitment drive in which 1.8 million new families were included to reach the first national target of 11.1 million households. Opinion polls revealed that the president's popularity was strongest among BF beneficiaries. This effect was most pronounced in the north-east, where he enjoyed a 21-point lead amongst those taking part in BF compared with a regional average of eight points (FSP, 2006). Hunter and Power (2007, p. 19) note that, 'an impressive state-level correlation exists between *Bolsa*'s penetration in 2006 and vote swing toward Lula compared to 2002'. Another study suggested that BF might have contributed up to five million votes in favour of the president (Zucco, 2010). Hunter and Power (2007, p. 20) conclude emphatically that, 'the social policy story is arguably the single most plausible explanation for Lula's re-election'.

For the first time in many years, Brazil's disadvantaged 'popular classes' felt that here at last was a president who delivered on his promises to assist the poor, directly boosting their household incomes. The electorate has in practice acquired new political influence through what could be described as a form of 'universalised clientelism'. This was based not on individual favours offered in direct exchange for traditional clientelistic votes. Rather, poorer voters expressed their collective gratitude in recognition of the cash benefits that have improved their livelihoods. As argued by Zucco (2008, p. 48), dependence on federal government transfers 'provides incentives for voters to support their benefactor (and is) an almost unbeatable strategy from the strictly electoral perspective'.

Brazil has a three-tier system of government at federal, state and municipal levels. The national Constitution of 1988 strongly advocated decentralisation policies under the new democracy. From the outset, implementation of BF was decentralised to municipal level, with operational responsibilities devolved to local management committees and mayors. These include beneficiary selection, registration on the central database, distribution of cash and monitoring of compliance with conditionalities. By 2006, all of Brazil's 5564 municipalities had adhered to the programme.

This direct link between federal and municipal authorities in the execution of BF has contributed to the bypassing of state administrations, helping to reduce the powers of patronage traditionally enjoyed by regional political bosses, along with their ability to constrain federal decision-making in areas such as social policy (Fenwick, 2009; Borges, 2011). In several north-eastern states, during the 2002 and 2006 gubernatorial elections, traditional bosses lost out to left and centre-left opposition. Thus, 'public policies implemented by Lula's government allowed the PT and its left-wing allies to obtain significant political rewards among the poor electorate' (Borges, 2011, p. 22). There is little evidence that BF benefits were distributed in an overtly clientelistic manner (Fried, 2011). However, BF has been particularly effective in helping to reduce regional income inequality, favouring the north and north-east, where poverty is concentrated. Thus, 'non-spatial social programs are really regional programs' (Silveira-Neto and Azzoni, 2012, p. 65). Unsurprisingly, the electorate has shown its appreciation.

It has been argued, furthermore, that this electoral strategy has contributed to a much wider process of political realignment in Brazil. Singer (2012) argues that the capturing of votes through BF is one significant element in a much wider plan to generate a new grass-roots political force amongst the very poor that is supportive of the PT, labelled 'Lulismo'. Based on higher incomes and improved living standards generated by economic growth, better wages and cash transfers, this 'new working class', it is alleged, will become a novel and dynamic actor in a more polarised party political system.

POLICY LOCK-IN

Bolsa Familia appears to have produced a marked path dependence on such social protection policies in Brazil. So strong is the effect of BF on voting patterns in Brazil that, nowadays, open criticism by those competing for office would be tantamount to committing political suicide. As BF coverage spreads to benefit an ever-expanding proportion of the poorer electorate, so this effect will become more pronounced. During the 2006 presidential campaign, for example, opposition candidates fell over themselves to stress the fact that under no circumstances would they cancel BF; on the contrary, they would invariably expand it!

Furthermore, social protection policies such as BF seem to be strengthening power at the federal centre in its links with municipalities, undermining old-style regional clientelistic politics. It has been argued that this 'bandwagon' outcome of political competition is benign since it has 'generated electoral incentives . . . (that have) . . . encouraged politicians to offer inclusive programmes with the characteristics of public goods' (Melo, 2007, p. 50).

Underscoring the continuing political importance of Bolsa Familia, President Dilma Rousseff has continued to provide strong government backing. There are plans to enlarge BF further to embrace the entire eligible population below the poverty line. At the same time, BF would gradually be incorporated into wider anti-poverty and development initiatives through the new umbrella programme *Brasil Sem Miséria* or 'Brazil Without Poverty' (*The Economist*, 2013). BF has remained free of public spending cuts and has continued to receive steady government financial support (Hall, 2008). Funding has risen steadily reaching R$17 billion (US$9 billion) or 0.6 per cent of GDP by 2011. It enjoys high social and political returns compared, for example, with the 11 per cent of GDP allocated for Brazil's mainstream pensions schemes. The country's experience is consistent with evidence from around the globe which suggests that government income transfers influence political choices (Arnold et al., 2011).

Bolsa Familia was originally conceived as the first step towards introducing a universal Citizen's Basic Income in Brazil, a cause championed for many years by PT Senator Eduardo Suplicy. Yet although the two programmes were introduced more or less simultaneously in 2004, they have remained fundamentally different in concept. Far from moving towards the principle of a universal basic income, the 34 bills introduced into Congress since 2004 have concentrated on increasing the effectiveness of targeting mechanisms to compensate the poorest and most vulnerable groups, enforcing conditionalities and strengthening social oversight in order to minimise the risk of clientelism. At present there is no sign of convergence in these supposedly complementary initiatives, with the universal basic income remaining a purely paper exercise (Britto and Soares, 2011).

STRUCTURAL TRENDS

Brazil's 1988 Constitution was meant to mark a watershed in the transition to post-authoritarian rule and the move towards equity enhancing reforms. Yet according to some observers, progress has been limited and reforms have remained modest. User benefits remain highly regressive and entrenched interests have blocked more fundamental changes from taking place. Bastagli and Soares (Chapter 12, in this volume) note, for instance, that social insurance accounts for over 47 per cent of federal social spending, with under 7 per cent going to social assistance for the poorest.

There are other tangible political dimensions to social protection, namely: (1) people's increasing reliance on cash transfers as a proportion of household income together with 'welfare-dependence' accusations, and (2) a gradual shift in policymaking towards safety nets at the possible expense of social investments into key development sectors such as basic education and health. There is a strong danger that, together, these tendencies may encourage a planning psychology based on short-termism, thus moving away from a longer-term strategic approach in which social welfare forms a fundamental pillar of economic growth rather than just a residual prop.

First, the high-profile nature of BF and its close association with Lula's electoral campaign led to widespread criticism, especially from the urban-based middle and elite classes in Brazil, that the programme was paternalistic and encouraged a 'culture of dependence'. Such allegations have long formed the basis of right-wing critiques of social protection policies in the West (Murray, 1984). During the planning phase of BF there was much opposition to the programme on these grounds, obliging policymakers to include education and health conditionalities as a mark of people's 'social responsibility', akin to the 'deserving poor' of old. There was a fear that grants could be 'perceived as entitlements and thus create negative incentives for beneficiaries to work' (Britto, 2008, p. 185).

Bolsa Familia is but one of a number of non-contributory cash transfer schemes in Brazil, alongside the PSR and the BPC. Overall, they account for around half of household income in the poorest areas and more than this in the most deprived rural regions in the north and north-east where job opportunities are scarce and federal transfers often form the mainstay of the local economy. Evidence from Brazil and Mexico suggests that membership of CCTs is not usually associated with employment decisions and that there is no such job disincentive effect (Bastagli, 2011).

Yet in some regions, such as São Paulo, for example, there is some evidence to suggest that BF might help reinforce growing informalisation of the economy since job registration would disqualify beneficiaries from the programme if household income exceeds the threshold (Figueiredo et al., 2006). At the level of municipal government, financial dependence on federal transfers can be pronounced and BF payments may account for up to 40 per cent of the budget, especially in the poorer north-east where the tax base is lower than in the more prosperous south (Marques, 2005).

Thus, the growing political popularity of cash transfers on the part of government and beneficiaries, especially Bolsa Familia, could lead to a subtle change in the way that social policy is conceptualised. Their growing importance in household budgets, whether or not they actually discourage people from seeking formal employment or create a 'hand-out' mentality, could lead to social protection becoming mainstreamed rather than it being seen as just a temporary measure to address chronic poverty, as originally conceived.

It could encourage the earmarking of CCTs as a specific social policy for the 'poor', while working against a more universalistic and equitable approach towards the provision of basic services (Kerstenetzsky, 2009; Costa, 2009). At the same time, it helps to keep wealthier social classes happy in the knowledge that no serious resource redistribution is being contemplated. Thus, given the high political pay-off, both in electoral and power distribution terms, this path could be a very tempting option for policymakers, since income transfers such as BF and BPC are quite effective in their own right and relatively inexpensive when compared with other social welfare programmes.

The other side of the short-termism coin would be a tendency to neglect investment into key sectors essential for economic and social welfare in the long run, such as education, health and sanitation. Although it is difficult at the present stage to reach any firm conclusions on this matter, there are some indications of a fall in longer-term basic investments at federal, state and municipal levels. Lavinas (2007, p. 1467) captured this contradiction well, noting a drop in government spending on basic sanitation, housing and education during the early 2000s, and observing that, 'there has been no coordinated effort at federal or sub-national levels to provide essential public services indispensable for the reduction of inequalities in lifestyle and improvements in welfare alongside improvements in individual and family income and consumption'.

Costa (2009, p. 704) also concluded that investment into BF together with growing social security expenditure and fiscal/macroeconomic adjustment to produce a primary surplus has restricted federal funding available for these basic social sectors, contributing to a 'high social deficit'. He notes that federal funding for health and education as a proportion of GDP fell steadily from 1995 to 2006, while sanitation suffered in particular.

Brazil has long been criticised for failing to invest sufficiently in primary and secondary education at levels commensurate with its growing global economic status (Birdsall and Sabot, 1996). Public investment into education in Brazil represents just 4.5 per cent of GDP, while adjusted per capita spending is just one-fifth that of Organisation for Economic Co-operation and Development (OECD) countries. Despite reforms to basic education finance and management since the late 1990s, the sector remains underfunded with major shortfalls in performance and quality (Hall, 2003; Kerstenetzsky, 2009).

Through Bolsa Escola and (later) Bolsa Família a demand-side solution has been attempted by encouraging greater participation through programme conditionalities on school attendance. Yet although enrolments have indeed been boosted on the road to achieving 'Education for All' and the Millennium Development Goals, there is no evidence that the quality of education delivered has been improved (MDS, 2010). Furthermore, there is little indication that, on its own, a demand-side approach targeting basic education for the poor is likely to stimulate an adequate response from policymakers (Handa and Davis, 2006). In Brazil's case, a supply-side response to the education crisis is also urgently needed. This would necessitate much greater levels of investment into school construction and maintenance, materials, equipment and teacher training as well as greater transparency and accountability in the management of resources (Hall, 2003; Hunter and Sugiyama, 2009; Sánchez-Ancochea and Mattei, 2011).

Brazil's cost-effective, non-contributory cash transfer policies, both conditional and unconditional, have been relatively successful in addressing absolute poverty and contributing to the slow reduction in economic inequality. Together with the high electoral and more fundamental political returns to social protection, this makes it doubly attractive to those in power. The danger is, however, that such advantages could induce a change in the mindset of politicians and policymakers towards the adoption of social assistance as an increasingly mainstream social policy at the expense of longer-term investment in social infrastructure. The opportunity costs of such a switch could be highly prejudicial for the country's economic development prospects.

While social protection policies may well be effective in establishing minimum income levels for the poor, they do nothing to encourage (and may actively discourage) more fundamental redistribution of investments towards meeting the basic health, education and other social sector needs of less privileged sectors of society. As one analysis observed, 'while Brazilian democracy has given rise to forces that help ensure a minimum level of social protection, it has also maintained and in some ways strengthened the forces that impose a low ceiling on living standards and human capital development among people with marginal levels of income and education' (Hunter and Sugiyama, 2009, p. 49). Any fundamental change in entitlements, they argue, would probably be dependent on poorer segments acquiring a stronger political voice in order to challenge more powerful vested interests.

Other observers who point out the distributional limitations of CCTs such as BF and argue in favour of a fundamental reallocation of public spending also reach similar conclusions (Sánchez-Ancochea and Mattei, 2011). However, they hold out some hope that CCTs may help to raise political awareness among the poor and stimulate a broader political debate over the challenge of widening and (finally) democratising access to social services, with health and education becoming key electoral issues in the future.

'SOFT' FOREIGN POLICY INFLUENCE

Another significant and growing political dimension of Brazil's social protection policy is its dissemination as a model to be emulated by poor countries in Africa and elsewhere. The wider political significance of Brazil's social protection framework is clearly reflected in the country's mounting presence on the international stage. Other BRIC countries such as Brazil, China and India are extending their aid and direct investment programmes to build up 'soft-power influence' in developing countries. Through its international aid programme, Brazil has become increasingly active in disseminating knowledge and experience acquired in key areas such as agricultural research, HIV/AIDS treatment, education and social protection. President Lula actively sought to expand Brazil's influence overseas. His emphasis on the 'war against hunger' rather than against terror formed a major pillar of this strategy (Nina, 2007). This has been allied to a proactive social development agenda that has helped fashion a 'soft-power' and flexible foreign policy role for Brazil as a leading nation in discussions over global poverty challenges (Sotero, 2010; Hurrell, 2010).

Some observers have commented that Brazil's aid-backed generosity is but part of a wider policy of extending its commercial influence, as well as being part of its strategy to secure a permanent seat on the UN Security Council. The country's assistance programme is currently worth around

US$1 billion a year. Yet the total annual figure could reach US$4 billion if commercial loans to Brazilian companies working in poor countries from the BNDES state development bank are included. This is less than China but comparable with Sweden and Canada (*The Economist*, 2010). Around US$480 million is spent on technical cooperation provided by numerous Brazilian institutions, including US$30 million from the Brazilian Co-operation Agency (ABC), part of the Foreign Ministry. This budget is growing steadily and is expected to reach US$38 million for 2012, with half allocated to Africa, especially the lusophone countries (Cabral and Weinstock, 2010).

'Technical cooperation is, therefore, emerging as an important operational instrument of Brazilian foreign policy' (Cabral and Weinstock, 2010, p. 2). Brazil has several advantages that make it an attractive donor. It can draw upon its own developmental and poverty alleviation experiences to pass on lessons to its partners, it has a high level of technical competence to offer poorer countries, it has a degree of political neutrality untainted by any recent colonial history and its aid carries no formal conditionalities (Cabral and Weinstock, 2010). Brazil's 'diplomacy of generosity' is based more on supporting agriculture, health, education and social policy, which account for half of its technical cooperation, rather than the heavy infrastructure investments favoured by the Chinese, for example.

Furthermore, Brazil's CCT dissemination strategy is also consistent with the high priority afforded to social protection as mainstream social policy by international financial institutions such as the World Bank, where such activities currently account for 6 per cent of its lending portfolio (World Bank, 2011). Social assistance 'resonates with the social protection agenda of neo-liberal organisations such as the World Bank' (Lloyd-Sherlock, 2008, p. 634). Social protection 'increasingly defines an agenda for social policy in developing countries' (Barrientos and Hulme, 2008, p. 3). Given Brazil's experience with CCTs such as BF, its expertise has been actively sought by poorer countries.

In 2006, with support from the UK Department of International Development (DFID) and the United Nations Development Programme's (UNDP) International Poverty Centre, a programme of technical cooperation and exchange commenced between the Ministries of Social Development and Social Security and a number of African countries; these include, Ghana, Mozambique, Nigeria, Guinea-Bissau, South Africa and Zambia. Brazil has also assisted other African nations in their health and social programmes, such as Angola, Kenya, Senegal, Cameroon, Tanzania and Mozambique, and São Tomé and Principe.

In 2007, as part of its 'Africa-Brazil Cooperation Programme on Social

Development', Brazil was instrumental in helping to establish a CCT programme in Ghana, the Livelihood Empowerment against Poverty or LEAP, within the National Social Protection Strategy (UNDP, 2012). Technical support has also been given to set up a pilot CCT programme in Benin (World Bank/IPEA, 2011). In Haiti, a post-earthquake dairy cooperative programme, *Lèt Agogo* (Lots of Milk), encourages mothers to take their children to school in exchange for free meals. This is also based on experience with BF and is being funded by the Brazilian aid programme (*The Economist*, 2010). Since Brazil's foreign aid budget is expanding steadily, it is highly likely that its global influence on the development of social protection programmes will grow as well, although how much 'soft power' will be generated in this process remains to be seen.

CONCLUSION: WHITHER SOCIAL PROTECTION IN BRAZIL?

Social assistance programmes in Brazil look set to occupy an increasingly prominent place within the country's evolving policy agenda. Their effectiveness in targeting some of the most needy and hitherto excluded sectors of the population with relatively low-cost interventions such as BF has been demonstrated. Yet it should be recognised that their momentum is due at least as much to political advantages as to their development impact. Within a new context of (albeit segmented) social citizenship, recognition of social rights and Brazil's increasingly prominent position on the world stage, two political dimensions stand out: electoral and distributional.

First, in terms of electoral rewards, there is little doubt that CCTs such as BF have yielded major gains in terms of votes and political capital to Brazil's ruling Workers' Party (PT) and in particular to former President Lula. His direct successor, Dilma Rousseff, has vowed to build upon this political heritage and expand BF to fully cover the country's absolute poor population, while supposedly integrating it into a wider national development programme. It is highly likely that CCTs will form part of mainstream social policy in Brazil for the foreseeable future.

Second, in distributional terms, social assistance could have both negative and positive consequences in political terms. There are fears, for example, that they might serve to reinforce Brazil's highly unequal social and economic structure, cementing existing skewed entitlement patterns. At the same time, there might be opportunity costs in terms of underinvestment in basic welfare, education, health and sanitation essential to underpin economic growth.

On the positive side, however, through the overt politicisation of social assistance as an anti-poverty strategy, the electorate has arguably acquired a new form of leverage through which it can collectively put pressure on politicians to deliver the goods rather than just empty promises. The path dependence created by BF, for example, is very evident in the invariable declarations of support for such social protection schemes right across the political spectrum. It remains to be seen whether they could stimulate wider discussions capable of inducing more fundamental changes. Beneficiaries will increasingly come to regard cash transfers as an entitlement rather than an act of charity or patronage. This factor could become increasingly important should there be a longer-term realignment of political forces in Brazil. In addition, although still modest by global standards, Brazil's overseas aid programme is growing fast. In particular, its anti-poverty social components are considered a significant element in the country's 'soft' foreign policy strategy.

Yet while all such social protection programmes invariably have a political dimension, policymakers must take care that the tempting quest for a fast political fix should not be allowed to distort longer-term development objectives. In some sense, providing social protection is a relatively easy option for policymakers and politicians. However, it is a necessary but not a sufficient prerequisite for enhancing economic and social development. It should not be regarded as a panacea for tackling poverty and inequality, merely the first step on a much longer journey.

REFERENCES

Abel, C. and C. Lewis (eds) (2002), *Exclusion and Engagement: Social Policy in Latin America*, London: Institute of Latin American Studies, University of London.

Arnold, C, T. Conway and M. Greenslade (2011), *Cash Transfers: Evidence Paper*, London: DFID, Policy Division.

Barrientos, A. and D. Hulme (eds) (2008), *Social Protection for the Poor and Poorest*, London: Palgrave.

Bastagli, F. (2011), 'Conditional cash transfers as a tool of social policy', *Economic and Political Weekly*, **46** (21), 61–6.

BBC News (2003), 'Brazil's Lula promises change', 2 January, accessed at http://news.bbc.co.uk/1/hi/world/americas/2621821.stm.

Birdsall, N. and R. H. Sabot (1996), *Opportunity Foregone: Education in Brazil*, Washington, DC: Inter-American Development Bank/Johns Hopkins University.

Borges, A. (2011), 'The political consequences of center-led redistributionism in Brazilian federalism', *Latin American Research Review*, **46** (3), 21–45.

Bourne, R. (2008), *Lula of Brazil*, London: Zed Books.

Brazil (1988), *Constituição da República Federativa do Brasil de 1988*, Presidência da República, Casa Civil, Subchefia para Assuntos Jurídicos, Brasília.

Brazil (2012), *Plano Brasil Sem Miséria*, Brasília: Ministry of Social Development, accessed on 23 February 2013 at www.brasilsemmiseria.gov.br/.

Britto, T. (2008), 'The emergence and popularity of conditional cash transfers in Latin America', in A. Barrientos and D. Hulme (eds), *Social Protection for the Poor and Poorest*, London: Palgrave pp. 181–93.

Britto, T. and F. V. Soares (2011), 'Bolsa Família and the Citizen's Basic Income: a misstep?', Working Paper No. 77, Brasília: IPEA, January.

Cabral, L. and J. Weinstock (2010), *Brazilian Technical Cooperation for Development: Drivers, Mechanics and Future Prospects*, London: Overseas Development Institute.

Costa, N. (2009), 'Social protection in Brazil: universalism and targeting in the FHC and Lula administrations', *Ciência e Saúde Coletiva*, **14** (3), 693–706.

Fenwick, T. (2009), 'Avoiding governors: the success of Bolsa Família', *Latin American Research Review*, **44** (1), 102–31.

Ferreira, F., P. Leite and M. Ravaillon (2010), 'Poverty reduction without economic growth? Explaining Brazil's poverty dynamics, 1985–2004', *Journal of Development Economics*, **93**, 20–36.

Figueiredo, A. and F. Limongi (2003), 'Congress and decision-making in democratic Brazil', in M. D'Alva Kinzo and J. Dunkerley (eds), *Brazil Since 1985: Economy, Polity and Society*, London: Institute of Latin American Studies, University of London, pp. 62–83.

Figueiredo, A., H. Torres and R. Bichir (2006), 'A conjuntura social brasileira revisitada', *Novos Estudos*, **75** (July), 173–83.

Fried, B. J. (2011), 'Distributive politics and conditional cash transfers: the case of Brazil's Bolsa Família', *World Development*, **40** (5), 1042–53.

FSP (2006), 'A 90 dias da eleição, Lula dá Bolsa Família a 1.8 milhão', *Folha de São Paulo*, 29 June.

Guimarães de Castro, M. H. (1993), 'Democratic transition and social policy in Brazil', in M. D. G. Kinzo (ed.), *Brazil: the Challenges of the 1990s*, London: British Academic Press, pp. 78–93.

Hall, A. (2003), 'Education reform in Brazil under democracy', in M. D'Alva Kinzo and J. Dunkerley (eds), *Brazil Since 1985: Economy, Polity and Society*, London: Institute of Latin American Studies, University of London, pp. 269–87.

Hall, A. (2006), 'From Fome Zero to Bolsa Família: social policies and poverty alleviation under Lula', *Journal of Latin American Studies*, **38**, 689–709.

Hall, A. (2008), 'Brazil's *Bolsa Família*: a double-edged sword?' *Development and Change*, **39** (5), 799–822.

Handa, S. and B. Davis (2006), 'The experience of conditional cash transfers in Latin America and the Caribbean', *Development Policy Review*, **24** (5), 513–36.

Hunter, W. and T. Power (2007), 'Rewarding Lula: executive power, social policy, and the Brazilian elections of 2006', *Latin American Politics and Society*, **49** (1), 1–30.

Hunter, W. and N. B. Sugiyama (2009), 'Democracy and social policy in Brazil: advancing basic needs, preserving privileged interests', *Latin American Politics and Society*, **51** (2), 29–58.

Hurrell, A. (2010), 'Brazil and the new global order', *Current History*, **109** (724), 60–6.

Jaccoud, L., P. Hadjab and J. Chaibub (2010), 'The consolidation of social assistance in Brazil and its challenges, 1988–2008', IPEA, Working Paper 76, December.

Kerstenetzsky, C. L. (2009), *DADOS – Revista de Ciências Sociais*, Rio de Janeiro, **52** (1), 53–83.

Lavinas, L. (2007), 'Gasto social no Brasil: Programas de transferência de renda *versus* investmento', *Ciência e Saúde Coletiva*, **12** (6), 1463–76.

Lewis, C. and P. Lloyd-Sherlock (2009), 'Social policy and economic development in South America: an historical approach to social insurance', *Economy and Society*, **38** (1), 109–31.

Lloyd-Sherlock, P. (2008), 'Doing a bit more for the poor? Social assistance in Latin America', *Journal of Social Policy*, **37** (4), 621–39.

Marques, R. M. (2005), 'A importância do Bolsa Família nos municípios brasileiros', *Cadernos de Estudos Desenvolvimento Social em Debate*, 1, Brasília: Ministry of Social Development.

MDS (2010), 'Síntese do 1º Relatório contendo os Principais Resultados da Pesquisa de Avaliação de Impacto do Bolsa Família – 2ª Rodada – AIBF II', Nota Técnica No. 110/2010/DA/SAGI/MDS, Brasília: Ministry of Social Development, August.

Melo, M. A. (2007), 'Political competition can be positive: embedding cash transfer programmes in Brazil', in A. Bebbington and W. McCourt (eds), *Development Success: Statecraft in the South*, London: Palgrave Macmillan, pp. 30–51.

Murray, C. A. (1984), *Losing Ground: American Social Policy, 1950–1980*, New York: Basic Books.

Nina, A. (2007), 'Action against hunger and poverty: Brazilian foreign policy in Lula's first term (2003–2006)', Working Paper Number CBS-83-07, Oxford: Centre for Brazilian Studies.

Sánchez-Ancochea, D. and L. Mattei (2011), 'Bolsa Família, poverty and inequality: political and economic effects in the short and long run', *Global Social Policy*, **11** (2–3), 299–318.

Silveira-Neto, R. M. and C. R. Azzoni (2012), 'Social programs, industrial deconcentration and the recent decrease in regional income inequality in Brazil', in W. Baer (ed.), *The Regional Impact of National Policies: The Case of Brazil*, Cheltenham, UK and Northampton, MA, USA: Edward Elgar, pp. 52–66.

Singer, A. (2012), *Os Sentidos do Lulismo: Reforma gradual e pacto conservador*, São Paulo: Companhia das Letras.

Sotero, P. (2010), 'Brazil's rising ambition in a shifting global balance of power', *Politics*, **30** (S1), 71–81.

The Economist (2010), 'Speak softly and carry a blank cheque', *The Economist*, 15 July.

The Economist, 2013, 'Social spending in Brazil: The end of poverty?' 28 February.

UNDP (2012), *Programa Africa-Brasil de Cooperação em Desenvolvimento Social*, Brasília: International Poverty Centre, UNDP, accessed on 25 February 2013 at www.ipc-undp.org/ipc/PageAfrica-Brazil2.do?id=21.

World Bank (2011), *An Evaluation of World Bank Support, 2000–10: Social Safety Nets*, Washington, DC: World Bank, Independent Evaluation Group (IEG).

World Bank/IPEA (2011), *Bridging the Atlantic, Brazil and Sub-Saharan Africa. South-South Partnering for Growth*, Washington, DC: World Bank/Brasília: IPEA.

Zucco, C. (2008), 'The president's "new" constituency: Lula and the pragmatic vote in Brazil's 2006 presidential elections', *Journal of Latin American Studies*, **40**, 29–49.

Zucco, C. (2010), 'Cash-transfers and voting behavior: an assessment of the political impacts of the Bolsa Família program', Mimeo, Woodrow Wilson School and Department of Politics, Princeton University.

12. The future of social protection in Brazil

Francesca Bastagli and Fabio Veras Soares

This chapter identifies Brazil's current social protection challenges and discusses the possible responses in moving forward, focusing on issues of coverage, adequacy and sustainability. The chapter is structured as follows. First, it identifies the primary imbalances and gaps of Brazil's social protection system today and discusses these against the primary objectives of social protection, which are understood to include both social assistance and insurance objectives such as poverty reduction and redistribution and income or consumption-smoothing over the lifetime. Second, it examines recent developments in three 'macro' areas of direct relevance to the future of social protection policy in Brazil: economic growth, demographic structure and the labour market. The third section reviews the main current debates around social protection design and financing in considering the future development of social protection in Brazil. The final section concludes.

BRAZIL'S SOCIAL PROTECTION: GAPS AND IMBALANCES

Over the last decades, improvements in Brazilian social protection policy coverage and adequacy have been achieved primarily through the implementation and expansion of contributory social insurance, non-contributory social insurance programmes (categorical benefits paid to individuals who have not matured an entitlement through payment of contributions, including means-tested benefits for the elderly and the disabled and universal rural old-age pensions) and means-tested social assistance cash transfers. Reforms in these areas have extended coverage to population groups that were previously excluded from formal social protection and have included increases in the generosity of public transfers for some population groups.

Despite these achievements, Brazil's social protection system continues to display characteristics and gaps that present current challenges and have important implications for future policy development and sustainability. Two features of Brazil's system stand out in particular: first, the persistent comparatively high levels of social insurance expenditure spending, relative both to the expenditure composition in other countries and to social assistance spending; and second, variations in the treatment (coverage and generosity) of different age, income, education and geographic groups.

HIGH LEVELS OF SOCIAL INSURANCE SPENDING IN A 'YOUNG' COUNTRY

Historically, social protection in Brazil has been dominated by social insurance policies for those formally employed and characterised by largely absent or weak social assistance policies (Draibe, 2002). This institutional configuration led to a system that guaranteed some provision to those in formal employment for the risks associated with the loss of formal employment, while leaving a large share of the population excluded from any form of social protection. The latter included the economically active population in informal employment and those out of work who had not matured an entitlement to the contributory-based policies, the poorest population groups (Barros and Foguel, 2000).

A glance at the composition of Brazilian social spending reflects this institutional arrangement. In 2010, according to the Institute for Applied Economic Research (IPEA, 2012a), social insurance accounted for 47.5 per cent of total federal social spending. This compares with 10.8 per cent spent on health, 7.2 per cent on education and 6.9 per cent on social assistance. (Note that federal social expenditure in IPEA's classification includes the following categories of spending: food and nutrition, social assistance, benefits to federal civil servants, culture, agricultural development, education, employment protection, housing, social insurance, sanitation and health.) A comparison with social insurance spending levels in other countries highlights Brazil's remarkably high levels of spending on social insurance. Brazil's social insurance spending as a percentage of gross domestic product (GDP) in 2005 was higher than in most Organisation of Economic Co-operation and Development (OECD) countries and at a level close to the highest OECD spenders, such as Italy (Rezende Rocha and Caetano, 2008). Comparisons with other emerging economies also reveal Brazil's exceptionality, its social insurance spending as a percentage of GDP at 11.8 per cent compared with that of India at 2.5 per cent and South Africa at 1.3 per cent (Rezende Rocha and Caetano, 2008).

Along with the high levels of social insurance spending, social protection in Brazil has historically been characterised by low levels of resources destined to social assistance. In 1995, social assistance spending accounted for 0.7 per cent of total social spending, compared with 44.3 per cent spent on social insurance (IPEA, 2012a).

A glance at trends over time in Brazilian federal social spending shows the growing importance of social protection in Brazil. The increase in federal social expenditures between 1995 and 2010, by 172 per cent in real terms, is almost entirely the result of increases in social insurance and social assistance spending (IPEA, 2012a). In fact, the two clearest patterns in social spending trends in recent decades show a marked increase in social assistance spending and a persistently and increasingly high share of spending on social insurance. These trends were accompanied by declining and then stable trends in spending in health and education as a percentage of total spending – with social assistance 'catching up' with education spending levels and surpassing them in 2005, when social assistance accounted for 6 per cent of total social spending against 5.6 per cent spent on education (IPEA, 2012a).

On the one hand, these trends reflect recent policy developments, including efforts to address the historic 'imbalance' towards the provision of protection against the risks associated with the loss of formal employment. On the other hand, they also arise from other factors such as the interactions of existing social protection policies with developments in the population-age structure and the labour market. Developments in both policy design and socio-economic and demographic circumstances have contributed to the increases in social insurance and social assistance spending observed in recent years through the increase in the number of beneficiaries and in the value of benefits paid.

In social insurance, reforms led to the introduction and expansion of non-contributory programmes, as mandated by the 1988 Constitution, with the objective of providing insurance and assistance to those unable to work and lead an independent life and previously excluded from formal social protection. An example is given by the *Beneficio de Prestacao Continuada* (BPC), a means-tested cash transfer paid to individuals above the age of 65 and to individuals with disabilities, paid in 2012 to 3.6 million beneficiaries. The expansion of the BPC programmes and regular increases in the benefit values linked to the minimum wage – which increased by 130 per cent in real terms between 1995 and 2003 (IPEA, 2012a) – together with the universal rural pensions, mainly paid to elderly smallholder farmers and rural workers, have contributed to increases in social insurance spending.

Yet this increase is also the result of higher numbers of beneficiaries of contributory benefits resulting from a combination of factors, including employment formalisation, as new workers joined the contributions-based system (Neri, 2010), as well as population ageing and old-age pension regulations facilitating early retirement (Queiroz and Bueno Figoli, 2011). According to Queiroz and Bueno Figoli (2011), the flexible retirement rules, allowing early retirement and leading to a fall in the economic participation of older workers, have played an especially important role in the rapid rise in the number of old-age pension beneficiaries.

Beyond the rise in beneficiary numbers, levels and trends in contributory social insurance spending are also determined by benefit amounts. Comparative studies highlight the generosity of Brazil's public pensions, the average pension benefit in Brazil is about 70 per cent of the average labour income, the highest in the sample of countries studied by Queiroz and Bueno Figoli (2011). This measure considers the ratio between average benefits of all retirees and average wage for all workers. Other countries in the study include the UK, the US, Canada, Japan, Germany, France and Italy. As concerns trends in benefit values over time, recent increases in the real value of the minimum wage have led to increases in the value of benefits linked to it, particularly the basic pension.

In the area of social assistance, the introduction and expansion of cash transfers paid directly to low-income families – the Bolsa Família and its predecessors starting in 2001 – marked an important turning point. Beneficiary numbers grew to 13.4 million families by 2011, equal to 26 per cent of Brazil's population. Upward revisions of the Bolsa Família income eligibility threshold, coupled with the extension of eligibility over time to new population groups (especially households with older and higher numbers of children and most recently with the introduction of Brasil Carinhoso, family specific transfers aimed at closing the extreme poverty gap for families with children under six), have resulted in the continuous increase of beneficiary numbers. Furthermore, the regular uprating of benefit values has contributed to an increase in the average value of the Bolsa Família benefit by 30 per cent in real terms between 2004 and 2012 (Bastagli, 2012).

Despite the policy efforts aimed at addressing the historical 'imbalance' in Brazil's social protection through the increases in coverage and in the benefit values of social assistance and non-contributory benefits, a clear feature of social protection in Brazil remains: the persistent, comparatively high spending on social insurance independent of increases in its non-contributory component.

In their international comparative study, Rezende Rocha and Caetano (2008) show that the non-contributory social insurance schemes (BPC and rural social pensions) – the 'redistributive' programmes of the social insurance system – account for a small share of Brazil's disproportionately high expenditures on social insurance. The main reasons for the substantial differences in Brazil's social insurance spending, compared with that of other countries, lie in the spending on retirement benefits based on time of contribution rather than on the age of beneficiary (*benefício programado*) and the survivors' pension.

This finding is particularly noteworthy when considered alongside the fact that, compared with other countries with similar social insurance spending levels (as a percentage of GDP), Brazil has a relatively young population – for example, as measured by the old-age dependency ratio. Brazil's exceptionality, then, rests in its high expenditure on old-age pensions and other elderly support compared with countries with similar population structures. Countries with a similar demographic composition to Brazil's spend about 4 per cent of their GDP on social insurance, compared with Brazil's 11 per cent (Rezende Rocha and Caetano, 2008).

Resources spent on social insurance also continue to remain high when compared with those destined to be spent on social assistance policies. Despite the recent considerable increase in the number of social assistance beneficiaries and in the real value of social assistance transfers, the latter continues to remain low when compared with the value of social insurance transfers (Lindert et al., 2006). The distributional implications of this are shown by Soares in Chapter 10 of this book. Although the Bolsa Família cash transfer is the most progressively distributed income source of families and the best-targeted public transfer (Soares et al., 2006), its distributional impact is lower than the impact achieved by social insurance programmes. The low value of the Bolsa Família benefit offsets its potential for poverty reduction. As was shown in Chapter 10, the highest impact on headcount poverty results from social insurance expenditures, mainly pensions. Despite being less progressively distributed, social insurance transfers (mainly pensions) achieve a higher distributional impact than social assistance transfers because of their higher transfer values.

GAPS IN SOCIAL PROTECTION COVERAGE AND VARIATIONS IN GENEROSITY

Despite efforts to extend the coverage of social protection to previously excluded groups and to address the imbalances in the generosity of different public transfers, gaps in coverage and variations in the adequacy of transfer levels remain. This section identifies the main gaps in social protection coverage and variations in treatments by socio-economic population group.

Given the objectives of social protection, the extent to which policy addresses different risks and needs over the lifecycle is of particular interest. A distinguishing feature of Brazil is that its social spending falls disproportionately on the older population groups. Whether we consider total social spending – understood as a broad category including health and education – or restrict our attention to social protection cash transfers, the distribution of social spending favours the elderly.

In comparative perspective, the share of public transfers accruing to the older population is high. Turra et al. (2011) compare the ratio of net per capita public transfers for the elderly (aged over 65) to net per capita public transfers for children (aged 0–15) and find that the ratio in Brazil of 9.96 is more than seven times that in the US and between 4.5 and 7.5 times larger than ratios in selected European countries. It is also 2.6 times larger than the ratio in Uruguay and 2.8 times larger than the one in Costa Rica – both Latin America and Caribbean countries that share social, economic and institutional arrangements similar to those in Brazil.

The comparison of poverty rates by age group with and without public cash transfers (including contributory, non-contributory and social assistance cash transfers) highlights how this type of spending also favours the elderly. Turra and Rocha (2010) report that in 1995 the incidence of poverty (post-cash transfers) among the elderly was 13.6 per cent compared with 40.8 per cent among children. They show that the lower poverty rate among the elderly was primarily achieved by public cash transfers, while the poverty estimates (with and without transfers) for children hardly changed. In 2008, poverty rates post-public transfers were lower for all age groups, the younger age groups benefiting from the introduction of targeted conditional cash transfers. However, the continuous expansion of social protection to the elderly over these years magnified relative differences in poverty incidence by age and for every old person in poverty there were still almost 16 poor children in 2008 (Turra and Rocha, 2010).

Social protection programmes help explain why Brazil has the lowest poverty rate among the over-65 population in Latin America: 18.5 per cent compared with an average of 31.8 per cent in the rest of the region (Rezende Rocha and Caetano, 2008). This is partly the result of Brazil's comparatively high social insurance coverage of the elderly. In 2009, 77 per cent of the elderly above 60 years of age received monthly social insurance pensions (IPEA, 2012b), compared to a regional average for Latin America of around one-third of the elderly population (Rezende Rocha and Caetano, 2003).

Despite the high levels of coverage of the elderly, social insurance coverage of the economically active population remains low at 49.4 per cent, though up from 38 per cent in 1995 (IPEA 2012b). In terms of coverage of the elderly, the expansion of non-contributory transfers such as the BPC for the elderly and the rural pensions has played an important role and has facilitated the high coverage levels. At the same time, the low coverage of the economically active population implies that there is a large proportion of workers outside the formal social insurance system with no access to contributory old-age pensions and to other contributory benefits such as maternity and sick leave.

Moreover, this gap in social insurance coverage depends on worker characteristics, with some categories at a considerably higher risk of exclusion. Using *Pesquisa Nacional por Amostra de Domicilios* (PNAD) 2011 household survey data, we examine the ratio of the number of contributors to the formal social insurance system to the number of workers by category or characteristic. We find that, in 2010, the share of workers paying social insurance contributions relative to the total number of workers in that category ranged: from 10 per cent of those with a per capita household income of up to half of the minimum wage, to 76 per cent of those with more than five minimum wages; from 18 per cent of those employed in agriculture, to 75 per cent of those employed in manufacturing; from 4 per cent of workers with no education, to 86 per cent of workers with a university degree; and from 24 per cent of workers in rural areas, to 65 per cent in urban areas.

In conclusion, this section has identified the main peculiarities of Brazil's social protection system and highlighted its gaps and imbalances, as summarised in the paragraphs that follow.

One of the defining features of Brazil is its high spending on social insurance, its levels reaching those of OECD countries with older populations. Recent policy efforts to improve the redistributive component of social protection have been partly offset by the low levels of social assistance transfers, when compared with social insurance benefits.

Brazil also stands out for its generous treatment of the elderly population relative to children in international comparisons. Social protection policies achieve a high coverage of the elderly and contribute to a substantial reduction of poverty among this age group, leading to Brazil having one of the lowest poverty rates among the elderly in the region. Conversely, Brazil's social protection policies have a much smaller impact on poverty among children. Although the recent expansion of cash transfers targeted at families with low incomes has improved the coverage and generosity of public transfers to children, this group continues to receive less favourable treatment than the elderly.

Finally, Brazil's high social protection coverage of the elderly population does not correspond to a high coverage of the economically active population. This is another peculiarity of the Brazilian system. Over 50 per cent of the working population does not contribute to the formal contributions-based social insurance system. While the expansion of non-contributory social insurance benefits has helped provide income support to most of the elderly, just over half of workers are not covered by formal social insurance. The risk of exclusion from formal social insurance varies by socio-economic group. Importantly, the share of workers in the lowest income groups contributing to social insurance is significantly smaller than the share in the highest income group. Workers in the agricultural sector as well as those in rural areas and with low education are also at a higher risk of under-coverage.

ECONOMIC GROWTH, POPULATION AGE AND LABOUR MARKETS

Three broad 'macro' trends accompanied the recent expansion of social protection in Brazil: sustained economic growth (2000–08), a young and growing working-age population, and increases in formal employment. Recent developments in these areas have signalled potentially significant change, with important implications for social protection.

Brazil's recent average growth rate has not been impressive when compared with the other emerging economies discussed in this book. Brazil is at the bottom of the BRICS (Brazil, Russia, India, China, South Africa) league table for growth (Neri et al., 2011). In fact, it has grown an average of 3.6 per cent per year between 2001 and 2010, which is a slight improvement over the decade 1991–2000 (2.5 per cent) and the 'lost decade' 1981–90 (1.6 per cent). But it is still well behind the 1971–80 average of 8.6 per cent. Moreover, recent data shows a gradual slowing down of the economy as captured by the recent reduction in real GDP growth – at 2.7 per cent in 2011 and at 1.6 per cent for 2012 according to a recent Central Bank projection (BCB, 2012). Several commentators have pointed to Brazil's sustained growth rates in 2007 and 2008 (6.1 per cent and 5.2 per cent respectively) as being central to the further expansion of social protection and the upward adjustments in benefit levels described earlier in this chapter (such as IPEA, 2012a). Brazil's moderate growth levels when compared with the other large emerging economies and recent evidence of declining trends raise questions regarding the adequacy of resources for the future financing of social protection. They also raise the issue of the role played by the expansion of social protection on growth itself. Are the moderate growth rates associated with the high and increasing social spending levels and related reductions in inequality?

Useful insight is provided by the comparison of the *type* of growth in the different emerging economies, beyond the GDP levels measure. In contrast with what has happened in other fast-growing economies, in Brazil the distribution of increases in household per capita income across income deciles has led to a decrease in income inequality over the past decade. Other BRICS countries have seen increased or constant income inequality. In Brazil, the poorest households have experienced a much faster increase in their income than the richest; the increase in the real income of the poor was higher than the GDP rates for India and just below China's, which illustrates the highly pro-poor nature of the recent growth process in Brazil (Neri et al., 2011).

These comparative trends highlight Brazil's more moderate but balanced and equitable growth path. The expansion of social protection and the associated reduction in inequality appear as key ingredients to this growth pattern. On the one hand, the expansion of Brazil's social protection has required increases in the tax burden. On the other hand, it was precisely the increase in the income of the lowest deciles through both a pro-poor labour market performance and pro-poor redistributive policies that provided the Brazilian economy with an additional source of dynamism to the external demand-driven growth. The high internal consumption is one of the factors that explain why the global financial crisis had a relatively mild impact in Brazil (Soares, 2012).

This inclusive growth path may support continuity in social protection and even its further expansion. Other factors that have characterised this growth pattern, such as the high (by international standards) interest rate and the overvalued exchange rate, which risk acting as limitations to its sustainability over time, have both been recently tackled by the Brazilian Central Bank (for example, through the reduction of the basic interest rates, bringing down the annualised real interest rate from 6 per cent to 2 per cent between 2011 and 2012). Such developments may improve the potential sustainability of this growth pattern.

A second factor that characterised the period of expansion of social protection in Brazil is the favourable population age structure given by the growing working-age population. This demographic structure is rapidly changing as fertility started to decline at the end of the 1960s at a much faster pace than mortality. Between 1999 and 2009, the number of the country's residents who were at least 60 years old grew from 9 per cent to 11 per cent (IBGE, 2011). Over the medium term, and starting in the 2020s, predictions show that Brazil will have a shrinking labour force and an ageing population. By 2050, at least 30 per cent of the Brazilian population will be aged 60 and older, compared with less than 10 per cent in 1980 (IBGE, 2011).

What is particularly striking is that the speed of population ageing is faster than what was experienced by affluent European societies. For instance, it took France more than a century for its population aged 65 and over to increase from 7 per cent to 14 per cent of the total population. The same demographic change will occur in the next two decades in Brazil (World Bank, 2011).

These shifts in population age structure will lead to substantial additional fiscal pressures on publicly financed health care and pensions. With regard to social protection specifically, the rapid process of population ageing has a number of implications for the sustainability of Brazil's pension system. A direct channel of impact is the increase in the number of beneficiaries depending on a smaller number of workers, leading to an increase in the old-age dependency ratio.

Yet this demographic change also interacts with the existing social insurance rules to further aggravate the problem. As mentioned in the earlier section, there has been a strong downward trend in labour force participation at older ages. Policy rules facilitating early retirement (that is, retirement plans based on years of contribution with weak age limits) have increased the dependency ratio by more than increases resulting from demographic change alone (Queiroz and Bueno Figoli, 2011). For instance, social security regulations based on the length of service and allowing retirement at the age of 55 have contributed to the significant decline in labour force participation of older men.

A third factor associated with Brazil's expansion of social protection over the last decade has been the steady increase in labour market participation. Starting in the early 2000s, growth in employment was especially strong for formal jobs; the share of informal work, measured as the sum of self-employment, informal and unpaid employment, fell from 55.1 per cent to 45.4 per cent between 2001 and 2011 (IPEA, 2012b).

Such increases in formal employment have played a central role in improvements in social insurance coverage (Neri, 2010). Beyond coverage concerns and the large numbers of unprotected workers that high informality entails, future trends in formal employment have important implications for social protection financing as high informality implies fewer financing resources as a result of the smaller tax base and of forms of tax evasion associated with informality.

Recent figures indicate that future prospects are mixed at best. First of all, they point to a reduction in labour market participation in 2011 (IPEA, 2012b). Moreover, although gains in promoting formal employment have been made, informality remains high, especially in certain sectors. For instance, IPEA (2012b) shows that although the fall in informality was observed in both metropolitan and non-metropolitan areas, the latter continue to have considerably higher informality rates.

SOCIAL PROTECTION DESIGN AND FINANCING: CHALLENGES AND POSSIBLE RESPONSES

The previous sections identified the main gaps or imbalances in Brazil's social protection system and reviewed recent economic and socio-demographic changes with potentially important implications for the future of social protection in the country. Three main issues arise in considering the future of Brazil's social protection. First, the recent reforms of social assistance and non-contributory benefits and their growing importance in terms of coverage and spending raise the question of their future development. Second, the high and increasing costs of the old-age support system point to the threat posed to the sustainability of social protection. Third, the central role played by employment formalisation in the expansion of social insurance coverage, coupled with persistent high levels of informality, highlight the priority of promoting labour market participation, particularly in the formal sectors, as a key ingredient for the further expansion and sustainability of Brazil's social protection.

Recent policy debates in Brazil have flourished around the future of social assistance and non-contributory transfers. Sweeping institutional reforms regulating benefit administration and value are responsible for the increases in coverage and benefit amounts. These include the consolidation of existing public cash transfers, the creation of a single administrative registry for the administration of conditional cash transfers and related programmes, the detailed regulation of the responsibilities of different government bodies and the linkage of benefits to the minimum wage. Recent debates have addressed the questions of how to further enhance the efficiency and effectiveness of public transfers, while securing their sustainability over time.

As concerns the institutional design, several commentators are arguing in favour of a reform aimed at the further integration of existing benefits. Soares and Satyro (2010), for instance, suggest as one possible reform the integration of the means-tested BPC non-contributory transfers with the social assistance Bolsa Família transfers, with the objective of simplifying the administration of benefits and consolidating policies with a similar purpose. The rationale for a reform of this kind would be to address the high fragmentation and poor coordination in current policy design to free up resources.

With regard to the increase in the value of benefits, real increases in the minimum wage have played a central role and, looking forward, future trends in the minimum wage are crucial to the future values of benefits. According to some commentators, the minimum wage has reached its upper limits. They warn against future increases of the magnitude experienced in recent years. New upward adjustments of the minimum wage imply a mounting fiscal burden, while their positive redistributive effects are decreasing as the poorest groups remain outside the formal labour market and formal social insurance (Souza, 2012).

Yet protecting the value of social assistance and non-contributory transfers remains a priority, given the historic configuration of Brazil's social protection and the crucial role played by these policies in ensuring a social safety net, particularly for children. Recent changes in the amounts transferred by Bolsa Família to beneficiaries who live in extreme poverty and have children – the Brasil Carinhoso strategy – seem to reflect a compromise between the objective of eradicating extreme poverty and using young children as a tool to flag the most vulnerable households. This recent adjustment to Bolsa Família benefit rules, leading to a cash transfer of an amount which will tap the extreme poverty gap of all families with children under the age of six, points to a continuation in the move towards a more balanced distribution between the elderly and children initiated with the introduction and expansion of social assistance benefits. Some have warned against the further expansion and increase in benefit values because of the risk of generating additional disincentives to formality and related poverty traps. However, the government sees Bolsa Família's complementary programmes, designed to promote employment opportunities, as the tool to prevent such undesirable effects.

A second challenge highlighted by the previous sections concerns the threat to the sustainability of social protection brought about by the high and increasing costs of the old-age pension system. Existing policy regulation that facilitates early retirement, comparatively generous benefits and rapid population ageing are factors which have contributed to the comparatively high public spending on social insurance and threaten its sustainability.

Brazil's low effective retirement age, compared to that of most OECD countries and resulting from retirement policy rules based on years of contribution, even with the introduction of some penalties in recent reforms – such as the discount based on the difference between age of retirement and life expectancy – suggests that there is scope to reform the system. Options include reducing incentives to early retirement and revising the generosity of the survivors' pension to at least bring it closer to international standards (Rezende Rocha and Caetano, 2008).

Increases in formal employment and in the number of workers

contributing to social insurance could improve the age dependency ratio and social insurance sustainability (Queiroz and Bueno Figoli, 2011). This leads on to Brazil's third main social protection challenge: expanding social insurance coverage.

Improving the formalisation of work is one way forward. It can be achieved by promoting human capital accumulation, facilitating the participation of categories at a higher risk of exclusion, such as the self-employed and small employers, and mitigating policy disincentives that reduce the opportunity cost of informality.

Some analysts emphasise the role of education in increasing formal employment. For instance, Neri (2010) finds that the impact of years of schooling on formalisation trends is empirically the most important determinant. Educational policy, particularly policies aimed at reducing education disparities, may be especially effective. From this perspective, policies such as the Bolsa Família, which explicitly address educational inequalities, hold some promise in promoting formality.

A number of policy reforms have been enacted with the explicit objective of increasing formalisation in the labour market as well as stimulating and facilitating the contribution of self-employed and/or small employers to social security. As suggested by Cotta and Paiva (2010), initiatives such as Super-simples, implemented since 2006 for small firms that reduce tax bureaucracy, seem to have contributed to formalisation of small firms. The Individual Micro-Entrepreneur (MEI) scheme, approved in 2008, also simplifies and reduces taxes and guarantees access to some social security benefits such as maternity and sickness benefits, in addition to the retirement benefit. It is a scheme with clear subsidies, but that could attract informal sector workers whose only option for old-age support would be the means-tested BPC benefit.

Finally, some commentators have emphasised the role of existing social protection policy design in discouraging the formalisation of employment. Specifically, the recent introduction and expansion of policies for people with low incomes independently of their employment status, while strengthening the safety net, would also have weakened the incentives to enter formal employment. Levy (2008) raises this point for the case of Mexico, where the implementation of social assistance income transfers targeted at the poor since the late 1990s went hand in hand with persistent high informality and, he argues, subsidised low-productivity, informal jobs. In Brazil, the payment of old-age assistance pensions (equal to the monthly minimum wage) to minimum wage earners who have not contributed to formal social insurance lowers the opportunity cost of informality, according to some commentators (see OECD, 2006). Employment formalisation could be encouraged by adjusting the design of policies which generate incentives to remain informally employed (Cotta and Paiva, 2010).

Overall, it seems that the strategy of the Brazilian government includes piecemeal reforms to improve the sustainability of contributory social insurance, including measures to increase the average retirement age, incentives to formalisation and contributions by the informal self-employed. In the area of social assistance, the further consolidation of the administrative practices of different public transfers based on those successfully developed for the Bolsa Família promise to improve the efficiency and effectiveness of these benefits. The planned expansion of a Unified System for Social Assistance is expected to play a major role in this process. Finally, a better balance between protection for the elderly and for children will depend highly on how benefits will be adjusted and on the role that the minimum wage policy will play in this process.

REFERENCES

Barros, R. and M. N. Foguel (2000), 'A focalizacao dos gastos publicos sociais e erradicacao da pobreza no Brasil', in R. Henriques (ed.), *Desigualdade e Pobreza No Brasil*, Brasilia: IPEA, pp. 719–39.

Bastagli, F. (2012), 'Brazil's Bolsa Familia reform 2003–2012', paper prepared for the Latin American Studies Association (LASA) 2012 Annual Conference, San Francisco, 25–28 May.

BCB (2012), 'Relatorio de Inflacao', accessed at www.bcb.gov.br/htms/relinf/port/2012/09/ri201209b1p.pdf.

Cotta, T. C. and L. H. Paiva, (2010), 'O Programa Bolsa Familia e a Protecao Social no Brasil', in J. A. Castro and L. Modesto (eds), *Bolsa Familia 2003–2010 – avancos e desafios*, Brasilia: IPEA, pp. 57–99.

Draibe, S. (2002), 'The national social policy system in Brazil: construction and reform', Caderno N. 53, NEPP, UNICAMP, University of Campinas.

IBGE (2011), *Microdata, PNAD 2011*, accessed at www.ibge.gov.br/english/estatistica/populacao/trabalhoerendimento/pnad2011/microdados.shtm.

IPEA (2012a), 'Gasto social federal: prioridade macroeconomica no periodo 1995–2010', *Nota técnica* 9, September, accessed at www.ipea.gov.br/portal/index.php?option=com_content&view=article&id=15361&Itemid=9.

IPEA (2012b), 'PNAD 2011: Primeiras Analises sobre o Mercado de Trabalho Brasileiro', *Comunicados do Ipea* 156, Brasilia: IPEA.

Levy, S. (2008), *Good Intentions, Bad Outcomes: Social Policy, Informality and Economic Growth in Mexico*, Washington, DC: Brookings Institution Press.

Lindert, K., E. Skoufias and J. Shapiro (2006), 'Redistributing income to the poor and the rich: public transfers in Latin America and the Caribbean', SP Discussion Paper No. 0605, Washington, DC: The World Bank.

Neri, M. C. (2010), 'The decade of falling income inequality and formal employment generation in Brazil', in *Tackling Inequalities in Brazil, China, India and*

South Africa: The Role of Labour Market and Social Policies, Paris: OECD Publishing, pp. 57–107.
Neri, M., L. C. de Melo, S. Sacramento, T. Cavalcante, L. Moreira, P. Lipkin and M. Carvalho (2011), *Os emergentes dos emergentes: Reflexoes globais e acoes locais para a nova classe media brasileira*, Rio De Janiero: Fundacao Getulio VargasFGV/CPS.
OECD (2006), 'Economic survey of Brazil, 2006', Policy Brief, November, Paris: OECD Publishing.
Queiroz, B. L. and M. G. Bueno Figoli (2011), 'Population aging and the rising costs of public pension in Brazil', *Texto para discussao* 438, Belo Horizonte: Cedeplar.
Rezende Rocha, R. de and M. Caetano (2008), 'O sistema previdenciario brasileiro: uma avaliacao de desempenho comparada', *Texto para discussao* 1331, Brasilia: IPEA.
Soares, F. V. (2012), 'Can we say there is sustainable growth in Brazil?', paper prepared for the PEGNET conference, Hamburg, Germany, 8 September 2011.
Soares, F. V., S. D. Soares, M. Medeiros and R. Osorio (2006), 'Cash transfer programmes in Brazil: impacts on poverty and inequality', IPC-IG Working Paper 21, Brasilia: UNDP/IPC.
Soares, S. and N. Satyro (2010), 'O Programa Bolsa Familia: Desenho Institucional e Possibilidades Futuras', in J. A. Castro and L. Modesto (ed.), *Bolsa Familia 2003–2010 – avancos e desafios*, Brasilia: IPEA, pp. 25–55.
Souza, P. H. G. (2012), 'Poverty, inequality and social policies in Brazil, 1995–2009', IPC-IG Working Paper 87, Brasilia: UNDP/IPC.
Turra, C. M., B. L. Queiroz and E. L. G. Rios-Neto (2011), 'Idiosyncrasies of intergenerational transfers in Brazil', in R. Lee and A. Mason (eds), *Population Aging and the Generational Economy*, Cheltenham, UK and Northampton, MA, USA: Edward Elgar Publishing Limited, pp. 394–407.
Turra, C. M. and R. Rocha (2010), 'Public transfers among dependent age groups in Brazil', background paper prepared for the Workshop on Ageing in Brazil, 6–7 April, Brasilia: World Bank.
World Bank (2011), *Becoming Old in an Older Brazil*, Washington, DC: World Bank.

PART V

South Africa

13. Social protection in South Africa: history, goals and strategies

Leila Patel

The post-apartheid government inherited a society faced with mass poverty, inequality and underdevelopment which coincided with race, class, gender and place. Social protection policies together with other social and economic development strategies were devised to address the legacy of the country's past. The welfare system was significantly redesigned. The new system built on aspects of past policies that reflected the country's vision and values while simultaneously devising and implementing new policies to promote reconstruction and development of society. Social protection policies captured the aspirations and ideals of a future society featuring notions of reconciliation, redress, the creation of an inclusive, just, stable and caring society. Thus, a rights-based approach with a strong emphasis on redistribution and the building of human capabilities to improve the life chances of citizens featured prominently in social policy goals. Significant progress has been made in the development and implementation of social protection strategies and particularly in the expansion of non-contributory social assistance for the poor and vulnerable groups. However, gaps exist in mandatory contributory social protection provision.

This chapter first describes the development of social protection in South Africa and illustrates how contemporary social protection goals and strategies were influenced by the country's history of colonialisms and apartheid. Second, social protection rights and policies, including the human development situation that current policies seek to address, are discussed. Third, an overview of the goals and strategies is outlined, concluding with some of the challenges for reform of the system.

HISTORICAL DEVELOPMENT

Racial inequality can be traced to the country's legacy of colonialism and imperialism. South Africa was first a Dutch colony dating to the mid-seventeenth century and later it became a British colony. The country's history of colonialism is marked by conquest, violence and wars between the indigenous people and between the Dutch and British settlers in a struggle for power and control over land, natural resources and labour. Economic and political power of the colonial authorities entrenched white privilege and resulted in the deprivation of indigenous people who were reduced to exploitable labour as industrialization took off following the discovery of gold and diamonds in 1860. Black migrant labour was the backbone of economic development, based on cheap labour drawn from the reserves which were under the control of traditional authorities. Migrant labour of African men resulted in the decline of the reserve economies, which relied on subsistence agriculture and were the main repositories of the most vulnerable people, namely women and children, older persons and people with disabilities and those who were too ill to work. Influx control legislation and migrant labour were therefore central to the inequalities and distorted development that flowed from the form of racial capitalism that evolved in South Africa at the time. The labour reserves continue to be the poorest and most underdeveloped areas in contemporary South Africa.

By the 1920s, the impact of industrialization and urbanization affected all race groups. However, the plight of Afrikaners, who were driven off the land and into wage labour, received particular attention from the Pact government of 1910, which accommodated Afrikaner and English group interests with a view to building a stable white society. This gave rise to social welfare responses to the growing needs of poor whites and vulnerable individuals and groups. Services were initially provided by newly formed voluntary organizations such as the Afrikaner Women's Organizations and religious organizations, particularly of the Dutch Reformed Church. These social programmes were also fashioned on the English Poor Laws targeted at the most destitute. During this period the foundation of the partnership model of welfare service delivery evolved between the voluntary sector and the state. Social welfare policies and programmes formed an integral part of the state's strategy, which included the first state pension scheme established in 1928 that provided income protection for the white elderly. A further key development was the establishment of the Carnegie Commission of Enquiry to investigate the 'poor white problem' that culminated in the establishment of the first state welfare department in 1937. This marked the beginning of organized state intervention in social welfare. The first Children's Act of 1937 was passed, under which maintenance grants were paid to single-parent families and the social work profession was professionalized. Due to the increasing impoverishment of workers as a result of the depression, the

Unemployment Insurance Act of 1932 was passed, providing protection for white workers. Payments were extended to women in 1946 due to the growing number of women who were entering the labour market.

Race-based social policies introduced in colonial times and following the formation of the Union of South Africa in the early part of the twentieth century were institutionalized and further entrenched when the Afrikaner Nationalist Party government came to power in 1948 and introduced its policy of *apartheid* (meaning apart-ness), based on the idea of separate development for each race group, namely Whites, Coloureds (people of mixed race), Indians and Africans. Racial and social constructions of superiority provided a powerful justification for race-based welfare policies that privileged a 'white welfare elite' while providing rudimentary services and benefits for Blacks. Afrikaner ideologues and strategists devised welfare state policies fashioned on British post-war welfare policies for whites as part of an overall strategy to overcome white poverty and its effects. This strategy included the creation of employment opportunities, social security, social services, access to health and education, subsidization of 'white agriculture' and concerted state intervention in the economy. These measures, coupled with the political power of whites, secured significant improvements in their standard of living. By the late 1960s, whites reached a standard of living that was on par with that of the advanced industrial societies. A residual welfare system was created for Black South Africans, marked by a racial hierarchy of privilege, with Africans being the most disadvantaged. Racial differentiation in access to welfare services and benefits was an explicit principle of the South African welfare system (Department of Constitutional Development and Planning, 1985). Welfare expenditure for whites peaked in 1950 with them receiving 61 per cent of allocations, and this declined as the situation of whites improved over the years, reaching 23 per cent by 1990. Africans who made up three-quarters of the population received only 25 per cent of welfare resources in 1950. This increased to just over half of the allocations for Africans by 1990, while coloureds and Indians who made up 9 per cent and 3 per cent respectively of the population received 24 per cent of total welfare spending (Patel, 2011). These expenditure patterns for the different race groups illustrate the high levels of inequity in the allocation of public resources. Over the years, a vast backlog in service provision and benefits developed as a result of past neglect of provision, while the demands for social welfare more broadly defined increased with pressure from below.

Several of the reasons why there was some expansion of welfare provision for Blacks were due, first, to the decline of the reserve economies, resulting in increased rural poverty and the realization on the part of the state that there was a need to accept some of the social costs of social reproduction of labour. Previously, subsistence agriculture enabled corporations, particularly mining companies, to pay very low wages to migrant workers. At the same time, the government employed social control strategies to manage in-migration of Africans to urban areas through the strict application of influx control regulations. Second, growing opposition to apartheid resulted in increasing state repression of opposition movements and the adoption of authoritarian legislation to crush and stifle political opposition to the government. At various times, attempts were made to accommodate the political aspirations of the different non-white groups in separate political arrangements, stopping short of meeting their demands for full political representation. Although these structures were ineffective in tackling inequality, mass poverty and under-development, the government nevertheless had to respond to some of the pressure emanating from these structures, such as the Tricameral parliaments for Coloureds and Indians and the Black administration authorities for urban Africans. Consequently, increases were noted in social welfare, health and education expenditure for Coloureds and Indians and for urban Africans. The self-governing territories also continued to pay old-age pensions and disability grants for Africans, although the amounts paid were far less than those paid to other race groups. Thus social welfare expansion had less to do with the needs of those who were disadvantaged, but was an attempt to stifle unrest and limit demands for full political rights and to further entrench apartheid ideology (Patel, 2011, 2005).

By the 1980s, the economy was in deep structural crisis, the country was experiencing growing international isolation; political opposition was endemic, resulting in the creation of successive states of emergency accompanied by the increasing militarization of society. The government's security strategy at this time also included campaigns to 'win the hearts and minds' of the Black population and community development strategies were adopted in selected areas known as 'oil spots' to dampen the revolutionary fervour in some of the areas where unrest was endemic. Grass-roots opposition organizations and social, trade union and political movements advocated the political, economic and human rights of all South Africans in a common society and drew attention to the effects of this deprivation on their well-being. Welfare demands were subsumed in overall demands for the achievement of a just society that would promote human dignity and the well-being of all citizens in areas such as health, education and social welfare. These demands were contained in the Freedom Charter adopted by the liberation movements such as the Congress of the People in 1955. Interestingly, these demands were also influenced by the social democratic ideas emanating from the Beveridge Report of 1942. It was not until the mid-1980s that opposition welfare groupings that were part of the mass democratic movement in the country began to formulate explicitly what may be referred to as welfare demands which were based on the Freedom Charter. The demands of the Freedom Charter included a non-racial and unitary welfare system; equity in resource allocation, a democratic model of social service delivery and for decision-making in the allocation of resources, state intervention in the economy and the provision of social security, free compulsory education; a national health service, care of the aged, the sick and orphaned, crèches, social centres, rest and leisure, recreation, promotion of family life, housing and affordable rents. Social welfare was conceived of as a redistributive mechanism and as an instrument in the building of a national identity (Patel, 1988, 1992, 2005).

The idea of a 'welfare state' was therefore quite central in the early demands of liberation movements and subsequent welfare, civic, youth and women's organizations in the United Democratic Front (UDF), who popularized the idea of 'People's Welfare' (Patel, 1988). The UDF-aligned social worker organization – Concerned Social Workers – published a series of papers that promoted an alternative model of social welfare which later shaped welfare policy in a democratic society. A negotiated settlement was reached in 1994 between the Nationalist Party government and the liberation movements, paving the way for democratic elections, the dismantling of the old colonial and apartheid order and the creation of a constitutional democracy.

SOCIAL PROTECTION, RIGHTS AND SOCIAL DEVELOPMENT

The Constitution of the Republic of South Africa of 1996 and the Bill of Rights guarantee civil, political and social rights to all citizens in a common society. Not only does it seek to bring about political transformation, it also sought to achieve the social and economic transformation of society. Social rights are guaranteed that afford the individual the right to a minimum status and standard of living in society, including the right of equal access to services and benefits. The right to education, health care, social assistance and housing are also upheld by the constitution. These rights are however envisaged to be realized progressively, while the state is obliged to meet the needs and rights of children as set out in the Bill of Rights. The equality provisions of the constitution state in section 9(3) that no one shall be unfairly discriminated against on grounds of race, gender, sex, pregnancy, age, disability, religion, conscience, belief, culture, language and birth. Genuine equality is also envisaged by giving priority to meeting the needs of the least advantaged persons in society. Post-apartheid social policy is also infused with developmental thinking and priorities such as the reduction of poverty and inequality, employment creation, the promotion of economic growth and social redress, just some of the features of the liberal egalitarian approach to transformation outlined in various social policies. Developmental ideas such as the interrelation between economic and social development, active citizenship, citizen participation and an active role for the state in a pluralist policy framework are also emphasized. Social and economic policies are considered to be integral to national reconstruction and in healing the divisions of the past. In keeping with these ideas, a comprehensive system of social security was proposed by the *White Paper for Social Welfare* (Department of Welfare and Population Development, 1997) and the Taylor Committee of Enquiry (2002) which included not only social assistance, social insurance and social services but also a range of developmental initiatives undertaken by the state.

Over the past 18 years wide-ranging macroeconomic and social policies were adopted to address race, class and gender inequalities, including other forms of social divisions such as language, ethnicity, sexual orientation, disability and geography. These policies gave effect to the Bill of Rights and undergird South Africa's rights-based approach to social protection. The country's social package of services and benefits is made up theoretically, but not in practice, of universal access to primary health care and basic compulsory education up to 15 years. Although this does not amount to universal free education, 60 per cent of schools in poor areas are designated 'non fee paying' schools, and it is government policy that no child should be excluded from education because of an inability to pay. Social security and welfare services provide social protection for children, youth and families, the elderly, people with disabilities and people with chronic illnesses, among others. In addition to a large publicly funded social assistance programme with demonstrated redistributive impacts, selective targeted housing policies and public works programmes also exist. In all these areas, significant achievements have been noted in de-racializing public policy and delivery and in the introduction of legislation. Increasing access to basic education has been highly successful with more than 90 per cent of children of school-going age in school, although the quality of education remains poor. Social assistance has been significantly expanded from reaching three million beneficiaries in 1995 to 15.7 million in 2012.

There are many policy gaps, and significant delivery failures exist due to a range of interlocking factors of an institutional, fiscal, human resource, public management and delivery nature, the scope of which are beyond this chapter (Patel, 2012). Although gender equity features prominently across the board, with women identified in some of the key programmes – including public works, health and social welfare – as the targeted beneficiaries, a gendered analysis of social care did not undergird social welfare policies. The *White Paper for Social Welfare* (Department of Welfare and Population Development, 1997) was more focused on meeting women's needs rather than the social relations constraining women and the gendered nature of social reproduction in the private domain.

While significant progress has been achieved in creating a democratic society and in developing a social protection system, and in improving access to social and basic services, education and health care, poverty and inequality remain the country's greatest challenge. Over half of the country's population lived in poverty when the new society was inaugurated (Patel, 2005). There is agreement among researchers that there has been a decrease in poverty levels since then, particularly for the chronically poor (Leibbrandt et al., 2010). The expansion of the social grant system, amounting to over 3 per cent of gross domestic product (GDP) since 2000, is one of the main reasons for this decline. However, reducing poverty connected with unemployment remains a key challenge (van der Berg et al., 2007). Poverty intersects with race, gender, family type and spatial dimensions, with the majority of the poor being African and Coloured. A comparison of poverty levels and profiles between 1993 and 2008 indicates some changes (Leibbrandt et al., 2010, pp. 34–40). First, as a result of inward migration, urban poverty is rising (by 13 per cent in this period). Despite this, most of the poorest of the poor are still located in rural areas, which may be attributed to the country's legacy of apartheid and the under-development of these areas. Second, the proportion of poor people who live in households with low levels of education (incomplete high school education) increased substantially, which may be attributed to a lack of demand for lower levels of skill in the labour market due to the effects of economic globalization. Third, households with one or more children made up the largest share of poor households (95 per cent). Finally, over the period under review, aggregate poverty declined modestly among the African population, principally among African males, with a respective increase in the poverty share of African females.

Despite the country's classification as a lower middle-income country, South Africa's human development performance has also slowed down as a result of the HIV and AIDS pandemic, with a prevalence rate of 21.5 per cent (IndexMundi, 2008), which has far-reaching implications for the care of adults who are ill and the care of children and the elderly in need of care. The burden of care is borne largely by women, who carry a disproportionate share of the responsibilities in the domestic sphere, which remain unacknowledged in social and economic policies. South Africa has a medium range Human Development Index ranking of 0.674 and was placed 121 out of 177 countries in 2005 (UNDP, 2007/2008). The declining human development situation is also accompanied by increasing levels of income inequality in society and unacceptably high poverty rates as indicated above. The income Gini coefficient stood at 0.70 in 2008 (World Bank, 2012). This makes South Africa one of the most unequal societies in the world, with the top 10 per cent of the population accounting for 58 per cent of the country's income and the bottom half less than 8 per cent (World Bank, 2012). Lower growth rates are forecast for the future due to the impact of the global economic crisis and factors germane to the South African economy. Unemployment stands at 25.2 per cent, one of the highest in the world, and is one of the key reasons why income distribution is skewed to such a large extent (World Bank, 2012). It has been widely argued that inclusive growth is needed in order for economic growth to improve (World Bank, 2012; Woolard, 2003). And, without the country's large and growing social assistance programme, poverty levels would have worsened significantly. Social protection by itself appears to be insufficient and needs to work in concert with access to other public services. However, unequal access to basic services, health, quality education and employment opportunities between different classes and strata in society continue to fuel inequality in post-apartheid South Africa. This is further exacerbated by circumstances beyond people's control, such as where they live (a rural village, a township or an informal settlement) and due to their gender, race, family structure and background. This situation is particularly severe for young adults in the 20–34 years age group, which makes up 25.7 per cent of the population (Statistics South Africa, 2011).

GOALS AND STRATEGIES

The *White Paper for Social Welfare* (Department of Welfare and Population Development, 1997) defined the key domains of social security to include poverty prevention, poverty alleviation, social compensation and income distribution (Chapter 7). Thus the various social security programmes mirror these social goals. The rationale for the social security system was to overcome the legacy of social and economic exclusion through redressing past inequities and to promote reconciliation and healing. Social welfare policies more broadly defined were envisaged to contribute to a more 'humane, just and caring society which will uphold welfare rights, facilitate meeting of basic needs, release people's creative energies, help them achieve their aspirations, build human capacity and self-reliance and participate fully in all spheres of social, economic and political life' (Department of Welfare and Population Development, 1997, p. 7). Formal social protection strategies include social assistance, social insurance and private savings. Informal provision exists alongside the formal system and continues to play a critical role in complimenting formal provision. A brief overview is provided of the nature and scope of social protection with a focus on social assistance and social insurance.

Social Assistance

The post-apartheid government inherited a developed social assistance programme for children and families, the elderly and people with disabilities. This programme was significantly expanded after 1994; benefits were equalized between the different race groups and some elements of the system were redesigned, such as child and family support. Social assistance, also referred to as 'social grants', is a means-tested non-contributory cash transfer that is fully tax-funded and targeted at specific categories of people. Eligibility requirements are set for each type of grant and additional assessments of need are taken into account such as the nature and extent of a person's disability and age. In April 2012, a total of 15.7 million people received social assistance, reaching an estimated 31 per cent of a population of 50.5 million based on 2011 estimates (Statistics South Africa, 2011). Table 13.1 provides a breakdown of the number of beneficiaries for each of the types of social assistance grants. The three social grants with the highest reach are child support grants (70 per cent), followed by old-age pensions (18 per cent) and disability grants (8 per cent). The remaining social grants reach much smaller numbers of beneficiaries (5 per cent), of which foster care grants are the largest in beneficiary numbers (3 per cent). The amounts received are variable, ranging from R1200 per month (US$153.84) for old-age pensions (OAP) and disability grants (DG) to R280 per month per child (US$35) for up to six children in the case of the child support grant (CSG). The amount paid for the care of foster children is considerably more than the CSG; it was initially established as a child protection measure, providing support for out-of-home care for children following a Children's Court Enquiry. The number of beneficiaries has increased significantly in recent years due to the HIV/AIDS epidemic and the growing number of children who have been orphaned due to the death of one or both parents. This is one instance where there has been a tension between the child protection goals of the foster care grant and the poverty reduction goals of the CSG.

Old age pensions are paid to persons aged 60 years and over who meet the requirements of a means test. There is a very high uptake of the OAP, reaching 2.7 million people, which is approximately 68 per cent of the total population over the age of 60 years. In 2010, OAPs made up 1.2 per cent of GDP (Department of Social Development, undated). The OAP empowers older persons (Moller, 2011) and is well targeted at the poor; it is gender sensitive, reaches far into rural areas and supports extended families and households (Ardington and Lund, 1995). Comparative research shows that between 2002 and 2009 improvements in material living standards and well-being were recorded in households with older persons, including higher levels of life satisfaction, particularly in rural areas where there are limited economic opportunities (Moller, 2011). The OAP is the largest social assistance programme in rand terms, but the CSG has the largest number of beneficiaries.

Disability grants are the second largest social assistance programme in rand terms. The number of grants has increased significantly, reaching approximately 3.5 per cent of the population between 17 and 66 years who are eligible for a grant (Republic of South Africa National Treasury, 2003). The rising numbers are due again to the impact of the HIV/AIDS epidemic, as chronically ill persons are eligible for benefits (Nattrass, 2007). In addition, poverty, a lack of access to education, discrimination in the labour market, a lack of appropriate employment opportunities for people with disabilities who are able to work, violence and road accidents are some of the reasons for the growing numbers of people who are receiving the DG. However, it is evident from research in an urban context that there are large numbers of disabled persons who are not accessing the grant due to not meeting the requirements of the means test, a lack of awareness of the grant and a lack of documentation (Graham et al., 2010). The means test does not take into account the social and care needs associated with a disability; it therefore acts only as a form of income support to poor households with a disabled person (Nattrass, 2007). There is therefore a need to review the means test as well as to assess the particular needs of chronically ill persons in a context where there is high HIV and AIDS prevalence.

Lastly, the CSG was instituted in 1998 to provide support to the caregiver of a child up to six years of age. In view of the success of the programme, it was scaled up and expanded to include children up to 18 years of age who meet the requirements of a means test. The CSG accounts for 3.5 per cent of GDP. Although the amount of the grant is small, the CSG supplements household income and, together with other earnings, Posel and Rogan (2012) found that the grant reduced poverty by five percentage points among women between 1997 and 2006. Other significant social developmental outcomes for children and women have also been noted in other studies (Patel et al., 2012; Neves et al., 2009; Delany et al., 2008;

Vorster and de Waal, 2008; Case et al., 2005; van der Berg et al., 2005; Ardington and Lund, 1995). Based on an analysis of the National Income Dynamics Survey for 2008, Hall and Wright (2010) demonstrate that the CSG by itself had a relatively small impact on child poverty because the amount given is small relative to other grants such as pensions and disability grants. These authors also found that child poverty, including limited access to services and inadequate living environments, remains most severe in rural areas under traditional authorities of the former homelands. Thus, child well-being is most compromised in these areas. Table 13.1 sets out the types of grants, amounts received and the number of beneficiaries for the different types of grants based on 2011 data. However, the Minister of Finance, Pravin Gordhan, indicated in his budget speech in 2012 that nearly 16 million beneficiaries are now receiving social grants.

Table 13.1 South Africa: types of grants, amounts received and number of beneficiaries

Social assistance	Target group	Amount of grant (2012)	Number of beneficiaries (2012)
Social pensions	Persons over the age of 60 years	R1200	2 761 120
Disability grants	Persons medically diagnosed disabled over the age of 18	R1200	1 188 604
Care dependency grants	Parents, the primary caregiver or foster parent of a disabled child who requires permanent care or support at home by another person	R1200	116 101
Child support grants	Paid to the primary caregiver of a child/children up to 18 years	R280	11 022 722
Foster-care grants	Foster families of children under 18 years old	R770	544 968
War veterans' grant	Veterans of the two world wars, Zulu uprising and the Korean War	R1220	735
Grants-in-aid	A person with a physical or mental condition requiring regular attendance by another person	R280	66 949

Source: Department of Social Development, SOCPEN system, 30 April 2012.

Finance of Social Assistance

Expenditure on social grants will grow from R105 billion in 2012–13 to R122 billion in 2014–15 (Minister of Finance Budget Speech, 2012). In his budget speech to parliament, the minister of finance also indicated that in 2012 social spending comprised 58 per cent of government expenditure, up from 49 per cent a decade previously. The budget provides social support to almost a third of the population, including social assistance, free services at public health facilities and no-fee schools for 60 per cent of learners, and it pays for housing, water and electricity in poor communities. Overall social protection in 2010–11 was estimated to be 15 per cent of government expenditure and 5 per cent of GDP, a figure that is somewhat lower than earlier estimates by the Taylor Commission of Enquiry and the International Labour Organization (Oxford Policy Management Africa, 2011). Despite the rapid growth in the number of social grant beneficiaries in recent years, spending on grants may decline from 3.5 per cent to 3.2 per cent of GDP in 2015 (Minister of Finance Budget Speech, 2012) due largely to the declining global economic situation. There are also concerns about the effect of the growth of social assistance on social spending on health, education and welfare services. The question of fiscal sustainability of social assistance remains high on the public agenda. There remains strong civil society support for social protection and there is now considerable debate about the extent to which receipt of a social grant has an impact on voter behaviour.

Social Insurance

South Africa also has contributory social insurance, whereby employers and employees contribute to a scheme to protect employees against contingencies which may interrupt their income-earning capacity due to ageing, sickness, disability, death, loss of employment and due to the birth of a child. Those who are not formally employed do not have access to occupational benefits, which is a significant gap in social protection provision in view of the country's high unemployment levels. These schemes are authorized by legislation and oversight is provided by statutory institutions that also regulate the viability of the different schemes operated by the financial and insurance industries. In 2008, there were 11 701 retirement funds with 10.8 million members according to the Registrar for Pension Funds (cited in Oxford Policy Management Africa, 2011). The current system is fragmented, a large proportion of employed workers do not have retirement provision due to the absence of a mandatory contributory system. The government's proposals for reform of retirement provision released in 2007 (Department of Social Development, undated) are still under discussion and aim to develop a comprehensive system made up of a combination of universal non-contributory provision and a contributory system.

Unemployment benefits are paid to employees who contribute to the Unemployment Insurance Fund. Employers and employees contribute 1 per cent of the employee's monthly earnings and, if the employee has accumulated sufficient credits, benefits are paid on a sliding scale for 34 weeks. The unemployment insurance system was reformed in 2001 and it is now more progressive as low-income workers, including domestic workers, benefit more than other categories of workers, with benefits paid up to 58 per cent of prior earnings. Approximately 45 per cent of the labour force is covered by the scheme (Patel, 2005). However, informal sector employees, independent contractors, the self-employed and the unemployed are not included in coverage. The fund has become more sustainable as higher income earners now contribute, but the current scheme does not provide adequate income protection for higher income earners. Compensation for injuries and diseases at work covers employees, although here again, those outside formal employment are excluded from claiming benefits.

CONCLUSIONS

South Africa has a well-developed social protection system made up of social assistance and social insurance which dates back to the last century. Its social assistance programme is widely regarded to be one of the largest publicly funded programmes in Africa with positive developmental outcomes. Despite significant reforms since the creation of a democratic society, the current system still has significant gaps in provision and coverage. This is largely due to the fact that various schemes developed over many decades and each of these was reformed in a piecemeal fashion. Consequently, structural efficiency of the system is compromised. The various public and private arrangements are not always in sync with one another, leading to a lack of universal coverage for particular target groups. A two-tier system exists with good public social provision for certain categories of the poor and social insurance for employed workers. Current arrangements do not cover those in informal employment and the unemployed, who are unable to participate in contributory schemes. Public provision is based on citizenship rights and in the future the question of how to incorporate migrant workers from the Southern Africa region into existing country and regional arrangements will be a significant challenge. The gendered nature of care and the lack of recognition of women's contribution to care and to the public good are poorly understood in current social protection arrangements. A further challenge is the absence of mandatory social insurance arrangements for the large numbers of people who are employed and who do not have retirement provision. Proposals for the reform of the retirement system are under discussion. This is however a complex issue as it impacts on the country's private insurance companies who stand to lose significantly from these reforms. There is ongoing contestation about the rapid growth of publicly funded social protection which enjoys support from civil society and the poor who are the main beneficiaries of the system. There are increasing tensions between the trade union movement and government about social protection initiatives that could adversely affect the position of employed workers. The potential for expansion of the social assistance system is also limited given concerns about fiscal viability and the country's small tax base. These competing interests make social protection reform a complex and politically sensitive issue. The outcome of various reform initiatives will have a significant impact on the direction and the scope of social protection reforms in the country and in the creation of a more comprehensive system.

REFERENCES

Ardington, E. and F. Lund (1995), 'Pensions and development: social security as complementary to programmes of reconstruction and development', *Development Southern Africa*, **12**, 557–78.

Case, A., V. Hosegood and F. Lund (2005), 'The reach and impact of child support grants: evidence from KwaZulu-Natal', *Development Southern Africa*, **22** (4), 467–82.

Delany, A., Z. Ismail, L. Graham and Y. Ramkissoon (2008), *Review of the Child Support Grant: Uses, Implementation and Obstacles*, Johannesburg: Community Agency for Social Enquiry.

Department of Constitutional Development and Planning (1985), *Report on an Investigation into the Present Welfare Policy in the Republic of South Africa*, Pretoria: Government Printer.

Department of Social Development (undated), *Reform of Retirement Provision*, Pretoria: Government Printers.

Department of Welfare and Population Development (1997), *The White Paper for Social Welfare*, General Notice 1108 of 1997, Pretoria: Government Printers.

Graham, L., L. Selipsky, J. Moodley and J. Maina and W. Rowland (2010), *Understanding Poverty and Disability in Johannesburg*, Johannesburg: Centre for Social Development in Africa, University of Johannesburg.

Hall, K. and G. Wright (2010), 'A profile of children living in South Africa in 2008', *Studies in Economics and Econometrics*, **34** (3), 45–68.

IndexMundi (2008), *South Africa HIV/AIDS – Adult Prevalence Rate*, accessed at http://indexmundi.com/south_africa/hiv_aids_adult_prevelance_rate.html.
Leibbrandt, M. V., A. Finn, J. Argent and I. D. Woolard (2010), 'Changes in income poverty over the post-apartheid period: an analysis based on data from the 1993 Project for Statistics on Living Standards and Development and the 2008 base wave of the National Income Dynamics Study', *Journal for Studies in Economics and Econometrics*, **34** (3), 25–43.
Minister of Finance Budget Speech (2012), Minister of Finance, Pravan Gordhan, MP, February 2012, Pretoria: National Treasury, Republic of South Africa.
Moller, V. (2011), *Perceptions of Fortune and Misfortune in Older South African Households: Social Pensions and the 'Good Life'*, Grahamstown: Institute of Social and Economic Research, Rhodes University.
Nattrass, N. (2007), 'Disability and welfare', in S. Buhlungu, J. Daniel, R. Southhall and J. Lutchman (eds), *State of the Nation of South Africa 2007*, Cape Town: HSRC, pp. 179–200.
Neves, D., M. Samson, I. v. Niekerk, S. Hlatshwayo and A. d. Toit (2009), *The Use and Effectiveness of Social Grants in South Africa*, Cape Town: FinMark Trust, Institute for Poverty, Land and Agrarian Studies, and Economic Policy Research Institute.
Oxford Policy Management Africa (2011), *South Africa – Social Budget: Phase 2 Report (1) Extract*, Pretoria: Oxford Policy Management Ltd.
Patel, L. (1988), 'Toward people's welfare', In Touch, Occasional Paper 1, Johannesburg: Concerned Social Workers.
Patel, L. (1992), *Restructuring Social Welfare – The Options for South Africa*, Johannesburg: Raven Press.
Patel, L. (2005), *Social Welfare and Social Development in South Africa*, Cape Town: Oxford University Press Southern Africa.
Patel, L. (2011), 'Race, inequality and social welfare: South Africa's imperial legacy', in J. Midgley and D. Piachaud (eds), *Colonialism and Welfare Social Policy and the British Imperial Legacy*, Cheltenham, UK and Northampton, MA, USA: Edward Elgar, pp. 71–84.
Patel, L. (2012), 'Poverty, gender and social protection: child support grants in Soweto, South Africa', *Journal of Policy Practice*, **11** (1–2), 106–20.
Patel, L., T. Hocfheld, J. Moodley and R. Mutwali (2012), *The Gender Dynamics and Impact of the Child Support Grant in Doornkop, Soweto*, Johannesburg: Centre for Social Development in Africa, University of Johannesburg, accessed at www.uj.ac.za/csda.
Posel, D. and M. Rogan (2012), 'Gendered trends in poverty in the post-apartheid period, 1997–2006', *Development Southern Africa*, **29** (1), 97–113.
Republic of South Africa National Treasury (2003), *Intergovernmental Fiscal Review*, Pretoria: National Treasury.
Statistics South Africa (2011), *Statistical Release*, Mid-Year Population Statistics, accessed at www.statssa.gov.za/publications/PO3022011.pdf.
Taylor Committee of Enquiry (2002), *Transforming the Present – Protecting the Future*, Committee of Enquiry into a Comprehensive Social Security System for South Africa, Pretoria: Department of Social Development.
UNDP (2007/2008), *Human Development Report 2007/2008 – Country Fact Sheets on South Africa*, accessed at http://hdrstats.undp./org/countries/country_fact_sheets/cty_fs_ZAF.html.
van der Berg, S., R. Burger, R. Burger, M. Louw and D. Yu (2005), 'Trends

in poverty and inequality since the political transition', Working Papers: 01/2005, Stellenbosch: Stellenbosch University, Bureau for Economic Research, Department of Economics.
van den Berg., S., R. Burger and M. Louw (2007), *Post-Apartheid South Africa: Poverty and Distribution Trends in an Era of Globalization*, accessed at http://mpra.ub.uni-muenchen.de/9065/.
Vorster, J. and L. de Waal (2008), 'Beneficiaries of the child support grant: findings from a national survey', *The Social Work Practitioner Researcher*, **20** (2), 233–49.
Woolard, I. (2003), *Impact of Government Programmes Using Administrative Data Sets: Social Assistance Grants. Project 6.2. of the Ten Year Review Research Programme*, accessed at www.sarpn.org/documents/d0000946/P1041-Woolard_10year_June2003.pdf.
World Bank (2012), *South Africa Economic Update Focus on Inequality of Opportunity*, The World Bank Group Africa Region Poverty Reduction and Economic Management, Issue 3, Washington, DC: International Bank for Reconstruction and Development.

14. Current approaches to social protection in the Republic of South Africa

Letlhokwa George Mpedi

South Africa's sad history of colonialism, racism, apartheid, sexism and oppressive labour practices is largely to be blamed for the majority of the social and economic woes experienced in that country today. These challenges, which include poverty and inequality as well as high unemployment, were identified in a number of policy documents developed by the post-apartheid government (see Ministry in the Office of the President, 1994; Department of Welfare and Population Development, 1997; Taylor Committee, 2002). In addition, proposals were made on how to rid South Africa of such challenges. With this background in mind, this chapter seeks to analyse the current approaches to social protection in South Africa. It commences by providing an overview of the South African social protection system. It proceeds by discussing the existent social protection approaches in South Africa with a particular focus on key groups of vulnerable persons such as children and old people, as well as labour market challenges (for example, employment, unemployment and low pay), poverty, income inequality and gender issues. This is followed by some concluding observations.

THE SOUTH AFRICAN SOCIAL PROTECTION SYSTEM: AN OVERVIEW

Social Protection and Comprehensive Social Protection: A Conceptual Perspective

Social protection is generally defined with reference to its key features and/or purpose. For example, in terms of the Asian Development Bank (2012), social protection '... consists of policies and programmes designed to reduce poverty and vulnerability by promoting efficient labour markets, diminishing people's exposure to risks, enhancing their capacity to protect themselves against hazards and interruption/loss of income'. It can thus be averred that social protection is primarily geared towards the prevention or minimization of social risks in the sense that it amplifies competences and opportunities for individuals to take advantage of improving their social and economic positions in society. This observation is very plausible, particularly when one takes into account the United Nations Commission for Social Development's (2000) viewpoint on the overall purpose of social protection:

> The ultimate purpose of social protection is to increase capabilities and opportunities and, thereby, human development. While by its very nature social protection aims at providing at least minimum standards of well-being to people in dire circumstances enabling them to live with dignity, one should not overlook that social protection should not simply be seen as a residual policy function of assuring the welfare of the poorest – but as a foundation at a societal level for promoting social justice and social cohesion, developing human capabilities and promoting economic dynamism and creativity.

South Africa's National Planning Commission (2011, pp. 327–8) enumerates the five functions of social protection as follows:

> Protective – Measures are introduced to save lives and reduce levels of deprivation. Preventive – Acts as an economic stabiliser that seeks to help people avoid falling into deeper poverty and reduce vulnerability to natural disasters, crop failure, accidents and illness. Promotive – Aims to enhance the capabilities of individuals, communities and institutions to participate in all spheres of activity. Transformative – Tackles inequities and vulnerabilities through changes in policies, laws, budgetary allocations and redistributive measures. Developmental and generative – Increases consumption patterns of the poor, promoting local economic development and enabling poor people to access economic and social opportunities.

It continues by observing that these functions and objectives resonate with South Africa's 'developmental approach to eradicating poverty and reducing inequality' (National Planning Commission, 2011, p. 328). Notwithstanding the aforesaid pronouncements, it should be noted that South Africa has, for its social provisioning policy purposes, adopted a concept called 'comprehensive social protection'. The comprehensive social protection idea was initially embraced by the Committee of Inquiry into a Comprehensive System of Social Security for South Africa (Taylor Committee, 2002, p. 41). Before the committee decided to settle for this concept, it took note of the description afforded by the United Nations Commission on Social Development, namely that: 'Social protection embodies society's responses to levels of either risk or deprivation . . .

These include secure access to income, livelihood, employment, health and education services, nutrition and shelter' (Taylor Committee, 2002, p. 40). The comprehensive social protection notion is a much broader approach to the concept of social protection. The reason being that:

> Comprehensive social protection for South Africa seeks to provide the basic means for all people living in the country to effectively participate and advance in social and economic life, and in turn to contribute to social and economic development. Comprehensive social protection is broader than the traditional concept of social security, and incorporates developmental strategies and programmes designed to ensure, collectively, at least a minimum acceptable living standard for all citizens. It embraces the traditional measures of social insurance, social assistance and social services, but goes beyond that to focus on causality through an integrated policy approach including many of the developmental initiatives undertaken by the State. (Taylor Committee, 2002, p. 41)

The comprehensive social protection concept functions through an integrated package of social protection interventions and measures. These include the following:

1. Measures to address *income poverty* (provision of minimum income) – key components are the basic income grant, child support grant and state old-age grant.
2. Measures to address *capability poverty* (provision of certain basic services) – key components are publicly operated health care, primary and secondary education, sanitation, electricity, public transport, housing and jobs and skills training.
3. Measures to address *asset poverty* (income-generating assets) – key components are access to productive and income-generating assets such as land and credit and access to social assets such as community infrastructure.
4. Measures to address *special needs* (for example, disability or child support) – such as disability grant, foster care grant and care dependency grant.
5. Social insurance – covering old age, survivors, disability and health needs.

The package approach outlined above is beneficial in the sense that it 'enables one to achieve a degree of balance between measures focused on reducing income, services (capability) and asset poverty' (Taylor Committee, 2002, p. 41).

Social Protection and the Human Rights Approach

The 1996 Constitution of the Republic of South Africa is the bedrock from which the efforts to provide, transform and develop social protection in South Africa should be constructed (Mpedi, 2008, p. 11). This assertion stems from a number of factors. First, the Constitution constitutes South Africa as one sovereign, democratic state founded on values such as human dignity, the achievement of equality and the advancement of human rights and freedoms; non-racialism and non-sexism; as well as the supremacy of the Constitution and the rule of law. These values are important in the process of social security provision because they to a large extent give meaning to the socio-economic rights entrenched in the Constitution (Olivier et al., 2003, p. 61). They imply that South Africa follows a value-based approach to social protection provisioning. This is mainly due the fact that it embraces a normative value system which is closely linked to the objective of transformation (Chaskalson, 2002, p. 7). This should be understood within the context of a past built on apartheid policies and concomitant social, economic and political ills which South Africa had to move away from towards a future based on human dignity, equality and freedom, as well as the advancement of race and gender equality. In accordance with the principle of constitutional supremacy, law or conduct in the social provisioning endeavours of South Africa which is inconsistent with the Constitution is invalid to the extent of the inconsistency and, most importantly, the obligations imposed by the Constitution must be fulfilled. Second, Chapter 2 of the Constitution contains a Bill of Rights which it appropriately regards as 'a cornerstone of democracy in South Africa' in Section 7. The Bill of Rights has a wide scope of application. It applies to all law, and binds the legislature, the judiciary, and all organs of state. Another point to be noted is that, according to Section 8(2) of the Constitution, it 'binds a natural or juristic person if, and to the extent that, it is applicable'.

The Bill of Rights entrenches an assortment of fundamental rights germane to social protection. It provides every person with the right of access to 'health care services, including reproductive health care; sufficient food and water; and social security, including, if they are unable to support themselves and their dependents, appropriate social assistance' (S 27(1)(a–c)). The state has a constitutionally imposed duty to take reasonable legislative and other measures to achieve the progressive realization of the aforementioned rights; this is, however, subject to the availability of resources.

In addition, the right of access to social security is buttressed by human rights such as the rights to equality, human dignity, life, privacy, access to information, just administrative action and children's rights to basic nutrition, shelter, basic health care services and social services. A combination of these rights, viewed from constitutional and human rights perspectives, guarantees adequate social protection (Taylor Committee, 2002, p. 50). The state has a duty to respect, protect, promote and fulfil the right of access to social security as well as the aforementioned rights. Notwithstanding the duties imposed on the state, it should be noted that the rights encapsulated in the Bill of Rights are not absolute, as they can be limited in accordance with the limitation clause of Section 36.

Furthermore, the rights entrenched in the Bill of Rights are enforceable. This means that (an) affected person(s) or parties with an interest may 'approach a competent court, alleging that a right in the Bill of Rights has been infringed or threatened, and the court may grant appropriate relief, including a declaration of rights' (S 38). The enforceability of these rights has played an important role thus far in the development of the South African social protection system. For example, they have been used with positive results in the past to challenge unfair and unjustifiable discriminatory practices (see, for example, *Khosa v Minister of Social Development*, 2004), administrative injustice and unfairness (see, for example, *Bacela v Minister of the Eastern Cape for Welfare*, 1998) as well as the failure of the state to implement social security measures (see, for example, *Minister of Health v Treatment Action Campaign*, 2002). The conclusion to be made is that South Africa follows a human rights-based approach in its quest to protect its population against social risks. This view is informed by the fact that the Constitution does not differentiate between social, civil and political rights; instead, it places emphasis on 'the fact that these rights are interrelated, interdependent and indivisible' (Taylor Committee, 2002, p. 50). Social protection measures, particularly those that are financed through taxes, are not mere hand-outs which the public should be grateful for. Rather, they are entitlements that can be claimed.

Some Key Structural Features of the Social Protection System

South Africa has a well-developed social protection system for a developing country. Although the system is far from being perfect, it does make provision for the nine classical social security risks enumerated in the International Labour Organization Social Security (Minimum Standards) Convention 102 of 1952, namely: medical care, sickness, unemployment, old age, occupational injuries and diseases, family, maternity, invalidity, and survivors' benefits. The key structural features of the system can be bifurcated into two; that is, public schemes and private measures. Public measures comprise social assistance (for example, social grants), social welfare (for example, welfare services) and statutory social insurance funds (for example, unemployment insurance, compensation for occupational injuries and diseases as well as road accidents). Private measures consist of voluntary funds (medical aid and retirement funds) and traditional support mechanisms (for example, burial societies and credit rotating schemes).

The South African social protection system is financed through a variety of sources. Public measures, on the one hand, are financed as follows:

1. Social assistance and social welfare measures: These are financed by the state through monies appropriated by parliament for that purpose.
2. Statutory social insurance funds: The unemployment insurance scheme is financed through contributions from employers and their employees. The state does take care of any deficit that may accrue in any financial year. The compensation for occupational injuries and diseases scheme is funded through employers' contributions. Unlike the unemployment insurance scheme and compensation for occupational injuries and diseases, the road accident fund is financed by road users through a dedicated fuel levy.

Private measures, on the other hand, are financed as follows:

1. Medical and retirement funds are largely financed through contributions by employees and employers, and
2. traditional support mechanisms are financed by private persons through contributions and/or donations.

The responsibility for administering the social protection is spread mainly between the government and the private sector/persons. Social assistance measures are primarily administered by the South African Social Security Agency (SASSA). The Department of Social Development fulfils a regulatory function. It is responsible for policy development as well as the setting of norms and standards in the area of social assistance grant administration. Social welfare mechanisms fall under the administrative framework of the Department of Social Development. Statutory social insurance funds are administered by different funds. The unemployment insurance scheme is administered by the unemployment insurance fund. The fund falls under the Department of Labour. Compensation for occupational injuries and diseases is administered by the Compensation Fund and the Road Accidents Fund is responsible for the administration of the road accidents scheme. Private measures are administered by private funds (medical aid schemes and retirement funds) and private persons (traditional support mechanisms).

Lastly, the legislative framework for the social protection system is set out in a plethora of legislation. Thus the South African social protection laws are not consolidated in a single legislation or code. This is the case despite a call by the August 1997 *White Paper for Social Welfare* (Department of Welfare and Population Development, 1997) for legislation to be made accessible to the public by, inter alia, consolidating legislation on the same issue, to the extent possible, into one Act or set of regulations.

KEY GROUPS AND ISSUES

Children

The Constitution defines a child as a person below the age of 18 years (S 28(3)). This definition is consistent with the one found in a variety of international instruments concerning children's rights, such as the 1989 United Nations Convention on the Rights of the Child, which South Africa ratified in June 1995, and the 1990 African Charter on the Rights and Welfare of the Child.

There are several pieces of legislation making provision for children's social protection rights in South Africa. One of the key sources of such rights is the Constitution. It makes provision, in addition to everyone's right to have access to social security, for children's rights in Section 28. Chief among these rights is every child's right to basic nutrition, shelter, basic health care services and social services. These rights are given effect by the Children's Act and the Social Assistance Act. The Children's Act has been enacted to give effect to certain rights of children as contained in the Constitution, to set out principles relating to the care and protection of children, to define parental responsibilities and rights, to provide for partial care of children and to provide for early childhood development. The Social Assistance Act, on the other hand, makes provision for children's social grants, namely the child support grant, care dependency grant and foster child grant.

According to the South African Human Rights Commission and UNICEF South Africa (2011, p. 21), 11.9 million children (64 per cent of all children) live in income poverty in South Africa. There are racial disparities in child poverty; for instance, Black children are, in comparison with children from other race groups, the most afflicted by poverty (South African Human Rights Commission and UNICEF South Africa, 2011,

p. 14). Unemployment, which is one of the prevalent social risks in South Africa, has been cited as the most plausible key cause of child poverty, likely for the reason that it is estimated that almost four out of ten children live in households with no employed members. In addition, it is reported that among the poorest, seven out of ten children live in households without employed members (South African Human Rights Commission and UNICEF South Africa, 2011, p. 22). These telling statistics clearly underscore the need and importance of social protection interventions to free the vulnerable young members of the South African populace as well as those who live and/or (should) care for them in the grip of destitution.

The tax-financed children's grants are a component of the prime social protection interventions introduced to alleviate poverty, particularly among children in South Africa. The child support grant and care dependency grant are payable subject to, among other qualifying conditions, a means test. The foster care grant is, unlike the child support grant and care dependency grant, not means-tested. The means-test levels for children's grants from April 2012 were, for those in spousal relationships, R67 200 for the child support grant and R288 000 for the child dependency grant, and half these amounts for a single person.

The children's grants have grown significantly over the past few years in terms of the number of children covered and monetary value. For example, the child support grant in 1999 covered only 21 997 children and was limited to children below the age of seven; the grant value was R100 (South African Human Rights Commission and UNICEF South Africa, 2011, p. 24). According to the 2012 revised estimate, 10 903 000 children benefited from the grant, while the economic value has increased progressively over the years; in 2012 the monetary value of the child support grant was R280 (National Treasury, 2012, p. 85). In addition, the age threshold has increased significantly. The child support grant is now awarded to qualifying children up to the age of 18. This complies with the recommendation by the Committee of Inquiry into a Comprehensive System of Social Security for South Africa that child support be paid to deserving children up to the age of 18 (Taylor Committee, 2002, p. 81). The aforementioned number of children drawing this benefit makes it the largest grant by number of beneficiaries in South Africa. This translated to 69 per cent of the total number of social grant beneficiaries in South Africa during the 2010–11 financial year (National Treasury, 2011, p. 102). The care dependency grant increased from 16 835 beneficiaries in 1999 to a revised estimate of 126 000 beneficiaries in 2012 and the grant value increased from R520 in 1999 to R1200 in 2012 (National Treasury, 2012, p. 85). The foster care grant had 46 496 beneficiaries and its value was R374 in 1999 (South African Human Rights Commission and UNICEF

South Africa, 2011, p. 24). In accordance with the revised estimate, the foster care grant was disbursed to 598 000 beneficiaries and its value was R770 in 2012 (National Treasury, 2012, p. 85).

In addition to the aforementioned children's grants, South Africa has initiated several other policy responses such as the school nutrition programmes. Of learners attending public schools, 68.5 per cent were reported to receive food at school (Statistics South Africa, 2011a, p. 12). Second, medical facilities (such as clinics and community health centres) funded by the state have a legal duty to provide pregnant and lactating women and children below the age of six with free health services, provided they are not members of, or beneficiaries of, a medical aid scheme. Furthermore, free basic health care services in districts and local areas are challenged by the shortage of sufficient financial and human resources. It is for reasons such as these that the Committee on the Rights of the Child (2000) has recommended that the state should expedite greater access to primary health care in South Africa.

Labour Market Issues

The 'working-age population' consists of every person 'aged 15–64 years who fall into each of the three labour market components (employed, unemployed, not economically active)' (Statistics South Africa 2011b, pp. 2–3). Of these, 59 per cent were aged 15–34, 32 per cent aged 35–54 and 9 per cent aged 55–64 (Statistics South Africa, 2011b, pp. 2–3). The Black African population was even more youthful with 63 per cent aged 15–34.

Black Africans comprise 78 per cent of the working-age population. This group is under-represented in one labour market component, namely the employed (69.3 per cent), and over-represented in two labour market components, that is the unemployed (86 per cent) as well as the not economically active (83.4 per cent) (Statistics South Africa, 2011b, pp. 2–4).

According to Statistics South Africa (2012c), 'employed persons' are 'those aged 15–64 years who, during the reference week: did any work for at least one hour; or had a job or business but were not at work (temporarily absent)'. The key labour market indicators show that out of a labour force of 17 916 million, 13 447 million persons were employed in South Africa during the period April–June 2012; those in employment were spread between four sectors as follows: formal sector (non-agricultural) (9571 million), informal sector (non-agricultural) (2085 million), agriculture (638 000) and private households (1153 million).

South Africa has high unemployment. The unemployment rate during the period April–June 2012, based on a narrow definition of unemployment, hovered around 25 per cent; almost 4.5 million persons were presumed to be unemployed during the same period (Statistics South Africa, 2012c, p. v). Unemployment is not uniformly spread between gender groups, population groups and age groups. According to Statistics South Africa (2012b, p. xv), women are 1.2 times more likely to be without a job than men. Second, unemployment is more pronounced among Black Africans than among other population groups in South Africa. Statistics for the second quarter of 2012 showed that the unemployment rate among Black Africans stood at 28.7 per cent while the coloured population had the second highest rate of 24 per cent, while the Indian/Asian and white population groups had the lowest unemployment rates, which were estimated at 9.5 per cent and 5.7 per cent respectively (Statistics South Africa, 2012c, p. xvi). Furthermore, youth unemployment (that is, persons aged 15–34 years) has the highest rate when compared with other age groups in South Africa: the 2010 unemployment rate among persons aged 15–24 years was estimated at 50.5 per cent (although it must be pointed out that the preceding estimate takes into account young persons who are prevented from participating in the labour market due to the fact that they are still at school), while the unemployment rate for persons aged 25–34 years was assumed to be in the region of 28.9 per cent in the same year (Statistics South Africa, 2011c, pp. 3–7). The reasons for high youth unemployment in South Africa are multifaceted and they include the lack of the requisite education and training, work experience and appropriate skills for available job opportunities.

Unemployment is clearly one of the biggest challenges facing South Africa today. In light of the high unemployment rate (discussed in the following paragraph) it is imperative that employment is increased in South Africa. The government has acknowledged the importance of employment within the realm of social protection by declaring in its National Development Plan that '[e]mployment creation is the most effective form of social protection' (National Planning Commission, 2011, p. 327). Accordingly, it has set itself a goal of raising employment by 2014, with the hope of reaching a targeted figure of about 16 million employed persons in that year (National Planning Commission, 2011, p. 20).

The government intends to reduce unemployment by at least 14 per cent in 2014 (National Planning Commission, 2010, p. 21). Measures proposed include: youth employment incentives, training layoff schemes and expanded public works (National Treasury, 2011, p. 47).

Salaries are the largest source of income for most households in South Africa, followed by social grants, reported nationally as income sources by the highest percentages of households, at 62.6 per cent and 44.8 per cent respectively (Statistics South Africa, 2012a, p. 38). There were wide discrepancies in the median monthly earnings by population groups: white and Indian/Asian population groups had higher median monthly earnings than those of the coloured and Black African groups in 2010; and Black Africans earned 22 per cent of what the white population earned, 36.1 per cent of what Indians/Asians earned and 81.7 per cent of what the coloured population earned (Statistics South Africa, 2012a, p. viii). These statistics are not surprising since Black Africans have, generally speaking, low levels of education and are widely represented in vulnerable sectors of the economy such as the informal sector. It should also be noted that the informal sector is survivalist in nature (Statistics South Africa, 2011b, pp. 4–31).

The problem is that people who subsist on low pay invariably live from hand to mouth. Even if they somehow manage to survive, there is often very little left for such workers to take advantage of voluntary insurance products offered by private insurance houses such as health insurance and retirement insurance policies. For those who manage to pay the requisite premiums, there is a constant risk that they may have to surrender or let such policies lapse due to slight changes in their economic and personal circumstances. In addition, the low-wage category of workers invariably lacks the resources to save for retirement. Consequently, they are more concerned about immediate risks (for example, putting food on the table) than long-term risks (for example, retirement); the end result is a reliance on government support in old age. It is therefore of utmost importance that measures are investigated on how to broaden the scope of social protection coverage, particularly social insurance, to cover those with low pay to secure, within their means, themselves and their families against social risks. Therefore, current efforts by the government to establish a national health insurance scheme are to be welcomed.

Social Protection Measures

South Africa has various social protection strategies aimed at addressing most of the labour market challenges mentioned above. These strategies comprise tax-financed mechanisms and contributions-based interventions. The tax-financed measures are largely in the form of social grants. These comprise the old-age grant, disability grant, child support grant, foster care grant, care dependency grant and war veterans' grant. In addition, there is the so-called grant-in-aid and social relief of distress. These benefits are not unemployment assistance. However, in practice they do fulfil such a role. This is primarily due to the reason that they are targeted at persons who are too old, very young or seriously disabled to a degree that such persons cannot participate in the labour market to earn a living. Needy persons who do not fall within the aforementioned categories are largely left destitute. The Committee of Inquiry into a Comprehensive System of Social Security for South Africa proposed a phased introduction of the basic income grant to plug the holes in the social protection safety net. It argued that:

> Analysis indicates that the Basic Income Grant has the potential, more than any other possible social protection intervention, to reduce poverty and promote human development and sustainable livelihoods. A universal Basic Income Grant has the potential to fortify the ability of the poor to manage risk thus contributing to socio-economic multipliers effects related to improved household self-reliance of social capital and societal cohesiveness. (Taylor Committee, 2002, p. 62)

Notwithstanding the preceding arguments advanced by the committee, the government opted for an Extended Public Works Programme (EPWP). The EPWP is one of the government's short-to-medium term strategies to address unemployment in South Africa. The initial goals of the EPWP (2004) were to create one million temporary jobs (at least 40 per cent women, 30 per cent youth and 2 per cent disabled) in the first five years of the programme, promote economic growth and promote sustainable development. The initial core objectives of the EPWP were threefold. That is job creation, skills development and improved social services (Zuma, 2004). Several sectors were identified as having potential for creating EPWP employment opportunities. These sectors were the infrastructure sector, environmental and cultural sector, social sector and economic sector. The new expanded public works programme (the so-called EPWP II), which was introduced in 2009, retained the key aim of the programme, which is the intensive use of labour on infrastructure projects. In addition, it aspires to create two million work opportunities per annum by 2014. This, according to the National Planning Commission (2011, p. 335), would 'translate into 4.5 million work opportunities, averaging 100 days per opportunity, over five years to 2013/14'. The usefulness of the EPWP as a social protection measure cannot be doubted. However, the impact of this programme could be significantly enhanced if it were to be developed into a 'more rights programme guaranteeing a minimum number of days of employment to all those who have no other source of income, following the model of the National Rural Employment Guarantee Act in India' (de Schutter, 2012, p. 20).

Separate from the social grants and the EPWP, South Africa runs an unemployment insurance scheme. Participation in this scheme is compulsory to qualifying persons. Furthermore, it is funded through employers' and employees' contributions. It makes provision for the payment of the following short-term benefits to eligible persons: adoption benefits, unemployment benefits, illness benefits, maternity benefits and survivors' benefits. In 2010–11 a total number of 732 158 persons received benefits from the unemployment insurance fund – 578 266 for unemployment and 104 042 for maternity or adoption (Department of Labour, 2011, p. 28).

Old People

(a) Social assistance

The most common form of social assistance available in South Africa for old people is the old-age grant. The old-age grant is the largest social assistance programme by expenditure; its expenditure was R37 318 billion in 2011–12 and is projected to rise to R42 526 billion in 2013–14 (National Treasury, 2012, p. 86). The old-age grant is provided to just over 2.7 million elderly persons from the age of 60 years and above. It is disbursed subject to a means test and the thresholds, which have been increased over the years, in April 2012 were for those in a spousal relationship: R94 800 on income and R1 584 000 on assets; the thresholds were half these amounts for a single person.

The monetary value of the old-age grant in 2012 was R1200 for qualifying elderly persons. An additional R20 is payable to old-age grant recipients over the age of 75 years. The value of the old-age grant is modest. Despite that, the poverty alleviation role of this grant among the intended recipients and those who live with them should not be underestimated. This is mainly due to the reason that the old-age grant is in a majority of instances the only form of income for families which often comprise three generations. Another important point worth noting is that, according to the Committee of Inquiry into a Comprehensive System of Social Security for South Africa:

> The SOAP [State Old Age Pension] reduces the poverty gap for pensioners by 94 per cent. Poor households that include pensioners are on average significantly less poor than households without pensioners. 'Skip generation' households (comprising child and grandparent), on average, have their poverty gap closed by over 60 per cent. For three-generation households the poverty gap is closed by less than 50 per cent due to the burden of the working-age members. For the average poor household without a pension-eligible member, however, social security's impact is almost negligible. For households with no pensioners, the reduction is less than 10 per cent. (Taylor Committee, 2002, p. 59)

(b) Social insurance

South Africa does not have a statutory retirement fund. Thus, provision for income in retirement for employees is generally made through occupational schemes (such as pension funds) or private savings. In 2011 it was reported that South Africa had approximately 3200 active pension funds. There are a number of challenges associated with the contributory pension schemes in South Africa. For instance, there is no statutory duty for workers to belong to retirement schemes. However, such a duty could be imposed by means of a contract of employment and/or collective agreement. The problem with the absence of such an obligation is that myopic workers who neglect to prepare for their post-retirement needs end up relying on the old-age grant system. In addition, there are divergent coverage levels and saving rates, mainly due to '... [a] lack of preservation: workers often liquidate their savings when they leave a job rather than transfer them to a new fund' (National Treasury, 2011, p. 107). Furthermore, exorbitant fees and administrative levies imposed by pension, provident and retirement annuity funds invariably diminish the value of the member benefits. Lastly, it has been reported that members of the provident funds tend to neglect to convert their lump-sum benefit upon retirement to an annuity. This practice exposes such members to the risk of them living longer than their savings. To address these problems, the government – as part of the proposed social security reforms – plans to found a mandatory statutory fund to cater for pensions, life insurance as well as disability benefits. In addition, the government intends to 'encourage higher savings and improved retirement provision' (National Treasury 2012, p. 80). Proposed reforms in this regard will incorporate 'mandatory preservation and portability, harmonisation of tax treatment of contributions to retirement funds, reform of the annuities market and better incentives for saving' (National Treasury 2012, p. 80).

Traditional Support Mechanisms

Social assistance and social insurance programmes found in the South African social protection system play an important role in shielding individuals and their dependents against social risks. However, their limited scope of coverage does in some cases force those that they exclude and marginalize to rely on so-called 'goodwill transfers' from those who have income (National Planning Commission, 2011, p. 332). These traditional support mechanisms, which are often referred to as informal social security, operate alongside the formal social security provisioning mechanisms. Their importance and relevance have not gone unnoticed in policy debates in South Africa. The Committee of Inquiry into a Comprehensive System of Social Security for South Africa warned against the imposition of a social security that could undermine the traditional support mechanisms. It urged that reforms aimed at the current social security framework should strive at supporting and strengthening existing informal coping strategies:

> In the first instance this requires considering ways to integrate currently excluded groups into formal schemes. This includes embarking on pilot schemes aimed at supporting informal social security mechanisms; removing unnecessary legal restrictions in relation to access to schemes; devising tailor-made schemes to cater for these excluded and marginalised categories and groups; introducing compulsory membership of private or public social schemes; and campaigns to promote private insurance and savings. Further, there is a need to consider broader interventions and programmes that bolster the overall ability of communities and informal systems to cope with and manage increased levels of risk and hardship. (Taylor Committee, 2002, p. 74)

Very little has been done thus far to comply with the committee's progressive recommendations.

Gender Issues

To achieve equity in the South African social protection system, the August 1997 *White Paper for Social Welfare* (Department of Welfare and Population Development, 1997) mandated, as part of its agenda for action, that policies and programmes be devised to be more gender sensitive and to address the special needs and problems of women. Although much has been done towards the realization of this goal, women seem to be more vulnerable to certain social risks (for example, unemployment) than men. The labour market conditions seem to favour men more than women. For instance, the employment rate is higher among men when compared to women and the labour force participation rate of women is lower than that for men. Furthermore, the unemployment rate for women (27.5 per cent) outstrips that for men (22.8 per cent) (Statistics South Africa, 2012c, p. xv). Discrimination against women in the South African labour market has been raised as a source of concern by the Committee on the Elimination of Discrimination against Women (2011, p. 8) as follows:

> . . . the Committee is concerned about the persistence of discrimination against women in the labour market, in particular the high rate of unemployment affecting (30 per cent), the wide gender/wage gap, and occupational segregation. The Committee regrets that even though the Employment Equity Act (1998) and the Equality Act (2000) prohibit discrimination on the grounds of pregnancy, and the Basic Conditions of Employment Act (1997) protects maternity leave, there is no provision in domestic legislation for remunerated maternity leave.

Accordingly, the Committee on the Elimination of Discrimination against Women called upon the South African government to, among other things:

1. safeguard equal opportunities for women in the labour market in line with article 11 of the *Convention on the Elimination of All Forms of Discrimination against Women*;
2. adopt effective measures in the formal labour market to eliminate both horizontal and vertical occupational segregation, narrow and close the wage gap between women and men, and ensure the application of the principle of equal remuneration and equal opportunities at work; and
3. review the pertinent laws so as to ensure that all mothers receive leave with pay. (Committee on the Elimination of Discrimination against Women, 2011, pp. 8–9)

The tenacious gender disparities in the South African labour market can be traced back to the apartheid system. It should be remembered that women could not occupy certain positions in the labour market under apartheid (for example, working as underground miners). This has since changed. In addition, the migrant labour system meant that African women stayed at home, predominantly in rural areas, taking care of their families while their husbands eked out a living in urban areas (see African National Congress, 1980). This invariably left such women with no or only elementary education, deplorable labour market skills and second-rate employment opportunities.

The labour market bias towards men has a negative impact on women's access to certain social protection mechanisms, in particular social insurance. This problem is compounded by the fact that most women are engaged in jobs which exclude them from the scope of coverage of a majority of social insurance schemes. For instance, a great number of women are employed in the informal sector. As a result, they cannot claim maternity benefits which are or should be generally available to most women who work in the formal sector. According to Statistics South Africa (2011b, pp. 4–45), about 43 per cent of women in 2010 worked in jobs which had no provision for them to take maternity leave. The likelihood of such employees not having access to maternity benefits is high. Moreover, it is probable that female employees without maternity leave would feel pressed to report early for work or could be at risk of being discharged should they fall pregnant, despite the fact that this would be an unfair dismissal according to the Labour Relations Act 1995.

Another point worth noting is that statutory exclusions of certain categories of workers tend to affect women more than men. The Compensation for Occupational Injuries and Diseases Act 1993 specifically excludes domestic workers from its scope of coverage. In light of the high representation of women in that sector this means more women bear the brunt of the exclusion than men. It should be mentioned that domestic workers who suffer occupational injuries and/or contract occupational diseases could still institute a civil claim for damages against their employers. Nevertheless, this route is laden with challenges. In the first instance, domestic workers are among the lowest paid workers in South Africa. Thus, they are usually persons with limited means. This naturally elevates costly legal services above their reach. Another consideration is that, even if they were able to afford such services, through their own means or that of civil society, civil suits have the propensity to drag on for a long time before the dispute is resolved and there are no guarantees as to whose favour the court will find in. Even if victory in favour of the domestic workers was guaranteed, that does not assure (immediate) compliance with the judgment by the domestic employer. It is, therefore, crucial that options be explored regarding the extension of the workers' compensation system to domestic workers in South Africa.

The Impact of Current Social Protection Measures on Poverty

The role of the current social protection mechanism on poverty cannot be emphasized enough. The social assistance programme, which is one of the main social protection measures, is a crucial tool in South Africa's war on poverty in that it either reduces the level of poverty among the intended beneficiaries and those who live with them, prevents targeted persons from falling into destitution or it helps individuals cope with poverty. The impact of available social grants in South Africa has been well documented. For instance, the old-age grant and disability grant are reported by the *White Paper for Social Welfare* (Department of Welfare and Population Development, 1997) to have a major impact on the incomes of households which receive such grants. This is significant, particularly when it is remembered that social grants rank second to salaries as a source of income in households in South Africa. Another point to be noted is that social grants do not only benefit the intended beneficiary, they are often used for the welfare of the entire family. This is particularly the case in Black African families. As noted earlier, the Committee of Inquiry into a Comprehensive System of Social Security for South Africa has found that the old-age grant reduces the poverty gap among pensioners by 94 per cent and '[p]oor households that include pensioners are on average significantly less poor than households without pensioners' (Taylor Committee, 2002, p. 59). In addition, social grants have been found to have a positive impact on education, health and labour force participation. According to the National Treasury (2007, p. 105):

> Grants are associated with a greater share of household expenditure on food, and thus with improved nutrition, and the child support grants contributes

measurably to the health status of young children. Survey evidence also suggests that social assistance leads to increased participation in the labour force, in part through its contribution to nutrition and household mobility.

Apart from their favourable impact on poverty, social grants are also reported to have a significant impact on inequality. It is reported that South Africa's poverty and inequality would have been higher had there not been social assistance (National Planning Commission, 2011, p. 330). Furthermore, Leibbrandt et al. (2010, p. 66) found in their study that 'the Gini co-efficient on "pre-grant" income is 0.03 higher than when calculated in either reported income or simulated income'.

Contributory social protection mechanisms, on the other hand, provide temporary and, in some instances, long-term income support to eligible beneficiaries and/or their dependants facing social risks. These schemes as well as the benefits they disburse are not directly aimed at poverty alleviation *per se*. In spite of this, they do cushion the impact of social risks on affected individuals thereby reducing the prospect of such persons falling into poverty or helping them cope with destitution. This assertion should be understood within the perspective that there is a close relationship between poverty and the labour market in South Africa. Therefore, contributory social protection measures indirectly alleviate the impact of unemployment-induced poverty. Social protection schemes such as the unemployment insurance scheme do also, particularly in times of crisis, play a role in preventing people from falling into destitution by supporting initiatives aimed at boosting employment. For instance, during the recent economic crisis the unemployment insurance fund invested R1.2 billion in the training layoff scheme to safeguard workers at risk of retrenchment (National Treasury, 2012, p. 89).

SOCIAL PROTECTION MECHANISMS: SOME PROBLEMS AND CHALLENGES

Scope of Coverage

Non-contributory social protection measures are indeed the mainstay of South Africa's poverty alleviation measures. They have grown significantly over the years in terms of their coverage and value. Contributory social protection measures have also improved significantly, particularly regarding their coverage. For example, the scope of the unemployment insurance scheme has been widened to cover previously excluded groups of workers such as domestic workers and a variety of persons employed in the taxi sector. Despite these efforts, there are still scores of vulnerable persons who are yet to find solace against social risks from the present social protection programmes in South Africa. The issues here are multidimensional. In the area of non-contributory schemes, there are unemployed persons mentioned earlier in the chapter who do not fit within the categories that are eligible for social assistance grants: needy young persons below the age of 18, persons with disabilities and elderly people below 60 years of age. The dearth of social protection measures for unemployed persons falling outside the ambit of the aforementioned categories of persons is counterproductive in the sense that it exacerbates poverty and inequality. Moreover, it waters down the impact of other social protection measures, particularly the social assistance programme. To address this problem, it has been proposed that a basic income grant be established to shield persons between the ages 18 and 59 who are disqualified from claiming current social grants (de Schutter, 2012, p. 20). Other proposals made by de Schutter include a placement subsidy and staff retention schemes.

In addition, there is a category of persons comprising those individuals who fulfil the requisite eligibility conditions but nevertheless do not receive the social assistance grants. This is largely due to the fact that social assistance services are mainly situated in urban areas. Thus, the rural poor as well as persons who live in peri-urban areas and informal settlements are often not aware of their social assistance entitlements due to ignorance and high illiteracy rates. To address this problem, the South African Social Security Agency has launched a programme called the Integrated Community Registrations Outreach Programme (ICROP), which aims to combat poverty in accordance with the Millennium Development Goals. It entails the deployment of mobile offices in rural areas of South Africa, thereby bringing social services to remote and difficult to reach areas. A longer-term solution would be to establish permanent offices in rural areas and deploy more mobile units to service additional rural areas (de Schutter, 2012, p. 20). This would naturally require the employment of further personnel to support the new offices and the expanded ICROP.

Other suggestions on how to make the social protection system accessible proposed by the *White Paper for Social Welfare* (Department of Welfare and Population Development, 1997) include the rendering of relevant legislation accessible to the general public by:

> (a) Formulating legislation in a language that is clear and easily understood; (b) developing strategies to enhance the participation of grass-roots stakeholders in formulation of draft legislation; (c) developing strategies to communicate the content of legislation to the public on an ongoing basis; (d) ensuring that sources of information are effective, clear, understandable and readily available; (e) consolidating legislation on the same issue, as far as possible, into

> one Act or set of regulations; (f) utilising existing structures in civil society to participate in legislative processes, and (g) making the national and provincial department of welfare responsible for the facilitation of the abovementioned processes. Capacity-building programmes will also be provided.

In the field of contributory social programmes, the biggest obstacle to coverage is that those programmes cover individuals (as well as their dependants) who are engaged in the formal sector (Mpedi, 2008, p. 29). Access is chiefly dependent on the existence of an employer-employee relationship. A person has to be an 'employee' or 'contributor' as defined in the relevant social insurance legislation. Thus informal sector workers, some part-time workers, casual and temporary workers as well as the self-employed are often excluded and marginalized from coverage. To address the coverage gap currently discernible in the South Africa social protection system, policymakers need to establish special schemes that cater for the special needs of the identified groups and categories of excluded persons. Such schemes could include social insurance-type schemes for, among others, the self-employed and those employed in the informal sector. Second, the development of commercial insurance products targeted at specific categories of the excluded persons should be encouraged. Another alternative concerns the use of welfare funds. In this regard, much could be learnt from a fellow BRICS (Brazil, Russia, India, China and South Africa) member country, namely India, where the welfare fund model, an innovative method of extending social security to the marginalized (such as the unorganized sector workers), evolved. These funds are largely financed by means of earmarked tax levied on the production, sale or export of specified goods and are set up to cater for the social needs of those employed in the informal sector. The welfare fund approach bypasses, to some degree, the difficulties associated with the extension of 'contribution-oriented' or 'employer-liability-oriented' social protection schemes to the excluded, mainly because it operates outside the realm of the employer-employee relationship (Mpedi, 2008, pp. 32–3).

In addition to the formal sector bias, some social insurance programmes (such as pensions and provident funds) do not make provisions for a legal obligation to affiliate. Thus, persons employed in the formal sector need to be compelled, in accordance with their means, into participating in contributory schemes so as to safeguard themselves and their dependents against social risks.

Quality and Adequacy of Benefits

The quality and adequacy of the benefits as well as services are one source of concern in the social protection provisioning endeavours of South

Africa. The monetary value of the social assistance grants has grown significantly over the years (National Treasury, 2012, p. 85). However, they are meagre and, as a result, scarcely satisfy all the basic needs of those who receive them. The monetary value of the benefits disbursed under most social insurance schemes is also low. The reason for this situation is largely due to the fact that the government sets low contribution rates so as to accommodate the paltry pay received by the majority of the workforce (Kaseke, 2000). Another challenge associated with the benefits provided by some social insurance schemes (for example, the unemployment insurance scheme) is that the benefits provided are only available for a short period of time (S 13(3) of the Unemployment Insurance Act 2001 sets the rate of accrual of entitlement to benefits at one day's benefit for every six days of completed employment as a contributor, subject to a maximum accrual of 238 days' benefit in the four-year period immediately preceding the date of application for benefits). This is mainly due to a false assumption that certain risks they cover, such as unemployment, are transitory. This is not always the case as only 5 per cent of the unemployed receive unemployment benefits and 44 per cent of unemployed persons with previous work experience remain unemployed for a period longer than a year (National Planning Commission, 2011, p. 331). This implies that they shall have long exhausted their unemployment benefits. What is required to deal with the situation is to reinforce unemployment benefits with measures to (re-)integrate the unemployed into the labour market. It is therefore pleasing to note that, according to the *2010 Budget Review*, alternatives for improving the system currently under consideration by government include options for improving and extending benefits (for example, raising the income replacement) and extending coverage to public servants (National Treasury, 2010, p. 108).

Long-term Sustainability of the Social Protection Programmes

The sustainability of the social protection system is one of the guiding principles contained in the *White Paper for Social Welfare* (Department of Welfare and Population Development, 1997). Despite this, the South African social protection measures are more focussed on compensation rather than prevention of social risks and (re-)integration into the labour market. The problem in the social assistance sphere has been summed up as follows:

> Unlike most of Government's poverty alleviation measures, the social assistance programme was not specifically designed with exit strategies for beneficiaries, other than a change in their living circumstances and income levels. There

> is a lack of proactive and deliberate strategy to link social grant beneficiaries to opportunities for economic activity. Consequently, an intolerable proportion of able-bodied poor South Africans (inclusive of caregivers of children receiving the child support grant) and those persons with disabilities capable of rehabilitation continue to face particular barriers to entering into, remaining in and progressing in such employment. (Department of Social Development, 2006, p. 2)

The growth in reach and value of the social assistance grants has, as could be expected, been accompanied by an increase in social assistance grants expenditure. Social assistance grants expenditure is expected to grow from R70 715 billion in the 2008–09 financial year to R104 888 billion during the 2012–13 financial year (National Treasury, 2012, p. 86). According to this projection, the social assistance transfers are expected to amount to R113 208 million during the 2013–14 financial year. In view of the poverty alleviation role of the social assistance programmes, this trend is to be welcomed. On the other hand, this has generated some concerns regarding the continued sustainability of the programme (see Organization for Economic Co-operation and Development, 2010, p. 112). As a result, the National Treasury (2005, p. 56) has called for a better balance to be struck between the war on poverty through social grants and broad-based development and opportunities for the vulnerable members of the society to participate meaningfully in the mainstream economy.

Administrative and Operational Efficiency and Effectiveness

The administration and operational efficiency as well as the effectiveness of social protection programmes are undermined by a number of problems. First, corruption and fraud rank highly among the challenges facing the social assistance scheme and some social insurance schemes such as the Road Accident Fund (Reddy and Sokomani, 2008). Second, inefficiency is widespread in the administration of the social assistance scheme (Parliamentary Monitoring Group, undated). This problem is more common in the former Bantustans, where officials are particularly lacking in skills. Consequently, every so often some prospective social assistance beneficiaries institute court cases against the SASSA to enforce their right of access to social assistance benefits. These court cases are largely concerned with the failure of the SASSA to (properly) apprise the social grant applicants of the outcome of their applications and the lapsing of a disability grant. Third, the social protection institutional and administrative framework in South Africa is not integrated. The end result of this situation is that the available resources are lost due to an unnecessary duplication of processes and functions. This is inefficient and minimizes the effectiveness of the affected social security schemes. To remedy this problem, the inter-ministerial committee on social security reform and health finance proposed that the administrative functions be unified, benefits be aligned and policymaking across social protection agencies should be coordinated (National Treasury, 2011, p. 107), not the first time a call has been made for the integration of social security agencies in South Africa (Taylor Committee, 2002). The objects of the SASSA are threefold, according to the South African Social Security Agent Act 2004: 'to act, eventually, as the sole agent that will ensure the efficient and effective management, administration and payment of social assistance; serve as an agent for the prospective administration and payment of social security; and render services relating to such payments' (S 3). Furthermore, the National Planning Commission has recommended that different welfare databases be merged into one. It envisions that the following databases could form part of the initial attempt to merge the databases: Labour Centre data, SASSA data, unemployment insurance fund data, Sectoral Education Training Authority data, information on participants in Expanded Public Works Programme and Community Work Programme projects, indigent registers used by municipalities to provide free basic services and the National Housing Subsidy Scheme database (National Planning Commission, 2011, pp. 347–8).

CONCLUSIONS

It is almost 20 years since the end of apartheid in South Africa. Great progress has been made through a range of social protection measures (both non-contributory and contributory) to alleviate the impact of social ills such as poverty and inequality as well as unemployment imposed by the apartheid system on the majority of the South African populace. The scope of coverage, the quality and value of benefits as well as the administrative and operational efficiency of the social protection schemes have been progressively improved. This is in line with the constitutional directive imposed on the government to strive towards the progressive realization of everyone's right of access to social security in South Africa. Despite these efforts, there are still a number of challenges in the social protection system that require urgent attention. These include poverty and inequality, high unemployment, gaps in the social protection safety net and systemic challenges such as corruption and fraud as well as the fragmented institutional and administrative framework. These challenges are acknowledged in a number of policy documents. In addition, a variety of policy proposals on how to remedy the aforementioned problems, thereby improving the current social protection approaches, have been comprehensively documented. Furthermore, the South African government has professed its continued commitment to a major overhaul of the social protection arrangements so as to eliminate the gaps in coverage and improve service delivery (National Treasury, 2012, p. 90). Nonetheless, it remains to be seen *if* and *when* the governments' resolve and policy proposals will translate into reality.

REFERENCES

African National Congress (1980), 'Effects of apartheid on the status of women in South Africa', 15 July, accessed at www.anc.org.za/show.php?id=4668&t=ES.

Asian Development Bank (2012), 'Social protection: reducing risks, increasing opportunities', accessed 19 October 2012 at www.adb.org/SocialProtection/default.asp.

Bacela v MEC for Welfare (Eastern Cape Provincial Government) (1998), 1 All SA 525 (E).

Chaskalson, A. (2002), 'The impact of seven years of constitutionalism on law and government in South Africa', in K. A. Stiftung (ed.), *Constitution and Law IV: Colloquium on Local Government Law*, Johannesburg: Konrad-Adenauer Stiftung, pp. 7–11.

Committee on the Elimination of Discrimination against Women (CEDAW) (2011), *Concluding Observations of the Committee on the Elimination of Discrimination against Women – South Africa*, 16 December, accessed at www.unhcr.org/refworld/docid/4eeb5fbe2.html.

De Schutter, O. (2012), 'Mission to South Africa', Report of the Special Rapporteur on the Right to Food, United Nations General Assembly, 13 January, accessed at www.srfood.org/images/stories/pdf/officialreports/20120306_southafrica_en.pdf.

Department of Labour (2011), *Annual Report of the Unemployment Insurance Fund for the Year Ended 31 March 2011*, Pretoria: Department of Labour.

Department of Social Development (2006), *Linking Social Grants Beneficiaries to Poverty Alleviation and Economic Activity: Discussion Document*, accessed at www.sassa.gov.za/Portals/1/Documents/66505010-f30a-4426-ba15-990ccd6c71ae.pdf.

Department of Welfare and Population Development (1997), *The White Paper for Social Welfare*, General Notice 1108 of 1997, Pretoria: Government Printers.

Extended Public Works Programme (2004), *Second Quarterly Report: Financial Year 2004/05*, accessed at www.epwp.gov.za/Downloads/report_2004-05_Q2_narrative.pdf.

Kaseke, E. (2000), 'The challenge of extending social security to the poor: an African perspective', paper presented at the 29th ICSW International Conference on Social Welfare, Cape Town, South Africa, 23–27 October, accessed at www.icsw.org/global-conferences/challenges-extending.htm.

Khosa and Others v Minister of Social Development and Others, Mahlaule and Another v Minister of Social Development (1994), 6 BCLR 569 (CC).

Leibbrandt, M., I. Woolard, A. Finn and J. Argent (2010), *Trends in South African Income Distribution and Poverty since the Fall of Apartheid*, Paris: OECD Publishing.

Minister of Health v Treatment Action Campaign (2002), 10 BCLR 1033 (CC).

Ministry in the Office of the President (1994), *White Paper on Reconstruction and Development*, General Notice 1954 of 1994, Pretoria: Government Printers.

Mpedi, L. G. (2008), *Pertinent Social Security Issues in South Africa*, Bellville: Community Law Centre (University of Western Cape).

National Planning Commission (2010), *Development Indicators*, accessed at www.info.gov.za/view/DownloadFileAction?id=137217.

National Planning Commission (2011), *National Development Plan: Vision for 2030*, accessed at www.npconline.co.za/medialib/downloads/home/NPC%20National%20Development%20Plan%20Vision%202030%20-lo-res.pdf.

National Treasury (Republic of South Africa) (2005), *Provincial Budgets and Expenditure Review: 2001/02–2007/08*, accessed at www.treasury.gov.za/publications/igfr/2005/prov/14.%20Prov%20Budgets%20&%20Exp%20Trends%20-%202001-02%20-%202007-08%20-%20Full%20Document.pdf.

National Treasury (Republic of South Africa) (2007), *2007 Budget Review*, accessed at www.treasury.gov.za/documents/national%20budget/2007/review/isbn.pdf.

National Treasury (Republic of South Africa) (2010), *2010 Budget Review*, accessed at www.treasury.gov.za/documents/national%20budget/2010/review/Budget%20Review.pdf.

National Treasury (Republic of South Africa) (2011), *2011 Budget Review*, accessed at www.treasury.gov.za/documents/national%20budget/2011/review/Budget%20Review.pdf.

National Treasury (Republic of South Africa) (2012), *2012 Budget Review*, accessed at www.treasury.gov.za/documents/national%20budget/2012/review/Prelims%202012.pdf.

Olivier, M. P., J. F. Khoza, L. Jansen van Rensburg and E. Klinck (2003), 'Constitutional issues', in M. P. Olivier, N. Smit and E. R. Kalula (eds), *Social Security: A Legal Analysis*, Durban: LexisNexis Butterworths, pp. 49–121.

Organization for Economic Co-Operation and Development (2010), *OECD Economic Surveys: South Africa*, Paris: OECD Publishing.

Parliamentary Monitoring Group (undated), 'Minister of Social Development address, South African Security Agency and National Development Agency: 2008/9 strategic plan and budget', accessed at www.pmg.org.za.

Reddy, T. and A. Sokomani (2008), *Corruption and Social Grants in South Africa*, South Africa: Institute for Security Studies.

South African Human Rights Commission and UNICEF South Africa (2011), *South Africa's Children: A Review of Equity and Child Rights*, accessed at www.unicef.org/southafrica/resources_8101.html.

Statistics South Africa (2011a), *General Household Survey 2010*, accessed at www.statssa.gov.za/publications/P0318/P0318June2010.pdf.

Statistics South Africa (2011b), *Labour Market Dynamics in South Africa 2010*, accessed at www.statssa.gov.za/publications/Report-02-11-02/Report-02-11-022010.pdf.

Statistics South Africa (2012a), *General Household Survey 2011*, accessed at www.statssa.gov.za/publications/statsdownload.asp?PPN=P0318&SCH=5217.

Statistics South Africa (2012b), *Quarterly Labour Force Survey, Quarter 1, 2012*, accessed at www.statssa.gov.za/publications/P0211/P02111stQuarter2012.pdf.
Statistics South Africa (2012c), *Quarterly Labour Force Survey, Quarter 2, 2012*, accessed at www.statssa.gov.za/publications/P0211/P02112ndQuarter2012.pdf.
Taylor Committee (2002), *Transforming the Present – Protecting the Future: Report of the Committee of Inquiry into a Comprehensive System of Social Security for South Africa*, Pretoria: Department of Social Development.
The Constitution of the Republic of South Africa (1996), Act 108 of 1996.
United Nations (2000), *Enhancing Social Protection and Reducing Vulnerability in a Globalising World: Report of the Secretary-General*, 39th Session of the Commission for Social Development, accessed at www.icsw.org/un-news/pdfs/csdsocprotect.PDF.
Zuma, J. (2004), 'Address at the launch of the Extended Public Works Programme', at Nombika High School, Durban, 28 August, accessed at www.anc.org.za/ancdocs/history/zuma/2004jz0828.html.

15. Social protection in South Africa – recent achievements and future prospects

John Kruger

OVERVIEW

The last decade has seen the strong extension of social assistance (and hence social protection) in South Africa. Nonetheless, poverty has remained very high and inequality has not decreased.

While continued high levels of poverty and vulnerability may indicate a need for further expansion of the social protection system, there is a growing sense that other, more directly growth-focused, routes to poverty alleviation need to be found. The reference is often to the need for 'productive investments'.

For example, in its 2012 Budget Review, the National Treasury, under the heading 'Shifting the composition of spending', argues that '[o]ver the past decade, substantial increases in social service spending and social grant transfers have improved welfare and reduced poverty. In the period ahead, budgeting will give greater emphasis to infrastructure, employment and economic growth'.

This sceptical view of the scope for and wisdom of further social protection expansion is often echoed by economists (see Pauw and Mncube, 2007; Leibbrandt et al., 2010). This chapter sketches the background to these issues and points to potential driving forces and implications for the future. It argues that while increased investment in physical infrastructure, health and education is necessary, further reform of the social protection system, in particular in the area of social insurance, is necessary to ensure the competitiveness and dynamism of the South African economy – and future welfare.

THE COMING OF DEMOCRACY AND THE RAPID EXPANSION OF SOCIAL PROTECTION IN SOUTH AFRICA AFTER 1994

South Africa entered democracy in 1994 with very high levels of poverty and inequality as a result of the systematic rigging of the education system and labour market against Africans. There was also very uneven access to public services generally, growth had faltered and the government deficit and debt service levels were at critical levels.

The last roughly two decades after the political transformation have seen a strong reversal of many of these negative factors. There was a building of strong macroeconomic fundamentals through restraining the growth of government expenditure in the face of stable, if unspectacular, growth. Between 2000 and 2010 the economy grew by a real 3.5 per cent per year, following, on average, annual growth of 1.8 per cent between 1990 and 2000 (South African Reserve Bank, KBP 6006Y).

Population growth had also moderated to around 1.1 per cent per annum between 2000 and 2010 for the total population to reach 50.5 million in 2011. As a result, per capita income increased by more than 2 per cent per year for the decade to 2010.

While per capita income in South Africa is high compared to other African countries, placing it in the category of middle-income countries, severe income inequality means that per capita income is a bad indicator of average welfare and that South Africa's ranking on the Human Development Index (HDI) is far below what would be expected on the basis of per capita income. South Africa ranks close to India in terms of the HDI while its average per capita income approaches three times that of India.

Sustained economic growth and a conservative fiscal stance saw the reduction in deficits, debt levels, and eventually reduced debt-servicing costs. This, together with increasing tax revenues (in spite of a reduction in tax rates), saw government expenditure increase as a proportion of gross domestic product (GDP) from 25 per cent in 2000 to 31 per cent in 2010, government spending on goods and services grow by a real 5.5 per cent per year over the decade to 2010.

THE GROWTH IN SOCIAL PROTECTION

Solid economic performance and moderate fiscal space therefore provided a first set of factors that supported the rapid expansion of social protection after 2010. Another factor was the strong political pressure for fighting poverty and for redistributive solutions, given the context of inequality. The crumbling of some of the pillars of apartheid prior to 1994 had already seen the fundamental reform of labour relations and the equalisation of grant values for all population groups. While there was some surprise that the system of grants to all population groups survived apartheid, discriminatory payments to different groups was its hallmark. A new technocracy and a more focused government administration also saw a strong search for solutions.

As a result of these factors, social services and household services (access to electricity, clean water, sanitation and housing) received priority and led, in the words of Leibbrandt et al. (2010, p. 4), to 'continual improvement in non-monetary well-being'. While access to health and education services improved, quality remains a problem and the AIDS epidemic added severe pressure to the health system and resulted in mortality rates increasing. But social assistance was one of the biggest 'winners' in this period of rebuilding.

First, a child support grant was introduced in 1998 at a modest level and targeted a proportion of vulnerable children (the poorest one-third of children aged zero–six). Over the last 12 years the qualifying age has been increased in a stepwise fashion and currently children under the age of 18 qualify subject to a means test. The number of children in receipt of a child grant went from zero to 11 million over slightly more than a decade. In 2010 the grant covered approximately 50 per cent of children aged 0–17 at an average amount of R259 per month, below half of a $2 per day (R561 in 2010) poverty line.

A decision to equalise the eligibility age for men and women for the state old-age grant at the age of 60 (previously 65 for men) from 2007 onwards also led to a more rapid growth in the number of old-age beneficiaries, reaching 2.6 million by 2010, or 68 per cent of the population over age 60. While this is not particularly generous compared to average income in the country (24 per cent of per capita GDP in 2010), the average monthly payment for old-age grants in 2010 equalled 74 per cent of the minimum wage determination for domestic workers (or about twice the $2 per day poverty line in 2010).

Partly because of the AIDS epidemic and partly because of weak regulation and administration, the number of disability grant beneficiaries grew very rapidly between 2000 and 2008 (from around 600000 to 1.4 million), after which numbers declined for two consecutive years. AIDS, through its impact on the number of orphans, also led to growth in the number of foster grants (valued at about three times the child support grant), which were increasingly approved for orphans being cared for by close family.

The introduction of the new child support grant and continued growth in other grants saw the total number of state grant beneficiaries growing from 2.9 million in 2000 to 14.2 million in 2010, or from 7 per cent of the population to 28 per cent of the population. As a result, public expenditures were realigned significantly: Government social assistance spending grew as a proportion of GDP to about 3.5 per cent while education spending dropped below 6 per cent, social assistance spending in the process overtaking government health spending in relative importance.

The changes in the social assistance system after 2000 amounted to more than a mere extension of the number of beneficiaries and represent a fundamental change in the nature of the South African social system. Prior to 2000 social assistance was limited to those unable to work, namely the disabled and the elderly poor. In 2012 the biggest number of beneficiaries, although not the biggest expenditure, was on child support grants, which support families with children, representing a shift in focus from the old and disabled to (often working poor) families.

The child support grant is innovative in other ways. First, it introduced a much simplified means test. Second, it acknowledged the reality of South African household structures (mobility of children between the extended family and caring for children by others than the mother or father) by introducing the notion of 'following the child' (not a specific household or house or family) and paying the benefit to the 'primary caregiver'. In being payable mostly to women, it is also a major tool of empowerment.

Administrative reform is also a part of the story of social assistance expansion. First, establishing greater autonomy for and increasing efficiency at the South African Revenue Services from the late 1990s resulted in sustained growth in tax revenues and targets being exceeded on an ongoing basis, which assisted in providing the fiscal space for the rapid expansion of the social protection system. Second, ongoing concerns and litigation with regard to uneven social grant administration and delivery in second-tier government (provinces) led to the centralisation of administration in the South African Social Security Agency, a national public entity. While delivery processes and turnaround times have apparently improved (little monitoring data is publicly available), it is not clear that efficiency savings from centralisation have become a reality. Improvement in information management systems (and process re-engineering and simplification, spreading out from the much-maligned Eastern Cape government) also played a role in improving delivery.

So, in 2012, in terms of social protection, South Africa had the following in place:

1. An innovative social assistance system, providing a basic safety net in risk areas such as old age, disability and family and child

responsibilities. A gap in the system is that there is no safety net for those of working age who are able to work but cannot find work and cannot rely on contributory social protection, that is, those who have not had an association with the formal sector or whose formal sector benefits have run out. This group has to rely on relatives and friends to survive and is probably a partial source of South Africa's high crime statistics.

2. A social insurance system (unemployment insurance, work injury and illness compensation, road accident fund) that is small and unsatisfactory from two perspectives. First, it does not cover key risk areas of retirement and health and, second, the components that exist (especially unemployment insurance and employment injury) cater for only a small proportion of the population of working age, those who are employed in formal jobs. An important extension has, however, been the inclusion of domestic workers in the unemployment insurance fund (UIF) and a concerted drive to register domestic workers.
3. An occupational and private retirement, death and retirement (pensions, retirement annuities, long-term insurance) and medical scheme system that is large (assets of official pension funds and private self-administered pension and provident funds, excluding the large administered and retirement annuity sector, equalled 64 per cent of GDP in 2010) and dynamic from some perspectives. However, the sector (a) covers only the wealthiest 20 per cent of the population, (b) provides very high-cost services which often translate into (c) low service delivery (low replacement rates on retirement and uncovered contingencies in health care). While improved regulation of the medical scheme industry over the last decade has improved the efficiency of the sector, it remains high-cost and regulation is weak in the very large retirement and life business.

Recent estimates for the Department of Social Development confirm the very large size of the South African social protection system relative to the economy. It is estimated that in 2010 social protection expenditure, including administrative expenditure (comprising government social assistance, social insurance schemes and occupational and private retirement pension schemes), totalled R226 billion or 8.5 per cent of GDP.

Just over 51 per cent of this spending originated in the public sector (social assistance and social insurance) with the rest consisting of private and official pension funds. The largest component of social protection expenditure is government social grants or social assistance (40 per cent of total social protection) and private and occupational pension funds (30 per cent). The rest went to social insurance (10 per cent) and official pension funds created for public servants and employees of parastatals (18 per cent), according to initial estimates for a South African 'social budget' for the Department of Social Development.

Key aspects of the current system are the glaring absence of a second tier, mandatory retirement and health insurance system and regulatory weakness in the occupational and private pensions industry. In addition there is significant institutional fragmentation between the social insurance funds and the absence of a coherent perspective on the development of the social protection system.

While systematic analyses of the social, occupational and private insurance systems are few and far between there has been some analysis of the impact of the South African social grant system. Specifically, there is evidence of a positive impact of the child support grant on child health and somewhat more limited evidence of its impact on educational attendance and attainments. A review of this impact by Hall (2011, p. 2) found that the child support grant:

- decreases the child poverty headcount and contributes substantially to the income of the poorest households.
- increases school enrolment levels among child beneficiaries. There is also some evidence that it increases enrolment of the siblings of child beneficiaries.
- improves children's health and nutritional outcomes as measured by the well-known measure of height for age.
- reduces the incidence of child hunger.
- may reduce the likelihood of older children engaging in child labour.

In addition to the direct effect of the state old-age pension on poverty there is long-standing evidence of its impact on children in households receiving the grant. Recently Neves et al. (2010) have pointed to mechanisms through which social grants can invigorate informal networks and provide a web for the survival of, and sometimes a springboard to improved, economic opportunities and returns for some of the elderly and marginalised.

PERSISTENCE OF POVERTY AND INEQUALITY

In spite of the strong recent expansion of the South African social protection system, poverty has remained at a very high level and inequality has worsened. Table 15.1 provides evidence on poverty levels and the impact of the state social protection system. It shows, first, that social assistance grants reduce poverty: pushing the poverty headcount down from 0.6 to

Table 15.1 South Africa: change in poverty over time and the impact of the social assistance grants

Year	Poverty Headcount		Poverty Gap (P1)		Poverty Gap (P2)	
	before soc. ass.	after soc. ass.	before soc. ass.	after soc. ass.	before soc. ass.	after soc. ass.
1993	0.60	0.56	0.40	0.32	0.32	0.22
2000	0.57	0.56	0.37	0.29	0.29	0.19
2008	0.60	0.54	0.44	0.28	0.37	0.18

Source: Adapted from Leibbrandt et al. (2010).

0.54 in 2008, but also that they have a very strong impact on the poverty gap, reducing both measures P1 and P2 very significantly.

While the social assistance system is therefore effective at reducing poverty, poverty has reduced only slightly over the 15 years between 1993 and 2008. In fact, poverty increased from 1995 (22.9 million on less the $2/day) to 2000 (25.2 million under $2/day) but decreased somewhat after 2000 due to the child support grant extension 'but persisted at acute levels for Africans and Coloureds' (Leibbrandt et al., 2010, p. 4).

Between 1993 and 2008 inequality increased substantially with the South African Gini coefficient moving from 0.66 to 0.70 (Leibbrandt et al., 2010).

The stubbornness of poverty and inequality in South Africa has its causes in the labour market. Joblessness and low wages are endemic in South Africa. From highs of 30 per cent, narrowly defined unemployment has now dropped to around 25 per cent. In addition to this chronically high unemployment rate, there is also a significant component of discouraged workers. As indicated, in the context of this high unemployment burden there is no social assistance or social insurance for the bulk of the unemployed. The UIF only benefited about 600000 people in 2011, a small proportion of the estimated number of unemployed of just over four million. This is a result of the small percentage of the labour force contributing to UIF because of high youth unemployment (and thus no previous contribution record) and significant informal employment.

Facing the Future

South Africa's social protection system has expanded significantly over the last decade. Key questions going forward are whether the country will be able to afford and sustain the large system of cash grants. In addition, given the high level of poverty and inequality and the gaps identified in the social protection system, the question is what should be done to change the system and whether these changes are likely to happen. Here we therefore try to answer two broad sets of questions. How would the likely costs of the current system develop over the next two to three decades and what are the changes we are likely to see in the architecture and management of the system?

On the costs side there are objective determinants (demography, economy, socio-economics) to estimate costs into the future, although there will necessarily be a significant confidence margin. However, system reform is harder to anticipate. While it is hoped that policy will respond to objective problems in a fairly efficient way, a number of complex aspects such as politics and political economy and bureaucratic capacity and innovation (in developing evidence-based responses to societal pressures) will intervene. With regard to system reform we therefore have to identify gaps and infer from current policy what likely trajectories could be.

The aim here cannot be to try and make detailed predictions. It is to identify high-level drivers and infer possible futures in broad terms.

COST OF THE CURRENT SOCIAL PROTECTION SYSTEM GOING FORWARD

Future costs of the current social protection system, assuming policy stability, will depend on demographic, economic and socio-economic change. The Department of Social Development has recently embarked on developing a social budget tool to use in support of medium-term planning and policymaking. A social budget, as developed by the International Labour Organization, consists of a systematic and consistent enumeration of social expenditure (the social accounting system) and a projection tool to project beneficiaries and expenditure and to use in analysing policy options (the social budget model). To date government and researchers have had limited tools for assessing the future of the system, tools mostly focused on social assistance expenditure.

The future cost of the current system will depend on demographics (the number of elderly people and children that will have to be catered for), income levels (affecting the means test and thus the number of eligible beneficiaries), the level of grant increases and interpretation and administration of rules.

Population growth has moderated in South Africa and, in spite of ageing, growth in the number of target beneficiaries by age group will not lead to sustainability issues. Moderate growth in the economy will be sufficient to maintain the current grant system. The total population has grown by an average 1.1 per cent annually between 2000 and 2010 and estimates by the Department of Social Development (based on the Actuarial Society of South Africa's 2008 projection model) project that population growth will slow to below 1 per cent per year during the current decade and average around half a per cent between 2010 and 2030. While the number of those older than 60 will grow by about 1.7 per cent per year between 2010 and 2030, those aged 0–18 are expected to decline by an average 0.1 per cent per year, leading to a decline in the overall dependency ratio.

In recent years, the government has endeavoured to keep the real values of grant payment stable, adjusting them in line with inflation. As a result, grant levels have declined somewhat relative to average incomes, given real economic growth. In spite of this there has been little pressure on government to push up grant values faster than inflation. It therefore seems unlikely that the growth of grant values will become a factor threatening sustainability.

In the past, weak regulation and administration of the grant system have led to the unsustainable expansion of beneficiary numbers in certain categories. This was the case for disability grants in the early 2000s. While HIV/AIDS and the resulting increase in temporary disability grants played a role, part of the problem was due to weak regulations (such as the definition of disability) but also to insufficient systems for monitoring decisions by medical practitioners and hence fraud and corruption.

The recent very rapid expansion of the foster care grant, which is impacting strongly on grant expenditure, is due to the increasing number of deaths of parents as a result of HIV/AIDS, a loosening up over the last decade in the interpretation by the Department of Social Development and courts of 'a child in need of care' and the fact that the foster care grant is nearly three times the value of the child support grant (R770 against R280 in 2012–13). While the phrase 'a child in need of care' (a requirement for accessing a foster care grant) was historically seen as indicating a child not able to stay with close family (grandparents and siblings – that is, those with a duty to care), the grant in recent years came to be awarded more and more to grandmothers looking after grandchildren where mothers had died. A recent High Court ruling, however, clarified that grandparents do have a duty to care (and therefore do not qualify for a foster care grant on behalf of a child's children). Some estimates indicate that this might affect as many as 350 000 orphans living with grandparents and accessing the foster care grant (Children's Institute in *Sowetan*, 3 September 2012).

The potential further rapid expansion of the foster care grant holds significant fiscal risk as, in spite of high recent growth, coverage is still quite uneven across provinces. Equalising access, currently held up by policy uncertainty, uncertainty about entitlements and bottlenecks in court processes (a court placement is necessary for a foster care grant) will escalate costs significantly (Children's Institutes have made estimates but these have not been published). It is to be seen whether this potential threat can be transformed into an opportunity, as was the case with the development of the child support grant as a response to a threatening fiscal crisis in the late 1990s. In this case the state maintenance grant (a grant that was payable to single parents at a relatively high level and had not been accessed to a significant extent by Africans) held the potential to be hugely expensive. The government's response was innovative, introducing the child support grant at a more modest level, and narrowly targeted, but significantly more fair, and provided the base for the progressive extension of the grant system (see Lund, 2008).

Past growth and future projections of social grant beneficiaries and spending are shown in Table 15.2 and Table 15.3. Continued rapid growth in spending is forecast, driven by the factors discussed above.

Fiscal sustainability of the current grant system given prudent administration and continued modest economic growth is therefore not likely to be a problem. Except for the foster care grant risks there are no explosive cost factors in the current social assistance mix (the elderly population growing from 7.5 per cent of the population in 2009 to 11.3 per cent in 2030, but the overall dependency ratio coming down because the number of children is declining).

FUTURE ISSUES WITH REGARD TO SOCIAL ASSISTANCE

There are a number of weaknesses or gaps in the system which require assessment, also in light of the constitutional promise of 'the right to have access to . . . social security, including if they are unable to support themselves and their dependents, appropriate social assistance'. The Constitution mandates the state to 'take reasonable legislative and other measures, within its available resources, to achieve the progressive realisation of each of its rights'. Three priority areas are: support for the unemployed able-bodied falling outside the unemployment insurance system and related mechanisms to deal with the very high rates of youth unemployment, and a potential kinship or similar grant to deal with the explosive growth in the foster care grant.

In spite of these gaps in the social assistance system, concerns have been raised about the further extension of the system. Pauw and Mncube (2007, p. 1) have argued against further expansion on the basis of fiscal space and the need to focus on other priorities. Specifically, they argue that 'in the past much of the increased expenditure on social security provisioning could be financed out of government revenue overruns, further increases are likely to be possible only through reallocation of government expenditures'. They argue that 'education and health expenditures have apparently declined in favour of increased welfare expenditures' and may 'harm the already weak education and health services in South Africa'. As we saw earlier, the National Treasury is also arguing for a shift in expenditure towards 'infrastructure, employment and economic growth'.

Leibbrandt et al. (2010, pp. 68–9) focus on the need to draw the unemployed into productive employment and that it would be '. . . imprudent to argue for permanent income support for the unemployed . . . the goal has to be . . . assimilation into the labour market'.

Table 15.2 South Africa: social grant beneficiary numbers 2008–09 to 2014–15

Thousands	2008/09	2009/10 Actual	2010/11	2011/12 Revised estimated	2012/13	2013/14 Projected	2014/15	% Growth per year
Type of grant								
Old age	2344	2490	2647	2724	2773	2835	2881	3.5%
War veterans	2	1	1	1	1	1	1	−10.9%
Disability	1372	1299	1212	1216	1192	1196	1196	−2.3%
Foster care	476	489	490	598	671	769	874	−10.7%
Care dependency	107	119	121	126	131	141	147	5.4%
Child support	8765	9381	10154	10903	11301	11549	11659	4.9%
Total	13066	13779	14625	15568	16069	16491	16758	4.2%

Source: National Treasury (2012).

Table 15.3 South Africa: social grant spending 2008–09 to 2014–15

RMillion	2008/09	2009/10 Actual	2010/11	2011/12 Revised estimated	2012/13	2013/14 Projected	2014/15	% Growth per year
Old age	25934	29826	33751	37318	39323	42526	45823	10.0%
War veterans	20	17	14	12	13	10	11	−9.8%
Disability	16474	16567	16840	17834	19152	20410	21992	4.9%
Foster care	3934	4434	4616	5245	5952	6216	6697	9.3%
Care dependency	1292	1434	1586	1948	1857	2107	2270	9.9%
Child support	22348	26670	30342	34036	38237	41553	44774	12.3%
Grant-in-aid	90	146	170	192	188	203	219	15.9%
Social relief of distress	623	165	174	118	165	183	197	−17.5%
Total	70715	79260	87493	96703	104888	113208	121982	9.5%

Source: National Treasury (2012).

In early 2011 the National Treasury reviewed options to create more jobs for youth (National Treasury, 2011) and proposed a wage subsidy which was scheduled for implementation in 2012 but has since been on hold because of criticism and resistance. It was proposed that the wages of workers between the ages of 18 and 29 earning less than R60 000 per year be subsidised through tax credits to employers through the pay as you earn (PAYE) system. The subsidy would be paid on a sliding scale equal to 50 per cent of monthly wages up to R2000 per month and reducing to zero at R5000 per month (see Bernstein and Altbeker, 2012). Over somewhat less than five years it was expected that 133 000 jobs would be created at a cost of R137 000 per job.

Further extending the arsenal to fight unemployment, the National Treasury also established in 2011 a R9 billion Jobs Fund, a challenge-type fund aimed at finding innovative ways of improving the working of the labour market (institutional capacity building), to bolster demand for labour (enterprise development; infrastructure development) and strengthen labour supply (support for job seekers). This fund extends a range of existing job creation initiatives which were further strengthened in the 2012 Budget, as set out below:

> Job creation is a central priority of government. An additional R4.8 billion over the 2012 period is provided for the expanded public works programme, bringing its allocations to a total of R77.8 billion.
>
> - The community work programme receives an additional R3.5 billion, enabling the number of people employed to increase to 332 000 in 2014/15 from 89 689 in March 2011. This initiative guarantees participants 100 days of work on local community priorities.
> - The natural resource management programme (Working for Water, Working on Fire) receives an additional R1.1 billion, providing for a total of 135 006 jobs over the medium term from 114 000 jobs in April 2011
> - The non-state sector programme receives an additional R345 million, which will fund about 127 009 cumulative short-term jobs by 2014/15 – up from 48 358 jobs in April 2011.
>
> The National Rural Youth Services Corps receives an additional R200 million over the next three years. This skills development programme for rural youth has enrolled 7500 participants and plans to enrol an additional 5000 per year over the next three years.
>
> An additional allocation of R300 million over the MTEF period will support the creation of about 16 000 short-term jobs through the Mzansi Golden Economy strategy in the arts and culture sector. (National Treasury, 2012, p. 116)

In its vision for the social protection system in South Africa in 2030, the National Planning Commission (2011, p. 328) sees a country ‘where the majority of working age South Africans are employed. . . . There is a defined social floor and households who have not achieved the basic standard of living are assisted. . . . Social protection also serves to protect against short term shocks and chronic vulnerabilities caused by labour market failures'. They also identify the '[l]ack of social protection for the unemployed' as 'the critical social protection gap'. With regard to this gap, the commission proposed the definition of a minimum social floor and monitoring of progress to reaching such a floor and expanding existing public employment programmes (as set out above). With regard to the expansion of the public employment programme they refer to India's National Rural Employment Guarantee Act and indicate that this has thrust public employment into the area of social protection.

What we therefore see is widespread scepticism about the further expansion of the social grant system and from both the National Treasury and the National Planning Commission a focus on direct job creation and a wage subsidy. In spite of this, the Department of Social Development has recently investigated the use of the grant system to impact youth unemployment. A youth grant could be argued to fulfil the same function as a youth wage subsidy, which has been proposed by the National Treasury in recent years. And indeed a youth grant could be seen as a wage subsidy payable not to employers but to the workseeker/employee.

What is clear is that future years will see the continuing exploration and experimentation of mechanisms to support the unemployed and draw them into productive employment.

In the past a basic income grant – a universal grant to all citizens – has been proposed in order to provide a social floor and cater for the able-bodied unemployed. This was seen by some as a straightforward way of creating a social floor without all the disincentives from a range of different means-tested grants. It has not gained traction, partly because of the assumed very significant cost and resulting increase in the tax burden and, arguably, because of continuing resistance against cash transfers or 'handouts' (consumption rather than investment as argued by Archer, 2007) as the main mechanism of alleviating poverty. It is worth noting that Archer also distinguishes between policies to *relieve poverty* and policies to *facilitate escape* from poverty.

In addition to the challenge to have an impact on the area of unemployment, social assistance policy will also have to resolve the current explosive growth and disruptive impact on the court system of the foster care grant. In this regard a 'kinship grant' has been proposed which would be payable to kin for looking after orphans, without having to go through a court process. Cost implications and its congruence with the child support grant system need to be investigated further.

THE FUTURE OF SOCIAL INSURANCE

Responding to the absence of a strong second tier of social protection providing mandatory retirement and health insurance, the South African government has been developing proposals for a mandatory retirement insurance scheme in the context of a comprehensive social security and retirement reform programme. The reform is aimed at 'strengthening labour market institutions and improving income security of low-income employees' (National Treasury, 2007b, p. 17).

The broad rationale, as expressed by the National Treasury, is that 'South Africans do not save adequately for retirement and only about half of the country's workers belong to a retirement fund'. In spite of the existence of the state social pension (social assistance) and occupational and private provision, the absence of a 'basic, pooled, mandatory contributory scheme' and high costs (partly because of regulatory issues) in the private sector, 'too few people have access to efficient and cost effective options for saving for retirement' (National Treasury, 2007b, p. 6) and there is a failure to 'provide adequate and quality coverage to a significant proportion of the population' (Department of Social Development, 2007, p. 13). The current system also raises significant equity issues, being built on large tax subsidies to high-income earners.

Initial options for reform were spelled out in documents from the National Treasury (2007a, 2007b, 2008) and the Social Cluster of Government (Department of Social Development, 2007). An interdepartmental task team submitted recommendations to political heads and decisions by Cabinet are awaited. While details are therefore not totally clear or final, the proposals are more comprehensive than mere retirement provision, also focusing on risk benefits and on integrating the fragmented social insurance apparatus (with the retirement fund regulator, the Financial Services Board, being supervised by the National Treasury and compensation, unemployment and accident insurance agencies reporting to three other departments – labour, health and transport – and the Department of Social Development having a mandate to lead in the development of social protection policy).

Proposals for a National Social Security Fund are expected to encompass:

1. The introduction of a mandatory retirement system with possible contribution subsidies at lower income levels.
2. The continuation of the non-contributory state old-age pension system and its harmonisation with the contributory system (inter alia relaxing the means test to remove disincentives to work).

3. In addition to retirement benefits, the inclusion of risk benefits (death and disability).
4. Harmonisation with the UIF to try to support preservation of benefits in the case of unemployment.
5. Building a stronger and coordinated platform for implementation of social protection through integrating key social protection funds into or under one administration, potentially a department of 'Comprehensive Social Security/Protection'.

At the same time, government is developing further its proposals for and piloting aspects of a national health insurance system. This is to deal with very large inequalities in access to and quality of health care, the equity issues associated with significant tax subsidies for private medical insurance and cost and affordability issues in private medical schemes.

Depending on how existing retirement funders and medical schemes are incorporated (or allowed to co-exist) with these two very substantial mandatory government schemes, the South African retirement and medical scheme landscape will be radically transformed.

CONCLUSIONS

The South African social protection system, and the social assistance component in particular, has expanded strongly in recent decades, providing a partial safety net for South Africans. While significantly reducing poverty (and being quite generous in comparative perspective), social assistance (and the limited unemployment insurance system) did not respond to the plight of the able-bodied unemployed – with narrowly defined unemployment running at more than 25 per cent for more than a decade.

Thus far the South African government has opted for or proposed what can be seen as ad hoc strategies to generate jobs – public employment programmes, challenge-type funds, wage subsidies – because of the perception that further expansion of the social assistance system will negatively impact on other priorities (such as investment/infrastructure, education and health) and aggravate the unemployment problem rather than reduce unemployment and promote growth.

With the introduction of the child support grant in the early 2000s, the South African state transformed a fiscal threat (the state maintenance grant) into an opportunity and very progressive extension of the social grant system, which arguably played a large role in stabilising a very unequal society. Social protection thinkers and policymakers currently have the challenge of forging new mechanisms of social protection that can address poverty and vulnerability through enhancing job creation.

It may seem as if the reform of the retirement and health insurance industry is not strongly related to this quest of getting more people into productive employment. However, the current sub-optimal social, occupational and private insurance systems – which are very large relative to the size of the economy – are wasteful and impose huge costs on the economy. If these costs can be reduced in real terms over time it will significantly enhance the competitiveness and capacity to employ of the South African economy.

While policymakers are therefore looking for solutions to the unemployment dilemma in the area of social assistance, public employment and job creation, reform of the costly social and private insurance system should be as much of a priority. Currently, delays in moving forward with regard to these social insurance reforms raise questions about the capacity of the South African state to transform this complex policy area. Nixon (2008, p. 15) has spoken of 'slow violence' as 'catastrophic acts that are low in instant spectacle but high in long-term effects'. Delays in reforming the South African social insurance system might be an example of such 'slow violence' – with part of the cost to be counted in excessively high unemployment and poverty.

REFERENCES

Archer, S. (2007), 'The basic homework on basic income grants in South Africa', CSSR Working Paper 122, Cape Town: University of Cape Town.

Bernstein, A. and A. Altbeker (2011), 'Jobs for young people: is a wage subsidy a good idea?', CDEW Roundtable 17, Johannesburg: Centre for Development and Enterprise.

Department of Social Development (2007), *Reform of Retirement Provisions – Discussion Document*, Pretoria: Department of Social Development.

Hall, K. (2011), *The Child Support Grant: Are Conditions Appropriate? Children Count Brief*, Cape Town: Children's Institute, University of Cape Town.

Leibbrandt, M., I. Woolard, A. Finn and J. Argent (2010), 'Trends in South African income distribution and poverty since the fall of apartheid', OECD Social, Employment and Migration Working Papers, Geneva: OECD.

Lund, F. (2008), *Changing Social Policy: The Child Support Grant in South Africa*, Pretoria: HSRC Press.

National Planning Commission (2011), *National Development Plan – Vision for 2030*, Pretoria: National Planning Commission.

National Treasury (2007a), 'Social security', in *Budget Review 2007*, RSA: National Treasury, pp. 99–116.

National Treasury (2007b), *Social Security and Retirement Reform – Second Discussion Paper*, RSA: National Treasury.

National Treasury (2008), 'Social security', in *Budget Review 2008*, RSA: National Treasury, pp. 91–104.

National Treasury (2011), 'Confronting youth unemployment: policy options for South Africa', discussion paper for public comment, RSA: National Treasury.

National Treasury (2012), *Strengthening Retirement Savings: An Overview of Proposals Announced in the 2012 Budget*, RSA: National Treasury.

Neves, D., M. Samson, I. van Niekerk, S. Hlatshwayo and A. du Toit (2010), *The Use and Effectiveness of Social Grants in South Africa*, Johannesburg: FinMark Trust.

Nixon, R. (2008), 'Slow violence, gender, and the environmentalism of the poor', *Journal of Commonwealth and Postcolonial Studies*, **13**, 14–37.

Pauw, K. and L. Mncube (2007), 'Expanding the social security net in South Africa: opportunities, challenges and constraints', International Poverty Centre, Country Studies of the Cash Transfer Research Programme.

South African Reserve Bank, KBP 6006Y, accessed 17 November 2012 at www.resbank.co.za/Research/Statistics/Pages/OnlineDownloadFacility.aspx

PART VI

Conclusion

16. Conclusion: experiences, issues and future possibilities

David Piachaud and James Midgley

In the preceding sections, experts on each of the four nations have discussed many different aspects of social protection. As mentioned in the introduction to this book, these countries were selected because they have all experienced rapid economic growth in recent times and have also expanded their social protection systems and, accordingly, present a good opportunity to examine the complex relationship between economic development and social protection. In addition to describing the history, features and future trajectory of social protection in their countries, the contributors have either directly or indirectly addressed this issue. The purpose of this final chapter is not to present a summary but rather to draw out some issues that are common, or not common, from all the nations to illuminate the future of social protection in these and other nations. As any painter knows, there is nothing like contrast to highlight the scene. The past, the present and the future have been perceived and discussed differently for each country. Another set of experts might have focussed on other aspects but there has been a substantial overlap of concerns and also substantial differences. Here some of these similarities and differences are discussed.

In this chapter we first outline some broad features and the experiences of each country with reference to social protection's development. We then consider some key issues in social protection that each country faces: these include the components of social protection, the needs of different population groups, organizational and administration issues and the goals and impact of social protection. The relationship between social protection and economic development is then considered with reference to the future and some lessons are drawn – perhaps questions is a more appropriate term – that all nations may wish to consider: what needs to be thought about, researched and discussed. What we do not do is prescribe a one-size-fits-all solution to how social protection should develop. That would be as arrogant as it would be inappropriate and unhelpful.

THE EXPERIENCE OF THE FOUR COUNTRIES

There are many differences in the history and current state of social protection in the four nations. That is not remotely surprising given their different histories, economies, societies, cultures and political systems. With a broad brush, certain broad features of each country can be described.

In China, the first two decades after the founding of the People's Republic of China (PRC) were characterized by a rigid egalitarian state within which social protection relied on state-owned enterprises and rural communes. Both were required by the state to pay benefits to their workers, but in time, as the number of retired workers and others in need increased, many were unable to meet their obligations. The shift to a liberalized economy and rapid economic growth has led to an expansion of formal social protection but there is still a major urban/rural divide and growing inequality. Another problem is the creation of different social protection schemes for different population groups, resulting in a fragmented system.

In India, the colonial heritage restricted any social protection to an urban elite. Social assistance was introduced at the state level to respond primarily to the needs of poor elderly people but it had a limited impact on poverty. The country's provident fund, which caters for workers in formal employment, is one of the largest in the world but still covers only a small proportion of the population. After independence, a short-lived aspiration to a Western model was followed by a regulatory state with extensive price controls and subsidies. Liberalization and rapid growth have brought more concern about poverty and employment but there is still great inequality and wide variations between states.

In Brazil, a limited state role for social protection, enforced through the military Juntas, provided for workers in formal employment and to some extent for the rural population, and in this regard the country was one of only a handful in the developing world to extend coverage to those in the countryside. In the 1990s, social protection expanded considerably, driven in part by a new Constitution embodying social commitments, carried out by a central, regulating government that has developed extensive social insurance and control of pension funds and has introduced non-contributory benefits subject to a loose conditionality. Brazil's conditional cash transfer scheme which covers more than 13 million families is one of the largest in the world and has received extensive international attention. But there is still an extensive informal, largely unprotected, sector.

In South Africa there was a dramatic shift with the advent of democracy from a system based on colonialism and apartheid. The social protection system, which was largely based on social assistance and the payment of retirement pensions, disproportionately favoured white elderly people, while the country's African population were neglected. The social insurance system catered primarily to white workers in formal employment. Since the transition, these inequities have been addressed and the government has used pensions and child benefits to alleviate poverty among poor African families, particularly in the rural areas. Now there is concern for poverty and rights but the economy is essentially liberal and remains highly unequal.

Despite these differences, there are similarities: All have economies that are growing fast, in the cases of China and India very fast indeed. On average the populations are better off. But economic inequality remains high in all of the four nations and in all save Brazil it has probably been increasing. The recent global recession has also had an effect and growth in all four countries has slowed. Poverty has generally fallen in absolute terms but risen in relative terms, except in Brazil. All have ageing populations, in the case of China ageing very rapidly. Social protection in India, Brazil and South Africa all show an abiding legacy of colonialism or colonial ideas. Social protection in all of them is primarily focussed on urban, formally employed populations. All have largely unprotected rural sectors. The beneficiaries of social protection differ substantially between countries.

Rapid growth has led to some expansion of the formal sector of employment that is covered by social insurance, but globalization and neoliberal economic policies have resulted in the growth of the informal employment sector lacking any developed social protection. As noted earlier, slower growth resulting from the global recession has also had a negative impact. More resources have gone into social protection but these are not substantial when expressed as a percentage of gross domestic product, except in Brazil. Generally growth in social protection has tended to reduce the extent of inequality. Most face challenges of government finance and concerns at the level of taxation. Most face problems in implementing social protection policies and concerns over corruption. All four countries have had and expect to have a growing role for social protection.

It is clear that the biggest changes in social protection have resulted from major political change: In China, the start of the PRC led to economic and social revolutions; about 20 years later, economic liberalization led to the end of occupationally-based social protection organized through state-owned enterprises and the introduction of urban social protection systems; only later did some limited rural social protection develop. In India, independence did not result in any major advance in social protection but more recently an increased emphasis on social rights has contributed to developments in social protection and in employment guarantees. In Brazil, a new Constitution enshrining social rights led to the rapid development of social protection. In South Africa, the coming of democracy led to the introduction of child support and aged grants.

ISSUES

In addition to the overriding issue of the relationship between social protection and economic development, many other important issues are raised by the authors in this collection; many were discussed by the participants from the four countries in the symposium. All inform the discussion later in this chapter on the role of social protection in countries experiencing rapid economic development. These may be grouped around the following key themes.

Components of Social Protection

Social protection means very different things. The development of social insurance, most marked in Brazil, has been largely confined in all four countries to those in formal employment who have been predominantly urban and in the upper echelons of the income distribution – those least likely to be poor. Social insurance has many merits but it is of limited effectiveness in terms of tackling poverty. By contrast, social assistance targeted at the poor can be an effective anti-poverty palliative, although how well it works depends on the effectiveness of the administrative structure; in some cases corruption seriously undermined effectiveness. Means-tested social grants for children (such as the child support grant in South Africa and Bolsa Família in Brazil) and for older people (such as South Africa's State Old Age Pension or SOAP) have proved effective in reaching many of the poor. They are clearly an important, relatively new component of social protection in the countries studied with the potential, if the groups targeted have a high incidence of poverty, to be more straightforward than social assistance. Yet the quality of administration in reaching the target group and in avoiding 'leakages' to those not eligible is again crucial. Innovative forms of social protection such as universal, non-means-tested pension programmes are only found in a few developing countries such as Botswana, Hong Kong, Lesotho, Mauritius and Namibia but their potential to extend social protection should be more widely considered.

Diversity of Need among Different Populations

In the course of the four country studies, situations regarding different population groups with different needs have repeatedly cropped up. Their diverse circumstances and needs pose challenges to social protection that need to be addressed; how social protection policies and programmes respond to them clearly affects their overall impact in the context of rapid economic growth.

First, in all four countries the elderly populations are rising. In terms of numbers, the devastation of HIV/AIDS in South Africa is limiting that growth as is the lower birth rate in Brazil. In India the birth rate, while reduced, is still high, so that despite longer life expectancy the dependency ratio will not rise greatly. It is in China, with a low birth rate and a rising life expectancy, that the dependency ratio will rise most dramatically; this is in large part due to the country's one-child policy, which has wider implications for the care of older people, and in part due to improved health. In combination, the prospective rise in the dependency ratio has huge implications for social protection. The choices this poses for social protection are stark. Either the working population will have to pay much more (either through taxes, compulsory insurance or inter-familial transfers) or they will have to continue working until substantially older ages than before or the elderly will face lower living standards relative to the working population. Western nations have reacted very slowly to rising life expectancy and have set a poor example of adjusting to changed circumstances. Whether newly industrializing nations do better remains to be seen.

Second, women are seriously disadvantaged by conventional social protection policies and programmes. Most policy and discussion of social protection in the West and also in the four nations studied has concentrated on men – implicitly adopting a male breadwinner model. This is clearly the case with social insurance schemes which cater primarily for those in regular wage employment, which generally means male workers in industry, commerce and services (including public services). But gender discrimination also operates in employer-mandate schemes and social assistance, which, despite being targeted at women, often pay small benefits under strict conditions. However, as Patel discusses in relation to South Africa in Chapter 13, this is misconceived in terms of the reality of actual employment patterns. Overall, the challenge of developing social protection in a gender-neutral form has barely begun to be considered. Clearly systems of grants based on individual rather than household status offer a way forward but these are still a small component of social protection in the four nations.

Third, the needs of unemployed people pose a major challenge. For South Africa the failure to bring down unemployment below 25 per cent for the last decade represents a major social and economic problem. Youth unemployment is a particularly serious problem, resulting not only in wasted opportunities for young people but a conspicuous failure for countries where human resources are emphasized as the crucial factor in development. Social protection has not accommodated this problem and maintained the incomes of those without jobs. At the same time there has been a growth in poverty among those in work. These problems have hit all the nations studied to differing degrees. There has not been a steady advance towards formal 'modern' employment, as was envisaged by some early writers on social security in developing countries; instead, many countries have experienced growing informal employment. The problem of providing for the unemployed is severe; many of those unemployed have been employed in low-paid jobs in the informal sector or have never been employed, so that social insurance schemes would be unlikely to help them. On the other hand, social assistance schemes assessed on a household basis could lead to serious disincentives to take work at all. Two ways out of this dilemma are to introduce employment guarantee schemes, such as India has done for rural areas, or to increase incentives to work by supplementing the incomes of low-paid workers. The former, which as Mutatkar writes in Chapter 8 may be extended to urban areas, provide an important complement to conventional social protection schemes. They provide a reminder that cash benefits can only alleviate poverty, they cannot remove the cause, in this case unemployment. Tackling the causes of poverty is at least as important as tackling its symptoms.

Next, migrants, ethnic minorities and indigenous people comprise a heterogeneous group that nevertheless shares common needs. With economic development, rural people and, particularly, young people have migrated to the cities of the developing world in search of work in huge numbers but most do not obtain formal wage employment and instead secure their livelihoods in the informal sector without access to the social protection system. Although the needs of workers in the informal sector have been recognized by many governments, academics and international organizations such as the International Labour Organization (ILO), little has been done to integrate them into the social protection system. Recent developments with regard to informal social security and microinsurance provide an opportunity for policymakers to address their needs. On the other hand, international migrants who are moving to high-growth developing countries in increasing numbers are often recognized in international social security treaties and by governments but their access to benefits is usually dependent on employment status; this means that only those who secure and maintain formal employment are likely to be covered. This is also the case with ethnic minorities and indigenous people who are often discriminated against and excluded from the social protection system. Writing about India, Mutatkar in Chapter 8 discusses the reasons for singling out certain castes and tribal groups for special treatment or affirmative action. He also considers the consequences, which he suggests may amount to segregation. Brazil faces such problems with respect to ethnic groups which live almost entirely separated from the mainstream economy and society. How far social protection should assume or require social inclusion is a fundamental issue which is rarely faced up to.

Organization and Administration

The two largest nations studied – China and India – have complex relations between central and state or provincial governments. There is also great diversity between regions. The question therefore arises as to how far it makes sense to operate a unitary social protection system, setting the same benefit levels throughout these vast lands. On the other hand, variation in benefits can lead to serious border problems and issues over the fair treatment of internal migrants.

Differences in the treatment of rural and urban populations have been most marked in China, where movement itself has been restricted. It is easy to suggest that all should be covered by one urban/rural scheme but administration in rural areas where many have no formal contract or wage presents formidable problems. Grants paid to individuals on the basis of age may be easier to administer but these are not linked to employment status. However, the existence of different social security systems for urban and rural people, which is found in Brazil and other countries as well, perpetuates the fragmentation of social protection which, as was noted in Chapter 2 of this book, is a major problem.

Another problem of administration is that of corruption. This was articulated only in the case of India but it is not suggested that the problem is limited to India or even to the developing countries, as is often assumed. The lure of claiming social protection for non-existent or deceased persons or claiming for benefits while employed may encourage fraud; limiting fraud without imposing harsh and stigmatizing tests of eligibility and severe sanctions on those who inadvertently claim to be eligible remains a severe administrative challenge.

A related problem which has long been a major issue is administrative effectiveness. Incompetence, delays in processing applications, poorly trained and motivated staff and indifference to the needs of consumers are just some of the issues that have been reported in many different countries over the years and although they are not highlighted in the book's country case studies their significance is recognized. If social protection schemes are to meet their goals, the challenge of administrative effectiveness needs to be given high priority. Fortunately, steps have been taken in some countries to address the challenge through, for example, improved staff training, better salaries and working conditions and more effective leadership. In some cases, electronic technologies have been effectively employed to process applications and the use of electronic cards that can be used at banks and post offices have speeded up the delivery of benefits. Another useful innovation is the creation of consumer groups to advise management. Obviously, managerial effectiveness can be enhanced if those receiving benefits are encouraged to give feedback and advocate for improvements. Although few countries have adopted this approach it should be more widely used.

The fragmentation of social protection into multiple schemes operated for different groups by different government agencies presents another challenge to administrative and organizational effectiveness and needs to be addressed. This issue applies to all the countries but to different degrees. If social protection policies and programmes are to meet their goals, steps need to be taken to improve coordination and formulate a more coherent approach that effectively links different schemes together so that they contribute systematically to people's well-being. This issue will be referred to again later.

THE GOALS AND IMPACT OF SOCIAL PROTECTION

As Midgley argued in Chapter 2 of this book, and as is clear in the book's country case study chapters, many goals are being pursued in social protection schemes. The extent to which these different goals are being met varies considerably. Social protection's impact is affected by funding, organizational effectiveness, coverage and benefit levels. This study highlights the fact that the goals of social protection differ substantially between countries and also between different social protection schemes within countries. Different goals call for different systems. It is not the role of the social scientist and analyst to determine what the goals should be. Seeking clarity as to what the goals are and evaluating effectiveness in meeting them are different tasks, which both have their value. Much more research is needed to fulfil these tasks for all four countries.

In all four countries, social protection is officially designed to maintain incomes in the event that contingencies – such as sickness, retirement, disability and death – interrupt, reduce or terminate income, but in general this approach involves membership of formal social insurance schemes which cater to those in formal employment and exclude the majority or a substantial proportion of the population.

Despite the limitations of social assistance, it is being used quite effectively in India, Brazil and South Africa to subsidize the incomes of poor families and to alleviate poverty. In these countries, social protection's poverty alleviation function has been emphasized in recent years through conditional cash transfers such as Bolsa Família, cash for work programmes such as India's National Rural Employment Guarantee scheme and South Africa's child support grants and retirement pensions, which use a relatively generous means test to subsidize the incomes of sizable numbers of poor people. These schemes also operate on the assumption that means-tested pensions and child benefit payments will circulate in the household, raising income as a whole and reducing poverty. Empirical evidence reported in several chapters suggests that social protection is indeed an effective way of achieving this goal.

Another goal of social protection is to reduce inequality and promote social justice. But, as was noted in Chapter 1, this goal is not given high priority in either the Western or developing countries. Since income and wealth inequalities as well as inequality between children, men, women, disabled people, older people, ethnic minorities and indigenous people are endemic in all four countries, and are believed to be detrimental to social and economic development as well as political stability, their governments have proposed that action be taken to tackle inequalities, but few commentators would claim that much has been achieved. Certainly, none of the governments have explicitly declared their intention to use the social protection system to promote equality. Nevertheless, as Soares reveals in his assessment of the impact of social protection in Brazil, the system has reduced inequalities (Chapter 10). Since empirical data on this question for other countries are limited, more research is needed. If it can be demonstrated that social protection not only alleviates poverty but reduces inequality, it can serve a powerful egalitarian function in countries experiencing rapid economic growth where income and wealth inequalities are especially marked. While contributory social insurance can contribute to horizontal equity, it is the other components of social protection that have the most direct impact on poverty. The findings of Soares on Brazil show, however, that social insurance has an 'impressive role' in combating poverty, particularly among the elderly; yet those most vulnerable to poverty are the least assisted. The focus on the elderly in social protection in all four countries, which reflects the priority shown in countries that industrialized earlier, does limit the impact on child poverty. However, for Brazil, Soares finds that the Bolsa Família has a strong impact on child poverty. This is also the case in South Africa, where the child support grant has been effectively targeted at poor families.

Other goals of social protection discussed in Chapter 2 include social protection's contribution to economic development and social and political stability. Although academic commentators in the West have made much of social protection's role in preserving existing power structures, it can contribute constructively to promoting social solidarity, stability and participation and this role should be more widely recognized. In addition, social protection's positive contribution to economic development through, for example, promoting social investments should form an integral part of a comprehensive plan to ensure that social protection plays a key role in both social and economic development. If social protection is to avoid fragmentation, duplication, confusion and chaos, and have a positive impact, more effective planning will be needed to clearly define goals, refine existing administrative systems and identify obstacles to implementation.

ECONOMIC DEVELOPMENT, SOCIAL PROTECTION AND SOCIAL CHANGE

Change is always present in all societies but over the past 20 years has been quite exceptional in the four nations studied here. Rapid economic growth has been accompanied by rapid urbanization and, except in Brazil, widening inequality. (Why Brazil is an exception in terms of inequality is a most interesting and important question but it is beyond the scope of this study.) In these circumstances the ability to afford social protection and the need for it have both increased and the result has been an increasing emphasis on social protection in recent years and anticipation of future growth. Yet claims for resources for social protection must compete with other demands and many countries are concerned that social protection develops in ways that promote economic growth and the development of human capital. Social protection is seen by some as potentially helping economic growth and by others as potentially damaging future growth. The conventional economic view has been that social protection reduces the incentive to work and harms economic growth. On the other hand, there is an alternative view which has been largely neglected: by maintaining and promoting human capital, by enhancing social capital and by maintaining aggregate economic demand, social protection can promote economic growth (see Piachaud, 2013). Evidence on both the negative and positive impacts of social protection is, however, in short supply.

LESSONS FOR THE FUTURE

There are numerous questions about the future which this study has not begun to resolve or even to suggest which way the future may develop

– although the insights offered about some of the factors and influences that will determine the future of social protection can only serve to make the future more understandable. Among the questions that must remain unanswered are: How will economic growth and change affect the future need and demand for social protection? How will changing needs and circumstances affect social protection – ageing, changing family structures and support systems, growing informal employment? How far will social protection continue to be concentrated on the urban, formal sector? Will the relatively unprotected rural sectors ever catch up? Will social protection become more targeted towards poverty or more contributory and insurance-based? Will social protection move from horizontal redistribution – over lifecycle, between employed and unemployed, between able-bodied and disabled – to being a significant promoter of social equity, including gender equality and inter-generational equity? What problems arise for government in terms of implementation and administration of social protection, the ability to raise finance, the regulation of the private sector, the public–private mix? How will the politics of social protection develop? Will more risks have to be borne by government? Will there be more or less trust of government?

Some things are clear. There has not been an end to history and the future will be dynamic. There is not one ideal model of social protection. From where we are now there is little that is predictable looking ahead one-quarter or one-half of a century – yet it is over these substantial time horizons that much of social protection is planned and operates. So anyone looking to this book for a forecast of the future development of social protection in the four nations will be disappointed.

What may guide answers to some of the questions posed are some lessons that can be drawn from the consideration of past developments, the analysis of current provisions and problems and the discussion of future challenges.

First, the diversity of social protection policies and programmes in the four countries needs to be recognized. In fact, it may be argued that there is no such thing as social protection. This may seem a strange lesson to draw from a book about 'social protection' but it is an important lesson, which is often neglected. There are hugely different schemes with wholly different effects which are loosely and misleadingly lumped together as 'social protection'.

It should also be remembered that all four countries have to some extent followed a model of social protection taken from the experience of the early industrialized nations. This model of provision – based on formal employment and deviations from it due to retirement, unemployment and sickness – is still highly influential. Yet it has left most of the populations of the four countries, indeed the whole world, totally excluded. Social protection is often thought of as benefiting the disadvantaged; the reality is that globally much has primarily benefited the advantaged.

Another lesson is the danger of a static view of social protection. Most discussions about extending social protection have approached it in a static fashion, when the reality is that economic and social conditions are constantly changing. This is most obvious in relation to ageing, where demographic change is perceived as posing a huge challenge for social protection. This is of course true if retirement ages are fixed at 60 or 65 and life expectancy increases. But this is to treat these arbitrary ages as somehow desirable and unchangeable.

It should also be noted that social protection is not an island. Linked to the previous lesson, social protection cannot be thought of in isolation as the sweeper that attempts to clean up all the problems left by economic and social changes and policies. It must be thought of in relation to other policies. Social protection has done and probably will do rather little to offset the changes in inequality that result from other changes. It cannot solve all problems.

The question of what priority should be given to social protection also needs to be addressed. Apart from needing clear goals that can form a basis for a coherent, integrated social protection system, it is not at all clear what priority should be given to social protection in relation to government's many other priorities. In none of the four countries studied did government appear to have a clear view on this. That is not surprising given the lack of relevant evidence comparing the impacts of social protection with other investments in education, job creation, water supply or any of the many alternative possible routes to promote economic growth or the incomes of those experiencing greatest poverty or those at most social risk.

THE IMPORTANCE OF SOCIAL PROTECTION

As stated in the introduction to this book, social protection is not a glamorous subject – it is complex in its goals, its politics, its structure and its consequences. Nevertheless, it is or can be very, very important. It can relieve suffering, it can provide opportunities, it can liberate and change lives, it can be transformational. Many closely involved with social protection treat the case for it as self-evident. This is altogether unhelpful. The case must be made in terms of who gains and who loses, and the consequences for each group and for societies as a whole. The ILO, in their pursuit of a social protection floor (ILO, 2011), make no clear distinction between different forms of social protection, indeed they extend their conception so far as to lose any meaning or policy bite – covering water supply, health and education. Nor do they discuss priorities or conflicting goals. They put forward a mush of high-sounding aims using language that offends no one. In reality the choices are stark, with life and death consequences for billions of people; warm words do not assist in facing up to these choices.

Given the extent of uncertainty that emerges from this volume, it may be useful to go back to the concept of social protection. What is it? What is the social security that many nations seek to promote? One thing is clear: there can be no protection from change. There have been huge changes in the last century as social protection has developed from being almost non-existent globally to being in some form virtually global. Change is unlikely to slow down. But this does not mean that social protection will continue to develop. It could contract so that social protection comes to be seen as a passing phenomenon of the twentieth century, just as alchemy was a phenomenon of previous centuries.

Nor is there a clear future for social protection if it is merely a political cosmetic, a gesture towards social justice, a veneer of concern that is used to legitimate the state. Those who, however humanely, clear battlefields of the dead and wounded do not shape history. Unless social protection is meshed with economic and social policies then its impact will be very limited. There needs to be greater clarity as to what social protection is trying to achieve. There are many possible goals and many possible trajectories. What is not in doubt, as this book hopefully makes clear, is the fundamental importance of social protection, the need to think about it in relation to the whole economy and society, and its potential to contribute to a more just future for humanity.

REFERENCES

ILO (2011), *Social Protection Floor For a Fair and Inclusive Globalization*, Geneva: International Labour Office.

Piachaud, D. (2013), 'Social protection, redistribution and economic growth', *Development in Southern Africa*, **30** (1), 24–38.

Index

This is primarily an index of subjects. Only authors specifically discussed in the text are included in the index; full references can be found at the end of each chapter.